Digital Era Governance

Digital Era Governance: IT Corporations, the State, and E-Government

Patrick Dunleavy, Helen Margetts,
Simon Bastow, and Jane Tinkler

OXFORD
UNIVERSITY PRESS

OXFORD
UNIVERSITY PRESS

Great Clarendon Street, Oxford OX2 6DP

Oxford University Press is a department of the University of Oxford.
It furthers the University's objective of excellence in research, scholarship,
and education by publishing worldwide in

Oxford New York

Auckland Cape Town Dar es Salaam Hong Kong Karachi
Kuala Lumpur Madrid Melbourne Mexico City Nairobi
New Delhi Shanghai Taipei Toronto

With offices in

Argentina Austria Brazil Chile Czech Republic France Greece
Guatemala Hungary Italy Japan Poland Portugal Singapore
South Korea Switzerland Thailand Turkey Ukraine Vietnam

Oxford is a registered trade mark of Oxford University Press
in the UK and in certain other countries

Published in the United States
by Oxford University Press Inc., New York

© Patrick Dunleavy and Helen Margetts 2006

The moral rights of the author have been asserted
Database right Oxford University Press (maker)

First published 2006

British Library Cataloguing in Publication Data
Data available

Library of Congress Cataloguing in Publication Data
Data available

Typeset by SPI Publisher Services, Pondicherry, India
Printed in Great Britain
on acid-free paper by
Biddles Ltd., King's Lynn, Norfolk

ISBN 0–19–929619–7   978–0–19–929619–4
1 3 5 7 9 10 8 6 4 2

Contents

List of Figures

List of Tables

Acknowledgements

This book is based on research carried out for the project, Public-private Partnerships in Central Government IT Systems, funded by the UK Economic and Social Research Council (grant no. no.L216 25 2030) and carried out by a joint UCL/LSE team based at the School of Public Policy at University College, London. It also draws extensively on experience gained in work carried out by LSE Public Policy Group and Helen Margetts for the UK National Audit Office's studies *Government on the Web* during 1998–9 and *Government on the Web II* during 2001.

Chapter 9 is a revised version of an article that was originally published by the *Journal of Public Administration Research and Theory*. We thank JPART and Oxford University Press for giving us permission to reproduce it here.

We are grateful to Ed Page, who directed the ESRC Future Governance programme of which this project formed a part: without this financial support comparative research of this kind would not be feasible. The other critical resource underpinning the whole book was the time and assistance of the 250 interviewees from both government departments and agencies, and from IT corporations, consultancies and interest groups. Without their unstinting help and generous openness to helping academic research, this book would not have been possible.

We would like to give warm and heartfelt thanks also to Nick Lacy and Michael Whitehouse of NAO for extensive helpful comments and advice on aspects of contracting and e-government programmes in the UK; Christine Butterfield (University of Canberra) and Bob Goodin (ANU) for invaluable help on the Australian research; Jonathan Boston (Victoria University, Wellington) for assistance on the New Zealand research; Paul Frissen (University of Tilburg, the Netherlands) for extensive help and hospitality on the programme of interviewing in the Netherlands; Tatsuo Igarashi and Kenichi Kondo (Tokyo) for the vital roles they played in the Japanese research; Sally Welham (School of Public Policy, UCL) for her invaluable help and unmatched administrative competence in numerous aspects of the project; Hala Yared for work on tax agencies and Hala and

Ruth Callaghan for work on *Government on the Web II*; Steve John and Don McCarthy for work on *Government on the Web*; Helen Margetts' colleagues at the Oxford Internet Institute for providing a supportive and stimulating environment to write up some of the research; Patrick Dunleavy's colleagues on the LSE Identity Project, for expanding his knowledge of ID and government issues; and Oliver Pearce of LSE Public Policy Group for his many inputs.

For friendship, advice, support and (in some cases) putting up with our absence during study trips abroad during the course of the research, we thank also: Sheila Dunleavy, Pedro Mascuñán Pérez, Oscar Mascuñán Margetts, Dana Rooney, Christine, Malcolm and Karen Tinkler, and Sean Callaghan.

List of Abbreviations

ABN—Australian Business Register
ACSI—American Customer Satisfaction Index
ADP—Automatic data processing
AMB—Administrative Management Bureau
APIS—Advance Passenger Information Service
ASZ—Automatiserung Sociale Zekerheid
ATO—Australian Tax Office
CCIO—Council of Chief Information Officers
CCTA—Central Computer and Telecommunications Agency
CGEY—Cap Gemini–Ernst and Young
CIC—Citizenship and Immigration Canada
CIO—Chief Information Officer
CITU—Central Information Technology Unit
CPSU—Commonwealth and Public Sector Union
CRA—Canada Revenue Agency
CSC—Computer Science Corporation
DBFO—Design, build, finance and operate
DEG—Digital era governance
DHS—Department of Homeland Security
DHSS—Department of Health and Social Security
DIMIA—Department of Immigration and Multicultural and Indigenous Affairs
DSS—Department of Social Security
EDI—Electronic data interchange
EDS—Electronic Data Systems
EI—Employment insurance
ESD—Electronic service delivery
ESDN—Electronic service delivery network
FCO—Foreign and Commonwealth Office
FEAF—Federal Enterprise Architecture Framework
FEAP—Federal Enterprise Architecture Plan
GCMS—Global Case Management System
GOL—Government On-Line
GSA—General Services Administration

GST—Goods and Services Tax
GWACs—Government-wide acquisition contracts
HMRC—Her Majesty's Revenue and Customs
IB—Immigration Bureau
ICAO—International Civil Aviation Organisation
IND—Immigration and Nationality Directorate
INS—Immigration and Naturalization Service
IRD—Inland Revenue Department
IRS—Internal Revenue Service
IT—Information technology
JUG—Joined-up governance
LDP—Liberal Democratic Party
MLAs—Micro-local agencies
NAFTA—North American Free Trae Area
NAO—National Audit Office
NIIS—Non-Immigrant Information System
NIRS—National Insurance Recording System
NOIE—National Office of the Information Economy
NPM—New public management
NPR—National Performance Review
NTA—Natinal Tax Agency
OCR—Optical Character Recognition Work
OeE—Office of the e-Envoy
OMB—Office of Management and Budget
PAYE—Pay as you earn
PFI—Private Finance Initiative
PPPs—Public–Private Partnerships
PSAs—Public Service Agreements
RFID—Radio Frequency Identification
SEVIS—Student and Exchange Visitor Information System
SRA—Strategic Rail Authority
SSA—Social Security Administration
SSC—State Service Commission
SSI—Supplemental Security Income
SWIFTT—Social Welfare Information for Tomorrow Today
TCA—Tax and Customs Administration
TSM—Tax Service Modernization project
USCIS—US Citizenship and Immigration Services
US-VISIT—US Visitor and Immigrant Status Indicator Technology
WTO—World Trade Organisation
ZTT—Zero touch technology

Introduction

Information Technology and Public Policymaking

In advanced industrial countries, governments typically spend around 1 to 1.5 per cent of GDP on public sector information technology (IT) systems. (To put this in perspective the whole of agriculture now accounts for only 1.5 per cent of GDP in the UK.) In the 1960s and 1970s governments in many countries were pioneers in IT development, with their own highly skilled staffs and developed expertise, reflecting the huge impact that computerization and the basic automation of government services had on the modernization of public sector processes and productivity growth in the economy. Today the importance of government IT systems for societal development continues to grow. Tax systems and welfare benefits systems, for instance, increasingly define the public sphere in economic terms. And modern ICT systems based on the Internet increasingly underpin trade, economic exchanges, and collective services provision critical for advanced industrial economies. In core state functions like national security and control of inflows of people into the national territory, modern IT databases, networks, and communication are also fundamental, with developments like e-borders transforming traditional administrative and legal operations.

What has changed though, is that governments no longer run their own IT functions. To get their systems built, developed, and managed they increasingly rely on the global IT industry, specifically the giant 'systems integrator' companies such as Electronic data Systems (EDS), IBM-Accenture, Cap Gemini–Ernst and Young, Lockheed Martin, and their like. Some of these companies are now huge global players, with turnovers comparable to the GDP of sizeable states. (For instance, the well-known corporation EDS supports 2.5 million desktops in the public and private sectors across the worldwide, employs 126,000 staff and has a turnover of US$33 billion.) Individual contract sizes in major countries are also often huge, amounting to billions of pounds in contract value, lasting up to a decade and hence having a considerable potential to shape the configurations of contemporary government.

However, the government contracting market also differs considerably from one country to another, a variation which we have sought to capture using seven case study countries on which we focus analysis. In the UK, Australia, and New Zealand, the top few corporations have completely dominated the field, with the top contractor (EDS) regularly controlling up to 65 per cent of contract value in the UK at one stage and 80 per cent in New Zealand. In Japan the market is also concentrated but almost entirely 'home-grown', with Japanese IT corporations involved in long-term relationships with government ministries covering all aspects of information services. In the Netherlands, the large global players have also found it hard to gain more than a foothold in government IT, because a different and more 'state-corporatist' pattern of contract relationships has developed, with departments and agencies retaining more control over both projects' design and multiple providers. In the USA, legislation aimed at maintaining competition means that a much more diffuse market has emerged, with the top five companies holding only 20 per cent of central government IT contracts. Finally, in Canada the government has benefited from its proximity to the US market and has also retained a much stronger in-house capacity to manage IT functions.

This book provides the first comprehensive picture of the new world of big governments' IT functions and their relations with the global service providers and other kinds of IT companies. It shows how the Weberian model of rational bureaucracy has increasingly developed in the modern era so that the most foundational information processing and decision capabilities of the state now rest on public officials' ability to manage complex industrial contracts and advanced 'knowledge intensive' professions and occupations.

Traditionally academic public administration and most public management and organization theory texts have focused on the human side of government organizations—the selection, socialization, and management of personnel, the configuring of organizations construed as hierarchies of human actors, the operations of strategic management and leadership roles, the organization of physical processes of production, etc. But some organizational configurations have already transitioned beyond machine bureaucracies or professional bureaucracies into adhocracies with out-sourced operating cores, of which privately designed, built and run IT systems are key components. So this book not only captures the previously almost uncharted government–IT industry interaction, it also shows how these relationships are central to the development of rationalization and modernization processes critical for the whole economic and social performance of advanced industrial states. It introduces the concept of 'digital era governance' and shows how it is increasingly displacing the aged 'new public management' (NPM) orthodoxy of the 1990s and early 2000s.

Current trends are likely to intensify further in the next decade. In the near future, government (as well as private sector) organizations look set to transition again, perhaps beyond adhocracies and into situations where many agencies *'become* their websites'—where the electronic form of the organization increasingly defines the fundamentals of what it is and does. Many agencies may be able to transition to being fully or partly 'digital' in their operations. 'Zero-touch' technologies already take human interventions out of some key administrative processes altogether. And processes of radial 'disintermediation' and 'service aggregation' will significantly reduce and alter the traditional role of government bureaucracies in intermediating between citizens, enterprises, and the state. We have set out here to provide a range of key audiences with a critical theoretical and empirical updating to help them appreciate not only the extent of existing changes but the impact of modern IT systems and IT contracting on the future direction of democratic governance.

Summary of the Argument

The book stems from a research project spanning five years (conducted for the UK Economic and Social Research Council's 'Future Governance' programme) which looked at the development of central government contracting for IT systems and the growth of e-government in seven countries—the USA, Japan, the UK, Canada, Australia, Netherlands, and New Zealand. The research team visited all the countries and interviewed hundreds of civil servants, IT industry executives and professionals, as well as informed academics and observers (more than 250 senior experts in all). We conducted a close investigation of the government IT markets across the countries and undertook a market analysis of each industry. The research looked in particular detail at government IT systems contracting in taxation, social security, and immigration policy sectors, but it also followed the most pathbreaking and innovative developments in each country across civilian government policy areas, and on focused the areas of most acute stress in government–industry relations. Finally, the team investigated the comparative development of e-government programmes since 1996, which are increasingly critical in the 'digital governance' era. The analysis covers a fifteen-year period, from the early 1990s to 2005.

The first two chapters introduce the terrain, looking briefly first at the theory of modern bureaucracy and the role assigned within it to the development and management of information systems. Chapter 1 shows that long before Max Weber codified his ideal type of bureaucracy in the 1890s there was an appreciation that the planning, implementation, storage, and re-accessing of written records on larger and more systematic scales was transformative for modern organizations. The early development of IT systems by the 1930s did no more than index (at first) large or (later) vast paper documentation stores. The 1980s development of structured relational databases and later the breakthrough to fully electronic storage and accessing capability in the 1990s made a decisive change from this pattern and the advent of the Web as a universal route to knowledge completed the transformation. Throughout this period the significance of IT professionalism for government operations grew in a fluctuating mode with periods of rapid progress and routinization succeeding each other, and a shifting balance between state patronage and later corporate patronage.

Yet in the theory of public administration and public management a number of factors have contributed to the under-appreciation of the contemporary salience of IT. Weber's recognition of organizations as socio-technical systems never fed through into subsequent thinking for several reasons. The core concept of bureaucracy was almost immediately differentiated as empirical studies highlighted how varied were civil service systems across different countries. The Parsonian critique of Weber localized his model's application to the class of 'machine' bureaucracies, separating it from more professional bureaucracy patterns of organization in the most rapidly growing welfare state sectors, like education, health care, and social services. Political influences and corporate patronage of IT professionalism perpetuated this view more in IT areas than in other areas of expertise. And a process of 'displacement' tended to focus the attention of government decision-makers on the human and organizational aspects of socio-technical systems. Part of our purpose in this book is to counteract the historic neglect of information systems and

information access within public management and the theory of government organizations, so that the centrality of IT for modern governance
processes can be better appreciated.

The precise focus of this influence is now in the commissioning, design,
and implementation of large-scale IT systems in civil government
applications (on which we focus here) and additionally in defence sector
applications (about which we say relatively little). Chapter 2 explores the
growing role of contracting, and the decreasing role of in-house design
and implementation, in government systems. The modern state's sphere
of action is increasingly defined in terms of distinctive systems for raising
and dispersing financial (plus a few other) resources, including particular
modes of generating and organizing information. Yet (paradoxically
almost) in many advanced nation states the capability for defining and
developing these critical systems now lies outside the competence
of public officials. It is instead located with IT professionals who predominantly work for large corporations, often multinational or global in scale.
These firms often seem to monopolize (or are allowed even encouraged
to monopolize) the necessary expertise and organizational capacities to
service and develop the very large-scaled government systems of big
nation states. Chapter 2 shows how the context for government IT
contracting changed in three dimensions over the last fifteen years to
2005, on the government side, the corporate side, and in the nature of
the tasks for which systems were being designed.

A critical dependent variable for the comparative analysis is the performance of government IT systems, operationalized in Chapter 3 in terms of:

– the scrap rate of government IT projects;
– the price comparability of public sector to private sector IT;
– the relative modernity of government IT systems.

Given the complexity of making such assessments, we use a 'fuzzy set'
social science perspective to categorize countries' performance in terms of
very rich data and qualitative judgements (following Ragin 2000). We then
explore how the patterning of countries' performance can be explained in
terms of two sets of explanatory variables—government institutional
arrangements and the power of the IT industry in its dealings with
government agencies.

We operationalize the institutional background in Chapter 4 in terms of
four key, qualitatively set dimensions:

– checks and balances in fundamental governance arrangements: we
  expect the absence of checks to worsen government IT performance;

– the openness of bureaucratic culture to technical expertise: again a closed, non-technical bureaucracy should inhibit IT performance;

– the openness of each country to NPM reforms: we expect NPM to inhibit government IT performance because of its direct effects in fragmenting government and its indirect effects in boosting the power of the IT industry (see below);

– the presence of a strong, central, political-administrative push for e-government: we expect the absence of such an effort to impair government IT's development.

The institutional explanatory variables do indeed show some influence on the expected lines, but they also show considerable country variance and highlight multiple 'exceptions' and explanatory problems.

We next operationalize the power of the IT industry in Chapter 5 in terms of three key, qualitatively categorized dimensions:

– the extent to which government IT contracting has moved away from effective competition, which we expect to worsen performance;

– strong market dominance by the top five firms, which we expect to reduce performance; and

– government's lack of in-house capabilities: again we expect increased dependence upon contractors to worsen performance.

There are sharply varied patterns of government–industry IT relations across our seven countries. But using an aggregate measure of IT industry power shows a very close negative relationship with government IT performance, far stronger in its influence than the effects of government institutional factors. In other words, the greater the overall power of the IT industry in a country, the lower the performance of government IT systems.

We explore the workings of these relationships in more empirical detail in Chapters 6, 7, and 8, looking in turn at three areas of civilian government IT that are critical for defining modern state capacities. Taxation systems in countries like the USA and Japan are now some of the largest information processing operations ever undertaken in human endeavour. In all seven counties important problems have been created by paper-based administrative systems having been converted early on into giant IT systems, designed in a cost-intensive à la carte manner, which now have significant legacy problems. We show how recent e-revenue initiatives have been overlaid upon a history of poorly performing system modernization efforts. For social security systems the challenges have been somewhat different, assessing benefits eligibility using highly intrusive forms for distributing heavily siloed benefits. Existing systems are far removed from allowing agencies to take a 'whole person' perspective on their clients, and interfacing with partners to achieve fulfilment and financial transfers has also been complex. Finally, immigration systems have had to respond to highly variable patterns of demand, and have generally remained more human-intensive and poorly modernized compared with other internationally orientated systems facing increased demands (such as customs systems).

We conclude in Chapter 9 by drawing out the major lessons both for government and for the IT industry itself. For governments in our advanced industrial countries we argue that NPM is intellectually dead, an orthodoxy now played out and plagued by evidence of adverse by-product effects. NPM focused on disaggregation, competition, and incentivization changes. In its day it achieved many successes in advancing social problem-solving, introducing additional diversity into the mix of methods and options available and usefully boosting imitation and competition processes amongst a wider range of providers. But NPM also fragmented administrative institutions, dramatically increasing policy system institutional complexity and somewhat reducing citizens' autonomous capacities to solve their own problems. NPM impaired government IT modernization by hollowing out public sector staffs and capabilities and bringing new contractually based risks and barriers into cross-government policymaking. An emerging post-NPM agenda has 'digital era governance' changes at its core, focusing on the reintegration of services, holistic and 'joined-up' approaches to policymaking, and the extensive digitalization of administrative operations on lines mentioned in the Introduction above.

For the global IT industry, the Afterword also identifies some key lessons for future development. Most of the large firms and smaller providers have made a good living for the last three decades from providing relatively expensive à la carte and *sui generis* solutions to early automation projects and more recent legacy system modernization and integration work. But past patterns are not likely to persist into the near-future. With the growth of the Chinese, Indian and other industrializing economies the locus and character of governmental IT will need to change to simpler, cheaper, and more modular approaches, while a whole range of new, lower-cost players will enter the government IT market. And in the advanced countries the willingness of public sector decision-makers to continue putting resources into advanced digitalization changes will depend critically on routinizing and making more reliable existing governmental IT systems and networks. The challenge for the industry will be to adapt in ways that can offer both advanced and emerging economies better solutions than those available in the recent past for basic computing and IT operations, while shifting the focus forwards into properly developing 'digital era governance' capabilities. A shift from actively maintaining oligopolistic practices, and instead to recognizing the long-run, dynamic benefits produced by maintaining stronger competitive tension and more purposeful knowledge-development, is in the interests of the global IT industry as much as it can be beneficial for governments and citizens.

1

The Theory of Modern Bureaucracy and the Neglected Role of IT

Why does the contemporary public management and public administration literature look like movies or TV programmes showing office life before the late 1980s? Answer: there is no IT at all visible. Government decision-makers are pictured doing strategic thinking about issues, detecting problems, setting priorities, making policy choices, carrying through implementation, managing human relations, and treating citizens equally, but all using information that is mysteriously and unproblematically at their finger tips. The only visible indications of information systems in the literature suggest an anachronistic apparatus of paperwork, filing cabinets, and file registries. Sometimes undergraduate public administration or public management texts contain elusive references to the Internet, to the automation of routine administrative tasks or even now to e-government—all of which are conventionally commended as being a largely effortless 'good thing'. Postgraduate or professional books occasionally link the same fleeting positive references to information technologies with sketchy warnings that perhaps IT systems are not a panacea for organizational problems or cultural limits that have not been solved elsewhere.

In this chapter we first seek to rectify this past theoretical neglect by briefly drawing out the key roles of government IT in contemporary bureaucratic operations. The second section then shows how a number of different factors have combined to create and maintain this past neglect, blurring or obscuring the importance of information systems in the development of contemporary public management.

1.1 Why IT is Critical for Government Organizations

Government IT is at the focus of contemporary rationalization and modernization changes within a wide range of public service delivery systems. We argue in this book not just that IT has played a significant part in these changes but that it occupies a central role in modern public management. There are four components of this case:

- the importance of initially paper-based and later electronic information systems in constituting modern bureaucracies as a socio-technical system;

- the impact of IT on the organizational structure of 'machine bureaucracies' especially;

- the pervasive importance of IT for the contemporary tasks of government; and

- why most policy changes and public management reforms now focus in their timing and scope on shifts in IT and information infrastructures.

(i) *How information (technology) underpins organizations as socio-technical systems.* Max Weber's ideal type theory of bureaucracy and characterization of bureaucratization as an essential, rationalizing/improving element of modernity were critical developments in the sociology of bureaucracy. But the organizational studies and public administration literatures tend to attribute to him more originality than is justified in terms of identifying some detailed features of modern bureaucracies, especially a shift to relying on written documentation and hierarchical organization. As Albrow has pointed out, this association did not date from Weber's time but had already been noted many decades earlier. The German *Brockhaus* encyclopedia of 1819 complained:

The modern form of public administration executes with the pen everything which previously would have been done by word of mouth. Hence many pens are set in motion. In every branch of administration bureaux or offices have multiplied, and have been accorded so great a power over citizens that in many countries a veritable bureaucracy, rule by offices, has developed. This bureaucracy becomes increasingly dangerous as the previous custom of conducting business through *collegia* falls into disuse. The directors of a bureau, in addition to their authority over its personnel, have acquired an inordinate amount of power over citizens at large. (Albrow 1970: 28)

The distinctiveness of Weber's analysis lay rather in his acute insistence that a bureau could *only* be constituted by bringing together well-trained, qualified, and impersonally selected officials, in a corporate and systematized organization configuration, together with the written papers and rules needed to conduct business. It was this simultaneity which created the inherent rationality advantages of bureaucracy compared with other forms of organization at the turn of the nineteenth century. Unlike the encyclopaedist, Weber correctly saw that organizations are socio-technical systems where the documenting of decisions and considerations play a necessarily critical role in three main respects:

(a) *Official files and documents* (covering rules, memos, letters, decisions, and case folders) provide a key underpinning for the impersonality and consistency of modern administration. They codify and express a common understanding which ensures that similarly trained officials will make identical decisions.

(b) Well developed and *systematically organized file registries* provide what Montaigne called a 'paper memory', a collective capability many times larger and less fallible than any individual capacity. And as Pascal stressed: 'Memory is necessary for all the operations of reason' (Pascal 1909–14: 369). The critical facility here was the development of file registries with indexing systems allowing material to be reliably found, and later cross-indexing systems allowing data with different foci to be linked, along with the capacity to store and re-find huge volumes of documents and papers.

(c) The joint development of file registries along with the impersonal occupation of offices and strengthening of bureaucratic training and socialization essentially gave bureaucratic organizations *a capacity to operate continuously through time*. Weber assigned much of bureaucracy's impact in improving efficiency to this permanence, along with economies of scale and the knowledge-development consequent on being able to control more exactly larger hierarchical organizations. In the government sector turbulent competition between organizations is rarer and the selective culling of failing organizations is weaker than in the private sector, so that serious analysts have wondered: 'Are government organizations immortal?' (Kaufman 1976).

Essentially the paper-based systems that were perfected from the late nineteenth century through to the 1920s then lasted another six decades or so into the 1980s, when the first free-text forms of searching began to be widely feasible. Across this long period newer indexing and document storage methods were successively introduced, along with more developed government forms, statistics and codified means of seeking information. In the USA the New Deal years saw the introduction of punched card

systems and automatic sorting machines, a key element in the development of the world's largest social security system. In the Second World War
and its aftermath, first clockwork versions and then electronic early computers were critical for code breaking. In the 1950s the early mainframe
computers had immediate impacts in defence and science-intensive areas,
where professional staff could cope with their complex human interfaces.
Later in the 1960s more powerful and cheaper mainframes with less
complex interfaces inaugurated a push to centralize large administrative
operations around batch-processing locations. For the most part, even
into the 1980s, the drive towards automating storage and retrieval systems
changed only the size and capacity of administrative systems, but not their
fundamental operation. File registries became fewer and bigger and
their indexing and cross-indexing grew much more automated and
sophisticated. But their essential modus operandi did not change much.
In most cases paper files still remained the largest and most authoritative
record, with big governments storing tens of millions of case files for
long periods. (For example, to this day the US Congress requires the
storage of all citizenship documentation on paper for seventy-five years.)

The widespread use of computers for holding financial information
developed in government from the 1960s and contributed strongly
to the greater systematization and (generally) to the improvement of
government accounting systems. Financial management information
systems plus the development of networks and remote terminals opened
the way for computers to begin to penetrate a wider range of 'front' offices
or mainstream administrative settings, instead of being concentrated only
in self-contained 'back-office' enclaves, run and visited solely by technical
staff. The development of relational databases with structured query
capabilities from the 1980s had some transformational impact later on
how data was stored and how much was computerized. But even here most
existing large government administrative systems were surprisingly little
affected up to the mid-1990s. For instance, as late as 1995 the British
immigration division of the Home Office maintained a 'watch' list of
around 10,000 undesirable aliens who were not to be admitted to the
UK. The list was held and updated on a computer database, but it was
distributed to officials at ports and airports only in a large printed folder,
updated in print form every two weeks (see Chapter 8).

In most areas of public management and civilian government,
the spread of electronic methods of working (rather than basically
paper-based systems indexed by computer or linked to automated
payment systems) lagged behind changes in the private sector. The

invention of the IBM personal computer and the advent of MS Dos in 1981–3 started a trend towards desktop computing. PCs had their own processing power and storage capacities and they were critical in moving from monocolour to full colour displays and later (after 1995) in accessing the Internet using TC/IP protocols. The capacity of personal computers also increased dramatically and networks to link them together became available to most organizations. But there was a considerable lag in many countries where government organizations remained wedded to dumb-terminal network systems. In addition, managers and policymakers in government had low initial levels of computer literacy. So outside strongly scientific areas and some financial applications, agencies were slow to pick up on using PCs and software packages. This rate of progress also created some considerable lags in the extent to which public agencies developed websites and socialized their staff into using the Internet and Web. For instance, in 1998 we visited one British agency with 68,000 staff administering welfare payments. Four years after the launch of the first widely used Internet browser and seventeen years after the first IBM PC, the organization had only eight PCs with Internet access (Dunleavy and Margetts 1999, Part 2).

A key reason for this lag between public and private sectors is that government departments and agencies for much of this period struggled to acquire expertise in this relatively new area. To handle IT, contemporary organizations of all kinds have to acquire completely new skills, of which four types may be distinguished (OECD 2004: 219). First, from the 1960s onwards when financial systems spread throughout government, any medium to large agency needed IT specialists, who have the ability to develop, operate, and maintain IT systems. Second, many organizations require at least some 'advanced users'; competent users of advanced and often sector-specific, software tools. Third, since the spread of computer terminals and latterly personal computers across the desktops of any administrative organization, most white-collar workers are required to be 'basic users', that is, competent users of generic tools, such as word processing, spreadsheet packages and the Internet. Fourth, in the private sector the rise of e-commerce brought the requirement for new 'e-business' skills needed to exploit the unconventional business opportunities provided by IT, particularly the Internet, at the highest organizational levels. Use of the Internet has been shown to play an increasingly important role in a company's competitiveness (OECD 2004: 219). We argue below, however, that web and new media skills are equally important for contemporary policymaking.

All of these new skills requirements have posed distinct challenges to public sector organizations. The first group of staff, IT specialists, proved particularly difficult for any organization to attract and retain. In the early days, government agencies were more successful in doing so. From the Second World War onwards the largest countries involved in the cold war, especially the USA and to a lesser degree Britain, developed defence and high-tech computing applications that were forefront technology, although usually only in scientific or defence agencies at first. From the early 1960s to the early 1970s large government schemes using mainframes for civilian applications also sucked in staff keen to work on forefront projects. Because the US and UK governments in particular built up reputations as IT innovators in this period, it was easier for them to tempt staff at the cutting edge of the new IT occupations into government. Rather than re-training existing generalist staff, big departments started to establish large and organizationally separate IT divisions that could design, build, maintain, and develop their mainframe accounting and transaction processing systems. Public sector projects at this time were so large compared to business uses, the technology was so expensive and the required expertise so specialized, that governments were more likely than private businesses to be able to afford the necessary investment in infrastructure and training. So a career in government IT could be as attractive for professional staffs as working in private industry. (Japan was an important exception amongst our seven case study countries that is worth noting immediately here: see below.)

But these periods of government being in the forefront did not last. Universal shortages of the requisite skills meant that government agencies have often had to compete with the commercial world to attract personnel. Within two decades of the diffusion of financial computing, it became more difficult for any government to secure and maintain IT skills in house. As information systems spread across central bureaucracies, the need for IT staff in government was massive. By 1983 about 41 per cent of the American federal government's data processing budget was allocated to personnel (Grace Commission 1983: ii). Ten years later the federal government employed 113,300 IT staff, at a cost of US$5.5 billion (OMB 1994: 15). In the UK by 1993, £500 million was being spent annually on IT staff costs across central government departments, at that time amounting to 22 per cent of IT expenditure (Margetts 2006). Meanwhile, commercial firms and especially large IT systems integrator companies handling a rapid successions of major projects had overtaken governments in terms of innovation and were offering more interesting work, at far higher salaries than government agencies constrained by public sector pay scales. By the 1990s, in some countries, the most talented and innovative staff were working solely for private industry corporations specializing in IT systems. In those countries (but not everywhere) governments then began to find it almost impossible to recruit the services of such staff on any large scale except by contracting systems development to private industry, a development which in many ways forms a key nexus for our analysis.

At this point, the Weberian concept of a government organization as a self-contained, socio-technical system where agencies are defined by their in-house operations and technology no longer seems adequate. Via their IT needs (as well as in political and other ways) government organizations are increasingly defined and constituted also by their external relationships, partners, and dependencies. To get some view of how the deployment of much larger amounts of IT has changed modern government organizations we next use two different slants, first placing IT within the well-established focus of organizational theory on structures or morphologies, and then (in the next subsection) looking at IT's changing role in the 'toolkit' that government organizations deploy to achieve their ends.

(ii) *The impact of IT on agencies' organization structures.* Strongly hierarchical or Weberian-pattern bureaucracies are characterized as 'machine bureaucracies' in an influential analysis by Henry Mintzberg, who argues that they focus essentially on the standardization of procedures and processes. The organizational structure or morphology of machine bureaucracies is the most articulated and complex of any modern organizational type, consisting of three 'line' elements and two 'staff' elements shown in Figure 1.1. The line elements consist of:

- *the controlling apex* of the organization, which includes the top management board and other senior personnel. They supervise:
- *middle management* who supervise and control the detailed operation of the organization's essential mission. They are the main connection between the controlling apex and:
- *the operating core*, consisting of all the staffs (of whatever grade) who directly produce the final outputs of the organization. In mass manufacturing the operating core consists of the production workers. In service organizations the core is all those who carry out direct functions for clients, often including professional staffs.

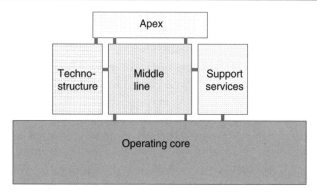

Figure 1.1. The organizational structure of a machine bureaucracy
Source: Mintzberg (1983).

Machine bureaucracies also have two 'staff' sections that do not stand within the main line hierarchy of the organization, but rather are offset in different ways:

- *the technostructure's* job is to scrutinize the organization's production process and evaluate its options for organizational change and improvement. In the private sector the technostructure are accountants, investment, IT and information analysts, design and marketing specialists, and more generalist change managers. They promote the continual process of cost reduction, reorganization, product development, and brand differentiation which sustains corporations' profitability in competitive conditions. In the public sector the technostructure are again accountants, organization and methods, business process and operational research specialists. Their role is again to grind out continuous improvements in agencies' efficiency or costs levels. Large public sector agencies in advanced industrial countries have moved a long way in the last half century from a previous pattern of being generally static in their modes of operating. Now the expectation is that agencies will generate annual 'efficiency dividends' in carrying out their core tasks. Typically central finance ministries will assume that a 2 to 4 per cent reduction in costs can be achieved every year by focusing on productivity improvements and accordingly may cut the agency's base budget by the same amount. Both to meet such demands, and to cope with a rapid external tempo of technological changes, the technostructure has become progressively more important inside government agencies. Meanwhile

- *the support services* provide ancillary goods needed for the organization to carry out its mission. Key examples of such functions are IT services, some kinds of marketing, and public relations, or other ancillary services like catering or cleaning which stand outside the organization's main line processes. Support services' essential feature is that they only indirectly contribute to bottomline profitability in corporations or to final outputs in government bureaucracies, by facilitating the work of the line departments—even though some servicing divisions' inputs (like IT) may be crucial for firms' or agencies' overall performance. In the modern public sector (as in large parts of the big corporations sector) many ancillary services are now hived out to separate private companies and hence are managed contractually.

Machine bureaucracies are one of two basic forms for medium or large government agencies, and this form is especially common amongst older delivery, taxing, or transfer agencies. (The other basic form is a 'professional bureaucracy' to which we return in Section 1.2.) Many of them focus either on the mass handling of forms, benefits claims, tax returns or other documentation submitted by citizens or enterprises; or on the delivery of labour-intensive but non-professionalized services, those of a more straightforward administrative or techno-bureaucratic kind. Machine bureaucracies tend to be the dominant organizational form for the biggest users of civilian government IT at national government level, like the taxing agencies, social security agencies and immigration control agencies on which we focus in Chapters 6 to 8. Arguably these three functions—requisitioning finance, redistributing incomes, and controlling entry into a territory—are all quintessentially state or governmental ones. In the modern world none could be easily feasible without massive amounts of investment in information and communications technology.

But it is significant that in the Mintzberg schema most IT staff in government organizations will not sit in the line elements. Instead they will often tend to be fragmented between the support services and the technostructure. The large majority of IT staff, doing routine care and maintenance for ongoing systems and business processes, will sit squarely in support services. In the public sector such staff are often fairly deskilled and hence can be located well away from the top echelons of the bureaucratic hierarchy. In order to keep staff costs to a minimum and to more evenly disperse government employees around the regions, most countries locate their big government IT centres outside capital cities, often in 'periphery' locations. New additions, such as Web-enabled call centres for phone-based services, have repeated this pattern. With contracting out, of course, this physical separation of most IT staff from the government organization often increases further, and a strong organizational boundary now also separates them from the client agency's hierarchy.

A minority of the most skilled IT staff fall into Mintzberg's technostructure, doing investment analysis, specification and change management for new business processes, as well as liaising with middle or top management. Hence these staff are typically more centrally located. Outsourcing IT services may cut into the government agency's technostructure staff, or it may not, depending on how it is done. Some agencies retain a substantial in-house capability to specify IT procurements and manage contracts actively and closely. Here outsourcing need not lead to the loss of many technostructure IT specialists and its impacts will be concentrated only in support services. Other agencies opt instead for an 'all-inclusive' approach to outsourcing, eschewing any role of specifying procurements in detail and not assigning serious management effort to contract monitoring. An agency taking this course may lose virtually all its IT-competent staff in the technostructure after outsourcing. Where this happens we can expect that the remaining IT-competent skeletal staff will do only episodic contract re-letting. Hence they will be lower-level people than before and will often lose regular contact with the strategic apex of the agency; for instance, there is unlikely to be a director of IT on the management board.

In the early modern era (the three decades after 1945) both the IT support services and the IT technostructure staffs tended to get larger in most government organizations as they built up in-house capabilities (except as noted in Japan). But since then support services have generally shrunk again as a result of technology improvements and the use of more standard components and packages, allowing staff numbers to be cut and considerable de-skilling of IT staffs' expertise. This effect is significant even where support services have not been outsourced to contractors. By contrast, the technostructure of IT, and the number of business change analysts, have tended to carry on growing in the period since the 1990s, as government agencies grapple with the need to shift legacy IT systems onto more modern systems and networks. Most recently this growth has been fuelled by agencies' efforts to come to terms with the impact of the Web and Internet on e-government and electronic services delivery. Where all-inclusive outsourcing strategies have been followed, the business given to consultants has also boomed.

The increased use of IT by civilian government agencies since the 1960s has also affected other parts of their internal structures, cumulatively 'flattening' their organizational hierarchies. The first wave of office automation in the 1960s and 1970s allowed considerable reductions to be made in the operating core by cutting out large numbers of clerical jobs, although often less in government organizations than in private sector companies making equivalent IT changes, as noted above. A second wave of automation changes from the 1980s and 1990s reflecting the introduction of more sophisticated IT-based procedures (e.g. the development of risk assessment techniques) also contributed to a thinning out of middle line positions, although again less radically than the flattening hierarchy of major business corporations.

Mintzberg's framework also encompasses a few very large 'divisionalized' bureaucracies, as in the US defence, intelligence, space, and nuclear energy sectors notable for their wartime and cold war growth. Here the top layer of the department is a kind of 'holding company' strategic apex supervising a wide range of component divisions or large agencies, themselves organized as semi-separate machine bureaucracies (and sometimes professional bureaucracies, see below). This kind of superministry set-up most closely resembles the large M-form, multi-firm holding companies that emerged at the same time in the American business sector. The highest form of divisionalized agencies, was and still is, the Pentagon core, where the Office of the Secretary of Defence is a 'holding company' apex overseeing the three military departments and a cluster of other major agencies. These big US divisionalized departments were strongly influenced by the parallel growth of an extensive American 'para-state' of major equipment contractors that brought them into closer contact with business practice, especially in technology areas. Here, IT professionals for a time played a more influential role, in the heyday of the cold war and the space race, as the divisionalized bureaucracies and IT-related techniques associated with them (such as Planning, Programming and Budgeting Systems) influenced administrative practices in civilian government. But this effect did not last long beyond the early 1970s.

Apart from the divisionalized defence and high-tech departments, the concentration of civilian government IT in machine bureaucracies with strong paperwork hangovers (and often lagging information systems compared to the private sector) had important consequences for the development of knowledge about government IT. The slow-moving machine bureaucracies were deeply unfashionable areas for organization theorists or even public management writers to study. Within these agencies, the concentration of IT functions in support services remote from top levels of power contributed to making them seem unpromising areas for study, despite their increasing salience for the operations of government, to which we now turn.

(iii) *IT and the tasks of government.* The role of computerized information systems in modern government operations is hard to capture briefly and in an interesting way, because their pervasiveness and centrality means that they are present and vital almost everywhere. Figure 1.2 shows a quick set of illustrative roles, categorized according to the useful 'tools of government' schema outlined by Hood (1983; and see Hood and Margetts 2006). This approach argues theoretically that all governments need 'detector' tools for finding things out and then 'effector' tools for getting things done. It also cross-groups these broad types of tools into

Type of government tool	Detectors: *finding things out*	Effectors: *getting things done*
Nodality: *government's central position in society's information networks*	Online Web and email facilities for benefits, taxation, or government inquiries; Web-enabled call centres; government media-monitoring systems	Government websites and information databases; 'broadcast' and 'specialist' messages sent out via government websites and mobile phone messaging
Authority: *the ability to make laws and regulations that coercively enforce outcomes on actors*	Databases on eligibility for benefits and liability for taxes; government records, including property rights databases; ID cards, immigration and citizenship records	Legal and regulatory databases; computerized courts and penalty systems; price and service information systems used in government regulation of financial or product markets
Treasure: *using finance and other government resources (like property or requisitioned labour) to secure the provision of goods and services*	Computerized tax forms used by firms and citizens; tax, income, profits and property registries	Tax system databases and payment systems; welfare state benefit payment systems, including direct debit payments; modern traffic-charging systems for cities
Organization: *the direct delivery of services by government bureaucracies*	Government agencies' management information systems, especially covering personnel and budget allocations	Grants systems sustaining public sector delivery chains; transfer systems
Expertise: *the accumulation of knowledge and professional expertise on how to handle social problems in government agencies*	Government risk registers and databases; risk-assessment systems; automated monitoring systems; computerized modelling, projection, and forecasting systems	Expert systems; monitoring systems for government events-handling and crisis interventions; medical records systems in public health care systems

Figure 1.2. Some illustrations of the contemporary role of IT in government functions

Note: Hood's original schema merged organization and expertise together, but because this is otherwise a very inclusive category we have split it into two here.

five categories shown in the first column of Figure 1.2. *Nodality* is the central position of government in society, such that other actors tell (a well-connected) government things for free and will also perhaps assign special credibility and attention to government messages or advice (e.g. about how to respond to a bird flu epidemic). In an era of digital communications it is hard to understate the importance of government websites for this function. But nowadays even calls to a government call centre depend completely on sophisticated IT for operators to be able to give correct information and to complete transactions like registering people for benefits online. *Authority* is the ability of government to requisition information or resources from other social actors and to mandate courses of action, using law and regulations. Increasingly the key databases on which government, businesses, and citizens make key decisions, such as the national registers of who owns what property, are online, as are all records of who owes what tax in relation to what income. *Treasure* is the use of finance or other resources (like property or requisitioned assets, such as conscription labour) to purchase information, effort or compliance, or to make resource transfers to particular social groups. Modern welfare state systems consume only about 5 per cent of the monies they expend on administrative costs, a demanding ratio which is sustained only by the massive use of IT. The *organization* category here includes the accumulation of an institutional capacity to process information and realize desired outcomes by employing staff, creating agencies, and building up standard operating procedures. Like every large private sector business, government is critically dependent upon its management information systems for its core operations, especially government intranets which now hold the authoritative copies of the rules and regulations by which state bureaucracies must operate. Finally, *expertise* denotes the often esoteric knowledge accumulation that occurs in highly professionalized agencies, which now goes far beyond the basic Weberian memory and consistency functions to condition what Douglas (1986) calls 'How institutions think'. At any given point in time much of this expertise is held informally or in 'oral wisdom' forms by staff members and organization sections. But the push in the modern age is increasingly to capture it in digital form, for instance, via constructing 'expert systems' that use complex modelling and decision algorithms to help inform experts' choices. The limitations of government information systems and information-finding algorithms increasingly determine the scope of what is feasible in policymaking terms (see the next sub-section below).

Something of the contemporary scope of modern government information systems did leak into some pioneering work by major political science and organization theory writers in the early post-War period, when the expansion of government activity during the Second World War and the rapid pace of technological change in defence fields during the cold war both impressed theorists with the 'complexity' of modern governance. For instance, Karl Deutsch's 'cybernetic' metaphor for government had some impact, as did general systems theory in the late 1960s—again partly responding to the influence of 'big science' and defence bureaucracies in the run-up to the Moon landings. But these high-level accounts then did not generally translate into more detailed pictures of information flows within government organizations, where an emphasis on the politics/administration interface and on organizational culture and the socialization of officials remained dominant (see below). And there were powerful models with countervailing impacts, such as Herbert Simon's influential account of organizations operating with bounded rationality. He stressed that there are necessarily severe cognitive limits on the ability of any actor or group of actors to process information. In the late 1950s, when his impact was greatest, Simon's cognitive pessimism was widely misappropriated by pluralist and public administration writers to imply that 'muddling through' was the best that could be achieved in government.

Yet in an interesting later article in 1973 called 'Applying information theory to organisational design', Herbert Simon offered a revisionist account of his own work in which IT now assumed a central role. He still emphasized that a push for comprehensive decision-making was flawed and that the key problem of organization design was to so factor out decision-making that the burden on any one node within the organization could be kept to a manageable level. But he stressed again that information processing and securing the right information for decision-making were critical determinants of all organizational performance and that the political sphere was in principle no different from business. Computers, he argued, could reshape organization design in three key ways. Two were fairly well known: creating a more accessible organizational 'memory', yielding a potential for more information and for grappling with the problems of information-rich, service-orientated, post-industrial societies; and increasing the total decision-processing capacity, radically. But Simon was far ahead of his time in delineating his third role, 'computer access to external information'. 'If we examine the kinds of information that executives use we find that a large proportion of it is simply natural language text—the pages of newspapers, trade magazines, technical journals and so on' (Simon 1973: 496). He noted that virtually all this text information went through machines at some point and speculated that if only it could be delivered electronically the capacity of business and political decision-making and management information systems could expand hugely, allowing computers to serve as 'initial filters for most of the information that enters the organisation from outside'. Yet despite being published in the leading American public administration journal, Simon's prescient anticipation of contemporary Web and Internet impacts, twenty to thirty years ahead of their realization, had little impact then on public management thought.

Perhaps the most cumulative effect of the last hundred years of enhancement of bureaucratic modes of storing records and data, especially in the successive waves of post-War IT changes, has been a widespread impact on the concept and quality of 'information' itself. Yet because these shifts in meaning have been very pervasive, diffuse, and gradual, some analysts have argued that they are amongst the least visible or well-appreciated of social changes. Government bureaucracies allied with newly expanded and powerful professions to advance the codification and certification of categories and classifications, are seen as enhancing the reliability and precision of this stored data. Some important results of these long-run developments have been charted by the sociological literature on the spread of a 'governmentality' orientation, in which human behaviour is seen as extensively reshaped by a range of technologies and strategies of power:

Thought becomes governmental to the extent that it becomes technical, it attaches itself to a technology for its realization. We are familiar with many uses of the term—high technology, new technology, information technology: here a technology seems to refer to an assembly of forms of knowledge with a variety of mechanical devices and an assortment of little techniques orientated to produce certain practical outcomes. In fact, if we consider any of these, for example, information technology, we can see that it entails more than computers, programmes, fibre optic cables, mobile telephones, and so forth. Every technology also requires the inculcation of a form of life, the reshaping of various roles for human practices, the mental techniques required in terms of certain practices of communication, the practices of the self orientated around the mobile telephone, the word processor, the World Wide Web, and so forth. Even in its conventional sense, then, technologies require, for their completion, a certain shaping of conduct, and are dependent upon the assembling together of lines of connection amongst a diversity of types of knowledge, forces, capacities, skills, dispositions and types of judgement. (Rose 1999: 51–2)

The combined political/official/professional/social science ambitions to monitor, categorize, control, or influence social behaviour have been greatly extended. The large-scale storage of data and enhancement of data-handling and manipulation technologies also fuelled the development of calculations upon or modelling of data, a feature that Weber also pointed out as distinctive to bureaucratic modernity a century ago. Increasingly official statistics and analysis underpin decisions made by all other actors in society, forming a key aspect of social capital. The latest turn of the twentieth century manifestation of this phenomenon has been an 'audit explosion' within the public sector itself, fuelled by a growth of internal regulators and the linking of key performance indicators (KPIs) to NPM reorganizations (Power 1994). For the governmentality literature, the push–pull links between these uses to which IT is put and its impact in driving forward new IT investments are not accidental or peripheral. They reflect a deep-rooted legitimation and intellectual drive for public authorities to not only get their analysis and prescriptions right but also to secure buy-in from a full range of societal stakeholders:

[I]n order to govern one needs some 'intellectual technology' for trying to work out what on earth one should do next—which involves criteria as to what one wants to do, what has succeeded in the past, what is the problem to be addressed. (Rose 1999: 26–7)

(iv) *IT, public management reforms, and major policy change.* The final dimension of IT's impact on public management is the extent to which major policy changes now necessitate, focus on and are timetabled around shifts in government IT systems. In traditional public administration theory the constitutional law distinction between legislation, 'executive action', and discretionary action denotes an important difference in likely timescales. *Legislative changes* inherently carry political costs, even in Westminster systems, and scarce legislative time-slots are carefully rationed by core executive actors, so that they are normally unavailable for making smaller or fine-tuning changes. In more competitive political systems, like the USA or the Netherlands, seeking new legislation is also an inherently risky activity, which may or may not deliver the intended effects. *Executive action changes* can be undertaken by governments without altering existing primary laws. They (normally) have a shorter time lag where the government takes steps to change regulations, usually involving publishing the intended rule changes, consulting stakeholders and then considering their reactions. Finally, *discretionary policy changes* are those that governments can implement immediately, because they are legal and permissible within an unchanged set of statutory instruments or regulations, as well as within primary legislation.

The broader significance of the inhibitions imposed by these legislation and regulation time delays has been stressed by recent rational choice theory. A current governing majority in the legislature will embody policy changes in legislation in order to better insulate the new measure from future changes of the political majority, thereby raising the value of the policy change to their constituents (Horn 1995). If the control of government or the legislature subsequently changes to a different political party or majority coalition then the new government or winning coalition can implement discretionary changes immediately, but must wait a short time for regulatory changes. They will normally anticipate some substantial possible delays before achieving primary legislation changes. The political role of an independent judiciary, and of a broader set of constitutional rules and political practices mandating consultation and allocating participation rights to interest groups and stakeholders, is to 'add value' to current policy changes by ensuring their perpetuation until and unless the current policy configuration can be legally changed (Pocock 1973; Horn 1995).

Now the salience of IT systems for modern policymaking and the levels of transition and transaction costs involved in changing major IT systems are in many contexts just as substantial and restrictive as the impacts of legal and regulatory constraints. Just as much as laws, the design of IT systems can have strong effects in embodying and freezing a particular set of administrative capabilities—literally 'embodying' since in 'legacy' systems a given set of procedures will be written up in millions of lines of programming or code, which then becomes expensive to change or modify at a later stage. The considerable costs of making a relatively fixed investment in a particular type of computer system, with a particular software and defined programmes and routines written within it, thus add a significant layer to the insulation of current policy orientations.

Of course, it is possible to argue (as current public management theory has implicitly done) that these effects of IT systems already have many parallels in simple administrative constraints. The inevitable fixing of rules and processes into 'standard operating procedures', the constraining impacts of staff skills, socialization, and training, and the limits of perception and action induced by organization structures, all add their own inertial weight to the continuation of the current operations. Seeking to push these administrative limits and implement changes without appropriate processes, properly trained staff or appropriate organizational structures will risk policy ineffectiveness or excess costs anyway. So does the fact that most contemporary policy shifts imply changes in IT systems add anything more or anything distinctive to these already well-recognized effects? There are five main grounds for arguing that it does:

(a) IT systems are often limiting for policy-makers' discretionary action in particularly *fixed and non-tradable ways*. Politicians can by-pass (or seek to by-pass) other limitations in departments and agencies, or can apply band-aids or administrative quick fixes to try and overcome purely organizational constraints. But if some goal A is non-attainable within an existing IT system, then there may not be any feasible way that policymakers can achieve A, short of redoing the IT system in a new investment, which may take years.

(b) The normal way for politicians or policymakers to overcome administrative limits is to bring into operation an exception-handling process that is more labour-intensive and costly than normal, which can supplement or replace established procedures for some cases. But the scale and scope of IT systems, and the extent to which modern administrative processes are now based on IT, means that *conventional short-term remedies are non-viable* as ways of coping with IT system constraints. 'Throwing money at the problem' will not help to overcome fundamental IT limits in the same way that it can do with normal administrative constraints. This effect selectively impacts on the largest scale IT-based processes, those handling the mass interactions between central governments and large numbers of citizens, businesses and other organizations. For instance, if the relevant current computer systems do not allow it, there is now no practicable way in which governments can collect broad-based taxation or distribute welfare benefits or regulate immigration into their country on a mass scale without first implementing the necessary IT changes. They no longer have the personnel or the expertise to accomplish these tasks without the IT.

(c) *The costs, complexity, and difficulty of IT investments* and renewals have all tended to grow over time. Like businesses, governments have enjoyed rapidly falling capital costs of IT equipment and physical technologies (especially the costs for processors) continuously since the 1980s. But these savings have been more than offset by the rising costs of software, networks, associated staff training and the disruption inevitable in major business process change; the spread of substantial IT into all aspects of organizational life; the rising scope and volume of the data that have to be processed and stored; and the complexities created in large systems by the cumulation of different 'legacy' systems, interconnections, and patches over time. Overall IT spending in central governments as a share of total administrative spending (including running costs and capital investment) has not declined over the decades since the 1980s. Government organizations have also recognized that technological change in IT is likely to be a continuous challenge.

(d) These three factors additionally have important feedback implications for administrators' behaviour. The special quality of IT limits and constraints creates a powerful dynamic in which officials hold back from trying to put through piecemeal changes. Instead agencies (especially large agencies) often adopt a practice of cumulating minor changes and improvements into *widely spaced and expensive big IT renewals or refreshes*. This dynamic can easily create a five to ten year 'big bang cycle' approach, in which short-term policy changes are frozen out and almost all change hangs on renewals of major IT infrastructures. This strong IT-periodization of planned policy changes and capabilities reflects both the considerable costs and risks of undertaking fundamental IT systems redesign and the normal political and administrative tendencies towards hyping up the 'transformational' impact of large-scale IT changes. The tendency of politicians and senior officials to tinker endlessly and recursively with the specification of new IT systems, right up to the last minute for commitment and the incentives for companies to 'gold-plate' new IT systems with every conceivable (but not always necessary) feature and capability both contribute to this big bang push to achieve the illusory 'perfect' new IT or 'complete' renewal or refresh.

(e) *Contracting out IT* makes these limits and constraints more clear-cut and apparent. Departments or agencies that outsource their IT operations, either piecemeal or in all-inclusive mode, have to pre-specify what they want in terms of IT services and capabilities. Newer and more flexible modes of IT contracting, such as specifying only numbers of desktops to be served by 'best, current technology', cannot take away the additional limits imposed by having a contractor with real-life cost and cash-flow problems of their own handling involved in the implementation of policy.

Of course, governments can and have repeatedly tried to ignore these five effects, and to behave as if the additional constraints of IT systems can be overcome by simply injecting more money or political capital into their solution. Thus, there is still a tendency for politicians to try and retrofit IT systems to policy changes, pushing the frontiers of what is technically feasible. Similarly top decision-makers often assume that if a given legislative or policy change is made then consequential IT changes will be obviously feasible. Nor does contracting out government IT necessarily make any difference to this syndrome. The global IT industry often encourages policymakers to aspire to a la carte, tailor-made solutions—for the very good reason that doing so only adds to the volume of their business. The last thing that major IT corporations and system integrators have wanted is for governments to do well-planned policy changes attainable via genuinely simpler or more modular forms of IT, for then where would be the need for their highly specialized and expensive services? Similarly outsourcing government IT need not necessarily lead to any cutback in goldplating of major IT projects, nor to fewer demands from politicians for 'after the fact' changes to IT systems. Indeed, as we see below, in the UK during the 1990s an informal rule of thumb was applied amongst major IT contractors that when companies won initial contracts for X amounts of money via initial competitive tendering, they could later expect to earn up to five or six times the X amount in negotiated add-on or re-contracts as a result of later political or policy changes that created new capacity needs or other specification changes. For in politics and government, everything is doable at a price. The chief effective limit on what ministers and governments are prepared to pay to avoid admitting mistakes is what they can get away with in terms of finance ministry or Treasury approvals, and what is politically tolerable within the constitutional framework of government accountability and audit arrangements. In Westminster system countries, like the UK and Australia, this latter limit is quite elastic, even while the costs of elasticity are inescapable.

1.2 Why IT Is Nonetheless Marginalized in Public Management Theory

Given the centrality of IT processes in the operations of government agencies charted above, how is it that IT features so little in the public administration and public management literature? We see three factors as important here:

- the emergence of different forms of the Weberian model, influenced by the pathways determining which kinds of officials become organizational leaders within government;
- the low salience of IT for many decades in professional bureaucracies, the kind of organization that grew most prominently with the expansion

of the welfare state, which tended to undermine the information insights in the basic Weberian model; and

- the weak professionalization of IT occupations themselves.

These influences have strengthened an already strong in-built tendency for public management theory and organization studies to minimize the importance of those areas of an organization's activity that are routinized or seen as technical operations. Instead social science has tended to focus attention upon those areas of organizations which remain most dependent upon continuous human interventions and most demanding of management attention.

(i) *How the pathways to leadership in Weberian public administration systems diverged and mostly excluded IT professionals from policy levels.* Government bureaucracies necessarily swim in a wider sea of political and cultural influences. In each country they must conform to generally accepted norms and expectations amongst elected politicians and the public about what a public service organization can legitimately be expected to do. Legislators, ministers, or an executive president and her staff collectively define and maintain general rules and norms that seek to ensure that public servants are socialized into respect for the public interest, so that in their discretionary behaviour they will do what society and the political elites expect. These norms are cross-organizational. Across the whole state sector they influence how the standardization of public service outputs is achieved and how different kinds of occupational groups rise to leadership ranks. These influences meant that Max Weber's apparently unitary model of bureaucracy failed to capture key differences between the public administration systems of different countries. Almost as soon as it was written the model seemed partial, because it apparently could not explain why the American, British, French, German, or Japanese bureaucracies each had a distinctive organizational culture of their own, that fundamentally conditioned how their departments and agencies operated.

There are many explanations of this differentiation, each of which appeals to varying sets of influences (Van de Walle et al. 2004). Silberman (1993) has argued that in countries where political elites mastered the arts of liberal constitutional politics and peaceful leadership succession early on, they created rather weak public administration systems that relied on educational socialization and a generally defined 'public service' ethos or moral code to keep control over bureaucrats. Already confident political elites, such as those in late nineteenth century Britain or USA set up their civil service systems mainly relying on a liberal university education to socialize new recruits destined for top-level positions into respect for the public interest. As Figure 1.3 shows, they also created cross-governmental civil service hierarchies and rules, which were in turn largely respected by politicians of all the main parties. Neither country developed anything equivalent to the European and specifically German *rechstaat* tradition of a strongly respected and separate public sphere. Instead political elites predominantly saw government intervention as a limited and necessary evil. This was the public administration tradition the British passed on to the 'white' Commonwealth countries, especially in Canada, Australia, and New Zealand.

Figure 1.3 also shows that countries in the British tradition stressed a generalist administrator class of civil servants recruited from top universities, moving across positions and departments as their lifelong career

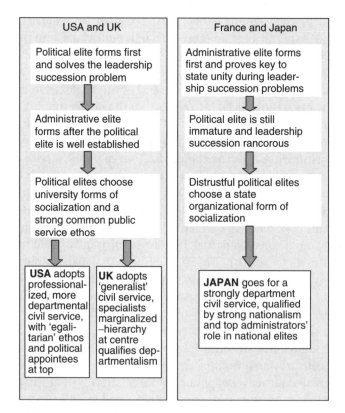

Figure 1.3. The divergence of central civil service systems in three of our case study countries, after Silberman

Source: Silberman (1993).

paths developed, focusing on political and administrative feasibilities rather than acquiring technical expertise, and effectively monopolizing the top positions across all government departments. Figure 1.4 shows that a high-flyer's typical career path would entail a tour of duty in a central coordinating agency like the Treasury or Cabinet Office, designed to give them a servicewide perspective. For a long period, until the 1980s, politicians who became ministers in Westminster system countries were required to seek advice almost exclusively from top civil servants. Generalist civil servants for a long time had high levels of IT illiteracy, however, typically downplaying in significance any technical issues that they did not understand. The obverse aspect of generalism was also that 'specialists' (including virtually all IT staffs) were normally separated out into separate, enclave professional streams and rarely became top managers. This exclusionary effect was compounded for IT occupations by their high degree of fragmentation and failure to cluster into a single 'IT

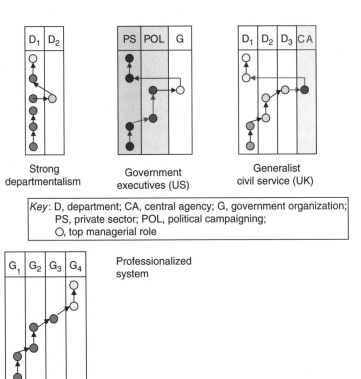

Figure 1.4. Typical career paths in four different central government/civil service systems

profession', so that in the UK they first secured distinct recognition as a civil service occupational group on a par with others only in 2004–5 (see below). Thus the generalist/specialist distinction was severely inimical for administrative elite's appreciation of IT and technology issues generally. The national UK pattern contrasts with local government, which was set up as a professionalized system from the start, one where (as Figure 1.4 shows) people move up in their careers by 'jumping' from one local authority to another. Yet even here IT functions were generally located with other services inside powerful central departments run by lawyers or public accountants, so that local government Directors of IT were rare.

By contrast, the USA developed a pattern of the civil service ranks in government organizations being controlled by the most relevant specialist professionals—for instance, the Department of Justice being run by lawyers, and NASA by engineers and rocket scientists. Figure 1.4 shows that officials would rise primarily within a single department over their career path. This more departmentalist system still relied on more general public service norms of impartiality and concern for social welfare. At the same time the US civil service ranks do not run right to the top of the main federal departments. Instead presidents coming into office (and governors at state level) bring with them a whole team of political appointees, who then staff the top echelons of departments, blurring the political/administrative divide more than in Westminster systems. Policy directions and top organizational decisions within the US executive are thus made by government executives, most of whom come from business, legal, lobbying, or other private sector backgrounds. The radically different career patterns for government executives spanning across business and government (shown in Figure 1.4) means that they are far more aware than other senior civil servants of private industry practices around the use of IT. While rarely being IT professionals themselves, US department and agency leaders are more in touch with modern technology and less patient with government lagging behind business practices.

The other pathway shown in Figure 1.3 was followed by countries like Japan (and France, not discussed here) where political elites mastered the liberal constitutional process and peaceful leadership succession *later* than the consolidation of the state apparatus in its modern administrative form. Without mature political elites, far more of the burden of ensuring state stability was placed on the civil service, which had to be a force for continuity coping with late emergence into modernity in Japan (and with successive revolutionary upheavals in France). Political elites were distrustful of allowing the national bureaucracy to control their own selection and socialization processes in the way that political elites in the UK and USA could tolerate. Instead Japan (and France) relied primarily on formal, organizational socialization processes within strongly defined ministries to educate and mould civil servants towards deference for the public interest. University education played a lesser role in recruitment; passage through state-run, internal education processes and competitions counted for far more. The result in Japan was a strong civil service, where administrative officials developed powerful loyalties to the ministries where they made life-long careers, and the main overarching affiliations were nationalism and loyalty to the Emperor, replaced in the post-war period by loyalty to the constitution. At the same time, Japanese ministries were dominated by generalist administrators (often lawyers from top universities like Tokyo). In many respects post-War Japanese culture assigns a lot of weight to scientific and technological experts. But this pattern was not generally followed within the powerful central government ministries on IT issues. Instead, administrative elites remained unversed in IT problems applying to their own work, and from the 1960s onwards outsourced IT provision very largely to major Japanese electronics and IT corporations. IT staff within government never rose near to the top.

The apparent importance of the politics/administration interface and of mechanisms for recruiting and socializing administrative elites in differentiating national civil service systems so strongly from each other suggested that Weber's insistence on the importance of information systems in modern bureaucracies was overdone. The continued predominance of generalist administrative elites with little detailed or professional knowledge of government IT issues encouraged the view that managing information issues was a relatively routine function. Both these influences boosted 'intitutionalist' interpretations of how government is run, which emphasized that administrative arrangements are path dependent, shaped by contingent arrangements and influenced chiefly by political and public expectations, rather than by technological or functional imperatives. So functional imperatives acting on government organizations were downplayed or ignored. Public administration and organization theory accounts became fixated by the task of identifying the character of national civil services, and neglected the more 'routinized' aspects of bureaucracies' operations. So key elements in Weber's initially unitary model, the ways in which paperwork and IT support government organizations as socio-technical systems, were pushed firmly into a 'taken-for-granted' background.

(ii) *The focus of state growth on professional bureaucracies, making little use of IT.* Weber's concept of bureaucracy as the cutting edge of modernization and rationalization processes also came under sustained attack from another direction, especially within sociology and organization theory, an attack that had important implications for modern welfare states. Studies in the sociology of the professions argued that Weber's prediction of the growing dominance of hierarchical bureaucracies was startlingly inaccurate as a characterization of trends in the advanced industrial countries during the twentieth century. Instead of machine bureaucracies policing giant rule books, the most rapidly growing forms of government organization were what Mintzberg terms 'professional bureaucracies'— like hospitals, health service organizations, universities, schools, and social services departments.

In addition, the key occupational groups running the new welfare state agencies were organized on a completely different basis, stressing the strong development of knowledge by an occupational community, the meritocratic and knowledge-based differentiation of ranks or influence within that community, the work autonomy of individual professionals, and commitment either to the welfare of the clients for professional services (patients, schoolchildren, or students) and/or to an impersonal ideal of scientific or technological progress. The reasons for these striking differences are not hard to find. The decision costs for politicians in trying to specify how the treatment of citizens or enterprises is to be organized or structured are typically much lower or more manageable in most areas handled by machine (or divisionalized) bureaucracies. In a sphere like taxation or welfare benefits, politicians can either retain control of key issues themselves (such as how much tax rates should be) or else require a bureaucracy to prepare under their supervision a detailed rule book on how to determine eligibility for transfers etc., which officials must then follow. By contrast, in professionalized policy areas politicians inherently cannot say how patients with particular symptoms are to be treated, nor can they decide themselves how to build safe nuclear power plants or which chemicals to license for industrial use. Instead they are forced to concentrate on just establishing the basic architecture of organizations and budgets in a policy sector and then specifying that professionally qualified staff be employed to decide on how service delivery is to be carried out in detail. These professional staff may make many detailed decisions largely autonomously, albeit operating within politically determined budgets and general public service rules.

These differences between the Weberian and professional models are well captured in Mintzberg's morphological analysis of the structure of a *professionalized bureaucracy,* shown in Figure 1. 5. Here the dominant part of the organization is the operating core, where individual professionals operate with more-than-ordinary levels of discretion, controlling their own work tasks and units. Such staffs mainly use professional collegiality and networks to achieve coordination among themselves. Only a small 'middle line' is shown in the Figure and a very restricted controlling apex, often run mainly by committees composed of senior professionals or staff internally seconded from the operating core. Within this organizational form the professional heads of sections or divisions may operate almost as feudal barons and be only weakly coordinated against their will. In the classical version of this pattern there is almost no technostructure, because interfering with professional autonomy (e.g. the clinical freedom of doctors or the professional behaviour of lawyers) is not permitted. But there are often extensive support services, run in very tightly controlled machine bureaucracy ways—because the professional staffs want to minimize any diversion of financial or other resources away from their organization's key mission.

Universities, schools systems, and hospital services in both the public and private sectors fit this pattern quite closely. Since the 1980s in some countries the public sector versions of professionally controlled agencies have tended to move somewhat towards the machine bureaucracy pattern, with stronger middle lines and technostructures and more substantial controlling apexes emerging. Other state agencies staffed by 'semi-professions', like social work agencies, have always been more ambiguously organized in ways intermediate between the machine and professional bureaucracy patterns.

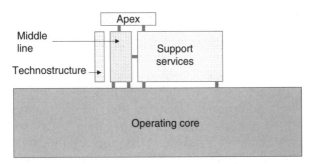

Figure 1.5. The structure of a professionalized bureaucracy, after Mintzberg
Source: Mintzberg (1983).

Professional groups grew fast under corporate and state patronage, and their characteristic bureaucracies concentrated power in the professional staffs within the operating core, close to the clients being served. So these kinds of organization were very slow to develop IT compared with private businesses and even compared with government machine bureaucracies. As late as the 1990s professional bureaucracies characteristically had simpler and more old-fashioned paperwork systems, which resisted computerization and automation for decades after large business corporations. Thus the pattern of post-War welfare state growth favoured organizations with much less developed IT systems and paper file registries. Alongside them, the Weberian machine bureaucracies with more developed information-processing routines seemed less modern and more residual to contemporary public management tasks. The decentralization of professional bureaucracies to state or regional governments and to local authorities contributed a further twist to the weighting of late twentieth century government growth towards less IT-intensive organizations. There has been a general and repeated pattern of a lower level of IT development in smaller government units than in large national bureaucracies.

This pattern also meant that IT had relatively less impact on a huge range of government tasks, in the deployment of organized expertise (the 'E' tool in the typology reviewed above). Much of the expertise in civilian government of the welfare state era remained steadily uninfluenced by computerization, office automation and even the financial IT waves—especially in law, in care sectors like public health care or social work, and for a long time in education. This process began to change rapidly from the mid-1990s onwards, first with the high-expertise sectors catching up with the general trend towards pervasive computing in basic organization activities, and later accepting an accounting and management information toolkit (see Kurunmaki 1999a, 1999b). The general Internet wave had a powerful effect on these services. But many professional sectors of the state are still developing their use of ICTs, a long lag which has had significant consequences for public management and organization theory as well.

The chief exceptions to this low weighting of IT occurred in those professionalized government agencies that formed component parts of divisionalized bureaucracies, often handling issues with a high-technology or scientific content. These organizations' fundamental missions made for an earlier and more intensive use of IT. But the US big science and big-tech agencies seemed in the cold war era, and still seem today, like special cases compared with the rest of American government.

They also have much more modest counterparts overseas, even in large countries like the UK (with a relatively large defence sector) or Japan (where the defence sector was constrained in the post-War period for other reasons). But even in apparently favourable contexts like these, the impact of occupational groups specializing in IT within organizations was often weak, compared with say physical scientists and technologists, or engineers—reflecting the difficulties that IT faced in getting recognized as a profession on its own within government.

(iii) *The slow development of IT professionalism.* A large part of the problem here reflects a more general condition for IT occupations—that they are highly fragmented from each other. In none of the countries that we studied are they typically constituted as any kind of cohesive or effective 'IT profession'. This is true generally and with additional lags and complexities in the public sector, where we might otherwise have expected that there was scope for IT professionalism to find a niche. Traditionalists' idea of the ultimate core IT occupational groups are computer science and computer engineering. But Denning (2001) lists nineteen occupations as 'IT-specific disciplines', sixteen 'IT-intensive disciplines' of which nine are primarily IT-focused, and an additional nine 'IT-supportive occupations' (such as computer technicians, help desk technicians, or web designers). Even amongst the IT-specific disciplines there are differences about the importance of different kinds of knowledge and organizations.

And variations in the make-up of differently weighted IT staffs seem to generate distinct patterns of performance, things that the organization is good at and things that it does not do well. The values, curricula, and roles of different IT professionals differ sharply, and their practices vary a great deal (even if they can agree on some basic principles of knowledge). In addition, the emphasis on clear standards of performance in classically successful professions is not evident in most IT contexts. Nor does the IT field have strong rules on ethics and responsibilities to the client. Instead of having well-developed and inclusive IT profession alignments, many people in these occupational groups have only an organizational orientation (more or less strong and public-interested), plus maybe a degree of client orientation or knowledge orientation. Technology professional staffs have a fuzzy sense of an alternative broader IT identity, mainly created and sustained by reading IT trade papers or specialist journals. 'So we are in a paradox. The IT profession is a historical necessity and yet we have progressed little beyond being a collection of crafts' (Denning 2001: 5). Many of the key inventions, such as the hypertext protocol that created the Web and the first browser were invented by non-IT professionals. And most progress in IT hard core areas or computational science now depends on computer scientists, engineers, and mathematicians working in mixed professional, sector-specific teams. In business (especially the big systems integrators and IT consultancies) and in many governmental contexts it is hard to see IT managers and workers as standing out much from the general run of techno-bureaucratic employees.

Within some government systems changes have been made more recently, discussed in detail in the next chapter, to develop a strong corps of IT professionals, give them greater cohesiveness and more of a common culture, extend their professionalism (partly to counter the loss of expertise to contractors), and to create a top-tier of IT jobs that better reflect the centrality of IT for agencies' operations and for the overall level of government investment in IT and e-government. There are some signs that these initiatives have had a degree of success, just as moves in private sector firms towards appointing chief information officers (CIOs) to sit alongside the better established chief technologists have done. By contrast the role of 'Chief Knowledge Officer' is much better developed and influential in firms. In government agencies the CKO role does not exist often, and where it does it is staffed mainly by lower-level staff. But these partly successful or promising innovations have been too recent to yet offset the basic pattern. IT has been far less important in most professionalized public sector organizations than in private business or even in government machine bureaucracies. And there is, as yet, no coherent IT profession either in general or in government.

To sum up these different influences, for much of the twentieth century the progress in IT automation and paperwork routinization was strongest in the older established machine bureaucracies and weakest in the rapidly growing and more fashionable professional bureaucracies. The importance of information factors was recognized in a few studies, but their influence was offset by the weight of work in public administration and public management focusing on what differentiates bureaucratic systems, rather than what makes them similar. The status of academic work (like professional work) is influenced by the power and status of its subjects, and the fact that IT staffs have been insulated from reaching the top positions in public agencies and generally confined to specialist staff enclaves contributed to government IT not being a fashionable area for study. Only in some of the large US federal departments and agencies with scientific or technological briefs created in the cold war were IT staff (or before them paperwork-handling staff) close to top-level decision-makers. Finally, with most governmental agencies lagging behind private sector corporations in their adoption of new IT systems (again with important exceptions in defence and intelligence computing), government IT has seemed intellectually and socially a backwater area.

Like most organizations government agencies reacted in an understandable but perhaps slightly perverse way to the post-war progress in the routinization of paperwork and later the advances in ICTs. In any organization where a function ceases to absorb human attention and operates in a stable and predictable way, that function will tend to move down the prioritization agenda for key decision-makers, however fundamental or 'mission critical' it may be for organizational success. For instance, pricing goods and stock control in supermarkets has become much easier and less demanding of human time and capacity since the introduction of electronic tills that can hold and change product price details and automatically reorder products from central warehouses or suppliers as they are sold to customers. Hence, store managers have to think about this function less and assign fewer staff to monitor it, moving it down their list of concerns. This trend cannot easily be reversed. Perhaps only a power blackout or an IT system collapse preventing the supermarket from selling any goods at all can actually bring home to the managers and staff involved how vital stock control still remains. In the same way within government organizations, the primary impact of new systems of well-functioning government IT, was a tendency for it to drop off top decision-makers' agenda in favour of continued, less routinized problems, chiefly human resource management, organizational culture issues, and managing crises.

Conclusions

'One evidence of the degree of novelty of the computer's capabilities', Simon wrote:

is the resistance it evokes from those who refuse to see in it anything more than an enlarged desk calculator. Not since the Darwinian controversy of the past century have we seen such a passionate defence of the uniqueness of man [sic] against claims of kinship by systems that don't belong to his species. (1973: 503)

Unhappily the closure of the Darwinian controversy that Simon saw as an accomplished fact in 1973 still looks far from obvious thirty three years on, under sustained political challenge from Christian and Islamic fundamentalists, both in the USA and in developing countries. The strong forces in public administration and public management combining to marginalize attention to the central role of IT processes in the government sector are not in any way comparable. But they do draw on a rather pervasive human response of overvaluing our own immediate roles above those of embedded background systems. We have argued that two key Weberian insights were lost sight of—that bureaucracies are socio-technical systems; and that the organization of information-processing is key to bureaucratization pushing ahead (for better or worse) the modernization and rationalization of human conduct. We turn next to exploring how some of the factors reviewed here have been involved in the acquiring and management of government IT in our seven case study countries, through our analysis period from 1994 to 2005.

Note

1. The collegia referred to here are those of the Prussian cameralist system, in which offices were controlled by a collective leadership.

2

Acquiring and Managing Government IT

In November 1998 the New Zealand government issued a guide to all the country's businesses entitled 'E-Commerce: The "Freezer Ship" of the Twenty-first Century'. This heading (obscure to an outsider) was explained by the Minister of Information Technology in his introduction:

Over a century ago, a breakthrough in technology brought increased wealth and prosperity to New Zealand when the *SS Dunedin* transported the first shipment of frozen meat to our major market in Britain. This brought about far reaching improvements to our economy and standard of living. Today, digital communications technology has the same potential. (NZ Ministry of Commerce 1998: 1)

Granted that both were technology shifts, in all other respects the analogy between the Internet and refrigeration ships is not a close one. Its use might be taken as rather neatly illustrating the institutionalist case that governments and officials tend to process new phenomena as far as they can in terms of what is already familiar.

Four years later when we visited Wellington the government had a few IT-related successes to chalk up (e.g. in electronic animation for movies on the back of *Lord of the Rings* being filmed there). But by then it seemed clear that New Zealand had largely missed the boat on the dot.com boom. Certainly by comparison with other small countries, such as Finland or Singapore, New Zealand's e-commerce and digital IT successes were limited. There were no doubt multiple reasons for this inability to exploit opportunities. But there were also some critical elements missing from the New Zealand policy mix in the 1990s. In particular, the government's verbal encouragement of e-commerce was clearly not backed by any effective e-government strategy for its own services nor any very substantial e-society initiatives—both were inaugurated only in late 2001, by which time the dot-com boom period was already past. Perhaps not coincidentally the New Zealand GDP in 2002 was second from bottom in the Organization for Economic Cooperation and Development (OECD) rankings (above Turkey).

This story mirrors a lesson that all the governments in our case study countries learnt and took to heart during the period from 1995 to 2002, that the arrival of the Internet and the digital era required governments to raise their game technologically if they were to have any chance of encouraging citizens and enterprises to do so as well. This connection was first made in a strong way by the Singapore government and appreciated early on in Australia and Canada, and in a somewhat uncoordinated way by US federal officials. The UK and the Netherlands followed close behind. Japan and New Zealand were slower to develop e-government initiatives related to the Internet.

By linking themes of national competitiveness, economic modernization and radical private sector change with how governments conducted their internal affairs, Internet and web changes transformed the context for government IT policymaking, producing new pressures for a degree of central coordination of government IT issues, discussed in the first section here. At the same time, changes in the contracting of IT pushed ahead the development of the global market in building and maintaining government IT systems, discussed in our second section.

2.1 The Internet and the Centralization of Government IT Policy

Earlier ITs were largely internally facing, with a clear potential for transforming administrative tasks and reducing costs but few possibilities for changing the way that government communicated with citizens. The Internet changed all that, as the World Wide Web system of hyperlinks offered citizens the opportunity to access information from any location. As citizens started to use the Internet, more organizations began offering information and other facilities online and a critical mass of users and suppliers rapidly developed. By 2003, more than 500 million people worldwide had Internet access. In the US and Canada the percentage of households with Internet access rose from below 10 per cent in 1997 to over 60 per cent in 2003. In the UK, penetration doubled between 2000 and 2002. By the turn of the century a bewildering range of global online organizations were leaping into the public eye: mortgage brokers (John Charcol), travel companies (easyjet.com), auctions (ebay), bookshops (Amazon.com). Although the bursting of the 'dot.com' bubble in 2000 brought the downfall of 5,000 Internet start-ups and the Nasdaq tech stock market fell 25 per cent in a week, the number of Internet users and e-commerce sales continued to grow strongly thereafter. By 2002, commentators were observing that buying habits had changed forever and the original predictions made at the peak of the dot.com boom were coming true. By 2002, online retail sales reached £8 billion annually in the UK (up 95 per cent on 2001) and US$48 billion (up 34 per cent) in the US. By this time too eBay had 60 million registered users worldwide and 40 per cent of America's 209 publicly quoted dot.com companies traded profitably (*Sunday Times* 24 March 2003). As citizens began to witness the transformation of their relationship with many private sector agencies (banks, shops, and travel agents, in particular) they began to expect to interact with government electronically also.

Governments too began to perceive the potential for new forms of government–citizen interactions. The development of the Internet and the World Wide Web presented a key opportunity for government to provide higher quality services directly to citizens in innovative ways at lower cost. It facilitated improvements in the provision of information to the public, especially allied with 'open government' and 'freedom of information' policies. Information can be made available via the Web 24 hours a day, whatever location people are accessing from. Customers who know their own personal circumstances in detail can search for exactly the information they require. There is scope for many citizens to conduct most of their business with government electronically. Web-based technologies can also be used to facilitate 'joined-up' government. Websites can provide virtual front-ends or entry points to otherwise fragmented organizational arrangements, allowing citizens to transact with several departments and agencies and across different tiers of government simultaneously. Someone newly out of work, for example, could use government websites to look for and apply for a job, but also claim and receive benefits, obtain information about starting up a small business, or find out about retraining and apply for educational courses. In general, governments have been much slower than commercial firms to realize the potential of the Internet and associated technologies. But from 2000 onwards the potential of e-government has been evident to most commentators, particularly given the phenomenal rise of e-commerce over the period 2000 to 2005.

With widespread use of the Internet, IT policy rose much higher up the political agenda in all of our case study countries and reached the attention of policymakers as it never had before. By the start of the twenty-first century, governments in all seven countries had some kind of e-government initiative. Three of our case study countries were particularly quick off the mark: the US, Australia, and Canada. In the UK a low key initiative in 1996 was transformed into a major government commitment by the new Labour government in autumn 1997. In the Netherlands, an effective government portal was operating by 2001. Japan apparently moved earlier than New Zealand in picking up the need for some e-government activity in 1999 as part of any effective e-society change push, but progress by 2002 was slow.

The new focus on e-government brought a revival of some kind of central IT policy in several of our countries. New initiatives were combined with existing arrangements, which in most cases had survived from the 1950s and 1960s, undergoing various reforms in line with more general technological and managerial change. In the 1950s, when government IT was seen as highly expensive and specialized, there was little central coordination because IT was seen as part of and specific to scientific or defence agencies' high-technology activity. The spread of computing in the 1960s and 1970s into many more agencies led to the creation of more centralized controls and checks. IT was still seen as an expensive and rarified element of administrative systems, so central departments wanted checks on what spending departments and agencies were doing, to control costs and to ensure that the agencies new to computerization were not behaving as naive customers, as well as to try and impose some sort of standardization. By the late 1970s and early 1980s there were central agencies checking IT bids from spending departments prior to authorization, paralleling the well-established budgetary and personnel control systems. And in many governments either the same agencies or central agencies with a servicing role were also running some specialized or common IT systems (like payrolls); providing IT advice and expertise and sometimes procurement services to smaller government agencies; and trying to maintain some standards in both the design of government computer systems and in IT contracting.

This centralization trend did not continue. Instead from the 1980s until the mid-1990s the apparatus of central controls of IT and central concentrations of IT expertise was radically reduced. Especially in the strong NPM countries like the UK, New Zealand, and Australia, IT was seen as solely the responsibility of the commissioning departments and agencies, to be run in a decentralized manner. Just as central controls of personnel and detailed budget allocations were thinned out in favour of controlling the total budget going to agencies, so specific IT controls were dismantled and central concentrations of IT expertise were closed down. The commodification of IT with the spread of low-cost PCs and falling prices for IT equipment spurred this trend along, making IT less of a special or costly feature and more of a routine part of agency business processes. The growth of a bigger government IT market, and the rise of large systems integrator firms, also leant weight to the argument that this was now a 'normal' procurement market, best left to agencies and departments to manage in a decentralized manner. A background factor also was the disengagement of many governments from having either explicit or tacit 'national champions' in the IT field. For instance, the UK government stopped supporting the British company ICL against IBM (as it had done in the 1970s), and later on in Canada the North American Free Trade Agreement (NAFTA) decreased government support for the Canadian company Corel against Microsoft in the office packages market. Even where the NPM movement made little distinctive impact, as in the USA, the normalization of IT procurement went ahead fast under the National Performance Review (NPR) process in the 1990s. Procurement restrictions on buying IT were eased and agency purchasing of IT was greatly simplified with the growth of governmentwide acquisition contracts (GWACs) that allowed one agency with IT arrangements to supply other agencies with smaller contract needs. Only in two countries did the decentralization period make little impact—in Japan and the Netherlands where there had never been a centralized IT capability, although in the latter there was still an overall concern with promoting the use of IT and analysing the impacts of 'informatization'.

By the mid-1990s when e-commerce began to grow fast and government websites first started mushrooming in the USA, there was little by way of centralized machinery for controlling government IT in most of our countries. So the e-business angle created some difficulties of coordination for governments. The encouragement of e-commerce devolved to industry or trade ministries, while separate departments or regulators were often in control of telecoms infrastructure policy (critical for the development of Internet service providers and later of broadband). At first there were commonly no central agencies responsible for public sector organizations picking up web-based methods, for encouraging or coordinating the provision of Internet-based information on government services, or for ensuring that issues of IT-literacy and Internet familiarization were tackled in schools and universities. Most countries at first responded to the Internet challenge by adapting the bits and pieces of machinery still available to them to centrally monitor or manage information systems in general.

In the USA, the Internet sparked immediate interest in the scientific and business communities. Even in government there was widespread interest—for instance, pre-Internet forms of messaging using mainframes and networks were already being used by some administrators and officials in the early 1990s. So it was no surprise that e-government targets were set early on. In the 1994, NPR Al Gore's Access America initiative promised to provide all citizens with electronic access to government by 2000, by connecting every classroom, library, hospital, and clinic to a national information infrastructure.

This apparently strong initiative was to be carried forward by a proliferation of central agencies, initiatives, and committees. The NPR established the Government Information Technology Services Board, which branched off in 1996 to promote cross-agency service applications. The General Services Administration (GSA) played a role in encryption and digital security and within GSA, the Federal Technology Service offered agencies various services through its 'smart government' and 'connected government' initiatives, such as systems integration support and outsourcing advice. The Office of Management and Budget (OMB) played a role in overseeing electronic service delivery (ESD) commitments, mandating agencies to offer all government services electronically by 2003, as part of legislation brought together in successive revisions of the Government Paperwork Reduction Act (1995). OMB was also responsible for overseeing implementation of a CIO initiative (part of the Clinger-Cohen Act of 1996) across the federal government, under which Cabinet agencies were mandated to name a CIO who reported directly to the agency head and had primary responsibility for all IT activities. These CIOs were brought together in a Interagency Chief Information Officers' Council, with six subcommittees and a budget allocation to formulate various aspects of online policy, which played a prominent role in the US government's handling of the Y2K (Year 2000) problem.

Australia was the next country after the USA to respond on e-government, developing an international reputation in the field that peaked around 1999. In December 1997, the prime minister set explicit targets for ESD by the Federal Government, promising that by 2001 'all appropriate services would be delivered electronically'. The social background was supportive, with 34 per cent of Australian households having home Internet access and 57 per cent PCs by 2001 (*Canberra Connect* 2001: 10–11).

In agency terms the Australian federal Department of Communications, Information Technology, and the Arts was a central player. Its creation meant that there was, in effect, a Minister for Information Technology. Within the Department, two units were created: the Office for Government On-line and the National Office for the Information Economy, providing advice and support to the government and matters which were Internet-specific. In addition, the On-line Council was established in 1997 as a Commonwealth initiative to foster cooperation on online issues between the commonwealth, states and territories.

Canada was also an early mover in terms of e-government, with the Government On-Line (GOL) initiative in 2000 promising to 'use information and communication technology to enhance Canadians' access to improved client-centred, clustered services, anytime anywhere and in the official language of their choice' (Accenture 2005: 60). It had an initial two-year funding of C$600 million and the aim was to complete the strategy by 2005. GOL also mandated that by 2002, all government websites must use common navigational tools and formats and conform to a 'Common Look and Feel': 'the intent is to make it easier for citizens and businesses to recognize, navigate and use federal websites and services' (*Government On-Line Report* January 2002). The GOL initiative was aided by the fact that Canadians were at the time amongst the most connected to the Internet in the world, second in overall connectivity only to the USA. Even by 2001, two-thirds of Canadians had Internet access, spending an average of nine hours per week on the Internet—more than any other nation (*Communication Canada* Spring 2001). Over half of Canadian Internet users had visited a Government of Canada website and 73 per cent believed that putting services and information online was a good use of tax dollars (*Listening to Canadians* 2001). The Canadian government viewed e-government as a potential stimulator for societal Internet usage and growth in the e-economy, rather than as a (late) by-product of Internet use by other organizations as in some of our other countries: 'We need to stimulate economic growth by investing more in moving government online, for everything from paying taxes to finalizing government purchases. Not only would this be a more effective use of taxpayers' money, the work of designing those systems would fall to Canadian e-business' (*E-Business Opportunities Roundtable* 7 December 2001). The government used a different, more user-focused, target regime to the other countries, undertaking a commitment to improve Canadians' satisfaction with its service delivery by a measure of 10 per cent by 2005.

The Canadian approach to administering these initiatives was a mixture of centralization and cross-agency 'buy-in'. The flagship GOL programme was centrally coordinated by the Treasury Board (acting as a 'cheerleader' for e-government) and led by the Government's CIO, a position created much earlier than in any of our other case study countries. Setting up this role seems to have created a key political champion for e-government, sending an important message both domestically and internationally. In addition, the particularly enthusiastic incumbent in the early 2000s, Mel Cap, clearly played a personal role in raising the profile of e-government in Canada and getting the GOL programme off the ground. The CIO coordinated the cross-agency and 'horizontal management' approach that has been central to Canada's 'whole of government' website design and was, according to our interviewees, 'one of the most effective governing structures in the Government of Canada'. A committee of deputy ministers provided further leadership, supported by a committee of departmental CIOs. Within the Treasury Board, the Board of Public Works has traditionally played a role rather similar to that of the Central Computer and Telecommunications Agency (CCTA) in the UK (see below), originally 'owning' all computers in government and still playing a role in procurement. For systems integration contracts, all departments have to go through Public Works who issue the request for procurement and charges an overhead. In the 2000s, the agency headed up the major Secure Channel project to create an intergovernmental network.

The UK was also quick off the mark with some rhetoric of e-government, but its concerted policy effort followed (and even mimicked) Australia and the USA. The theme of e-government was picked up by both Conservative and Labour governments during the election campaign of 1997 with politicians from both major parties claiming to be the 'British Al Gore' (Margetts 1999). In autumn 1997 Tony Blair used his Labour conference speech to pledge that by 2002 at least 25 per cent of all government interactions with citizens would be 'electronic'. By April 1999 the *Modernizing Government* white paper put in place later targets of 50 per cent 'electronic' interactions by 2005 and 100 per cent by 2008, a target later brought forward to 2005 after a study for the National Audit Office found that the 2008 date was untaxing (NAO 1999*a*).

IT policy and strategy in the UK became more centralized, with the old NPM stance of leaving departments and agencies to manage their own services slowly rolled back. Previously, there had been a kind of serial monogamy over time, with one agency—frequently changing name and organizational location—taking responsibility for IT systems in government. Until 1984, the responsible body was the CCTA (formerly CCA) which actually 'owned' around 80 per cent of administrative computers in government and played a major oversight role in IT projects throughout the 1980s. From 1984 the CCTA's role diminished to a minimal background role, running some government Web services for instance. Its various responsibilities mainly moved to the Treasury until 1995 when a small Central Information Technology Unit (CITU) was formed within the Cabinet Office to secure 'a strategic approach to IT across the government' (*Financial Times* 8 November 1995). Later, CITU was merged into the new Office of the e-Envoy (OeE), established in autumn 1999 with a high profile head reporting to the PM. OeE was charged to both make Britain 'the best place in the world to carry on e-commerce' and to marshal and direct the government's ESD efforts. The agency expanded rapidly (with 200 staff and running costs of around £50 million at its peak in 2001) and developed a new but not very successful government portal (called UK Online) which started operating in spring 2001. Control mechanisms for the e-Government targets ran through the OeE but also the Treasury's system of Public Service Agreements (PSAs) and subordinate service-level agreements which specify output and efficiency improvement targets for departments and agencies. By 2004, however, there was concern that the OeE was providing limited return on investment and the office was scaled down and remodelled as the e-Government Unit under a new Head of e-Government, also in the Cabinet Office. The new Unit has responsibility for IT systems across the government and the IT profession as a whole, but less of an emphasis on the front-end of e-Government. In 2005, its *Transformational Government* programme signalled a belated copying of many much earlier US and Canadian initiatives, including the expectation that all major IT-using agencies would have a CIO and the creation of a Council of CIOs for the first time in Britain. This aimed to promote a more collegial and less directive central learning and coordination of IT and the better development of professionalism amongst the UK's 50,000 central government IT staff.

In the Netherlands, both society and government have a long history of successful use of ICTs. Internet penetration in the Netherlands is high, 46 per cent in spring 2001 (compared with 34 per cent in the UK at the same time) and 77 per cent by 2002 (OECD 2004: 159). Even by 2001 more than 90 per cent of Dutch households reportedly had a PC at home, for example, a very high number relative to neighbouring European countries, partly due to an initiative in which citizens were given tax benefits for purchasing PCs through employers – something that was discussed in the UK only in the mid-2000s (*Guardian* 11 September 2004). The Netherlands has long prioritized the development of IT, for example, spending 2.3 per cent of GDP on IT in 1989 compared with 2 per cent in the UK and USA. At an academic conference in Den Haag in 1991, a minister in her opening address claimed 'I am responsible for all IT systems in the Dutch government', a claim it is hard to imagine her UK or US equivalent making at that time. The government of 2001 even announced in its coalition agreement its intention to 'devote attention to the processes of shaping the information society, as a whole' (Infodrome 1999: 3). The government's first major e-government programme, the *Dutch Digital Delta*, was a joint initiative by the Ministry of Economic Affairs, the Ministry of the Interior and Kingdom Relations, the Ministry of Finance, the Ministry of Justice, the Ministry of Education, Culture and Science, and the Ministry of Transport, Public Works and Water Management with 70 million gilder (about £20 million) spent on it every year, in 1999, 2000, and 2001. In addition, each department produced a policy paper and devoted further funding to initiatives contained in those. The Digital Delta document outlined the targets for ESD at 25 per cent by 2002, but the target was later played down by the government and there were no subsequent targets set.

The highly networked nature of Dutch public administration works against central control and coordination. The department with responsibility for e-government was the Ministry of the Interior and Kingdom Relations. The strongest measures it would admit to was a policy of 'keep it small' and 'open coordination'. But the Ministry (with three ministers and 3,000 civil servants) contained the Directorate-General for Public Administration which examined the options and dilemmas surrounding the use of IT in the relationship between citizens and government. From the mid-1980s the Minister for Urban Policy and Integration of Ethnic Minorities was also responsible for government information systems and related policy areas such as municipal personal records databases and travel documents (including passports). The incumbent in 2001 (Roger van Boxtel) was particularly enthusiastic about all IT innovations and had a chat page on his home site, where he encouraged citizens to give their views on e-government. The Ministry of the Interior and Kingdom Relations created the portal site www.overheid.nl–as well as providing a guide to citizens, it was used to stimulate web-based initiatives across governmental organizations. For example, the site included a report on the 'Web Wiser' award, a monthly ranking of local governments, ministries, and agencies, with a first prize awarded by the Minister. It seemed to be successful in encouraging innovation, as many local aldermen were keen to see their local government at the top of the list. The Ministry conducted a number of initiatives to stimulate societal use of the Internet, including provision of grants to local governments and agencies to work together. The 'Digital Playground' initiative involved creating public Internet cafes in the Netherlands' thirty biggest cities; each city got one cafe, funded half by the government and half by local private companies and the largest cities extended the initiative to create more. In Rotterdam, there was even an initiative to give homeless people email addresses, so that at least they had some form of contact address. Early in 2004, the government started a new programme called Andere Overheid (Different Government), emphasizing improving government services through cooperation with other agencies.

New Zealand was a small country with an agriculturally based economy confronting poor terms of trade and slipping rapidly down the OECD rankings. But with a well-educated, English-speaking, and technologically open population, it could have expected to gain much from e-commerce and e-government. More than 1,200 miles away from any other land mass, New Zealanders have always been quick to pick up on technological trends that enhance communication, and they were early converts to the Internet. But the Liberal-led coalition government elected in 1996 gave e-commerce scant attention and e-government none at all. Nor was e-commerce an early priority for the incoming Labour-led coalition in 1999, pre-occupied with its social agenda. A strategy was eventually unveiled only in April 2001, approximately four years after the UK and Australian political initiatives and more than five years after Singapore (NZ State Services Commission 2001). The strategy was mainly a kind of indicative planning or framework document, with agencies exhorted to consider Internet- and web-based systems and to work together jointly, but without there being any additional or tagged budget line for such developments.

New Zealand developed a highly fragmented structure of government under the NPM changes that it pioneered (see Chapter 4). So a centralized approach to e-government emerged only gradually. The Ministry of Economic Development began a slow process of gathering political and administrative support for e-commerce initiatives around 1999. In mid-2000, the State Services Commission (SSC) set up a unit with around forty staff to development a separate e-government strategy, reversing years of disengagement of the centre from IT policy issues in favour of agency autonomy. The e-government unit worked on a raft of background issues, coordinating the development of government-wide metadata and web protocols, fostering interoperability standards, working on a government portal to arrive in mid-2002, addressing public key infrastructure (PKI) issues, and encouraging the development of e-procurement.

The Japanese government also came late to developing systematic policies for the Internet era. Although it invested heavily, and as it turned out rather abortively, in encouraging 'fifth generation' computers in the mid-1980s, the hardware orientation of its technology ministries meant that it was slow to appreciate the possibilities of the new era. And in contrast to the Netherlands and perhaps surprisingly given its reputation as a 'high-tech' nation, IT was slow to diffuse in Japan. Even by 1999, only around 25 per cent of households had a personal computer (OECD 2004: 354). Japanese ministries had adopted mainframe computer systems relatively early but they remained strictly departmental specific until 1994. At this point, the Cabinet produced a 'Master Plan for the Promotion of Governmentwide Use of Information Technology' with revisions in 1997 and 1999. It promoted information-sharing across departments and the use of IT in the interface between society and the government. By 2000 all ministry and agency head offices had websites and there were over one PC per staff member across central offices. In some respects the image of government IT seemed advanced. Visiting government offices in 2002 we were struck by the prevalence of portable PCs, with not a single desktop PC to be seen across whole floors of offices, in a period when US or UK government offices uniformly relied on bulky desktop machines.

But in 2001, a damning report by the Ministry of Economy, Trade and Industry concluded from a white paper on international trade that Japanese companies' IT strategies were weak and that a lack of competition, high costs, and bad IT infrastructure needed to be addressed immediately if Japan was to catch up (*Financial Times* 22 May 2001). In response, the e-Japan strategy was announced in 2001, whereby all administrative procedures would be available electronically by 2003 as part of the Prime Minister's campaign to turn Japan into an 'IT superpower'. E-government was perceived as both supporting the administrative reform of 2001 and demanding it—that a revision of Japanese public administration would be necessary before introducing ICTs. An e-government portal site began operation in 2001, consisting of a homepage retrieval system, an administrative document management retrieval system, and an administrative procedure retrieval system (Furukawa 2001). It was not very citizen oriented, in spite of the claims of the e-Japan strategy and was geared mainly at providing government information rather than services (Accenture 2002). Internet use charges in Japan at the time were three times higher than in the USA and most of Europe, and the percentage of regular Internet users was relatively low at around 38 per cent (Accenture 2002) compared with the other countries covered here.

The highly departmentalized nature of Japanese government administration and the long running departmental IT contracts with favoured firms combined to ensure that there was little central control and coordination of IT policy up until the beginning of the 2000s. Even by 2003, central responsibility for Japanese government information systems, including information outsourcing and systems integration, was buried deep in the central bureaucracy, in the Information Planning Division within the Administrative Management Bureau (AMB) of the Ministry of Public Management, Home Affairs, Post and Telecommunications, a department created from three former ministries. From 1999, an Inter-Ministerial Council for Promoting Government-Wide Use of Information Technology, directed by the head of AMB, took responsibility for inter-ministerial coordination towards the development of e-government. But the council only encouraged each ministry to share experiences and it lacked authority to implement policy. Responsibility for the e-Japan Strategy was placed under a newly created IT Strategy Headquarters headed by Prime Minister Junichiro Koizumi, in the attempt to turn Japan into an 'IT nation'. The IT Strategy Headquarters was supposed to mandate every ministry to accomplish the policy goals of e-Japan, but it too seemed to suffer the same lack of authority as the other central bodies. Overall, commentators observed 'a lack of strong leadership ... and a lack of co-ordination' leading to 'poor implementation of policy initiatives concerning information provision' (Koga 2003: 58). For example, the revised IT plans of 1997 mandated that information locator systems would be operative in all ministries and agencies by March 2000. Yet even in July 2002, a very limited number provided data for the locator system on the central government portal and the Ministry of Public Management, Home Affairs, Posts and Telecommunications, the administrator of the portal, was not even providing their own data.

2.2 The Growth of Contracting and the Government IT Market

As IT in general, and the Internet in particular, became increasingly associated with competitiveness and productivity, so the demand for IT expertise accelerated. The size of the worldwide IT services sector was estimated at US$558 billion in 2005, having grown 3 per cent in 2004, a rise predicted to double in 2005. The computer services consultancy Accenture increased its staff by around 20 per cent in 2004 and was predicted to do the same in 2005 (*Business Week* 11 January 2005). This continual competition for technically skilled personnel posed a major challenge to most governments. In the UK, the supply of IT staff had been recognized as a 'recurrent problem' as early as 1978 (Civil Service Department 1978: 50).

By the early 2000s, governments in most of our case study countries were employing strategies to foster IT skills and to incentivize IT professionals to migrate from overseas (OECD 2004), to fill skills gaps across the economy in general and certain sectors in particular. As we discuss later, some governments (the Netherlands and Canada in particular) did retain significant in-house IT capability in all larger departments and agencies. The Australian Tax Office, the Canada Customs and Revenue Agency, and the US Social Security Administration are all examples of major transaction processing departments that maintained large IT divisions right up until the early 2000s. But there is no doubt that the need for new types of specialist technical skills and expertise and the increasing challenge of retaining them while operating in a continually changing technological environment caused most governmental organizations at least to consider other options.

One potential response to the need for new skills in government was to buy them from the private sector through some kind of contract arrangement, rather than entering the increasingly fierce competition to recruit IT staff under conventional employment contracts. In fact in all our countries, there had been some kind of private sector involvement from the early days of IT. In the USA, government by contract has in any case been a distinctive feature of federal administration throughout the twentieth century, fitting with the resistance to 'big government' and antagonism towards bureaucracy in general that has always prevailed in American political culture. The outsourcing of government computing has long been at the forefront of this trend, with commercial services as a percentage of IT expenditure in the federal government already being 39 per cent in 1982 and rising to 49 per cent by 1993 (Margetts 1999: 136).

From the 1980s onwards there were two additional drivers towards higher levels of contracting out, again varying across countries. First, across the world there was a growing trend towards outsourcing of IT in the private sector, which by the 1990s the public sector was starting to mimic. And second, in the countries where NPM style reforms were prevalent and included contracting out as a key theme, IT tended to be at the forefront of the trend.

Private sector practice

The first driver was private sector IT practice. From the early days of computing it was recognized that there were economies of scale to be achieved if some companies specialized in the production of computer systems to carry out functions common to most large companies; the earliest market developed for standardized payroll and pension systems and financial management and accounting systems. Over time, more bespoke services became popular, until by the 1980s it was possible to discern several variants of IT contracting (see Willcocks and Fitzgerald 1994: 15; Margetts 1999: 126–7):

- *Ad hoc consultancy*, where private sector consultants are brought in as and when required at any stage through a computer project;
- *Project tendering*, where an individual project is specified for competitive tendering, which the contract company will undertake to supply by a certain deadline;
- *Facilities management*, which typically involves a supplier taking over a specific operation or function on a long-term basis, for example a computer centre;
- *Systems integration*, meaning a company 'knitting together' an alliance of software and hardware, sometimes already existent within the customer's organization and sometimes bought in from third, fourth, and fifth parties;
- *Partnerships*, where a company agrees a 'strategic alliance' with another firm to provide all or a subset of their IT needs;
- *Preferred supplier agreements*, where a client agrees to turn to a given contractor first for IT needs.

In some of these arrangements, the contracting company may act alone but for larger contracts will probably act as a 'prime' contractor, with a number of 'subcontractors'; the prime contractor charges a premium for taking on a share of the risk of the project. Other users may contract a number of suppliers in parallel, one of whom might be charged with project management.

From the late 1980s onwards, the closer relationships between vendors and clients implied by 'systems integration', strategic alliances, and 'partnerships' became popular in the private sector. By the 1990s the average life of an IT contract in Britain and Europe was five to seven years; in the USA it was longer, often ten years. Systems integrators often aimed to develop expertise in a wider range of their clients' activities than merely information systems, since information systems intertwined closely with other service functions. Some of the contracts were seen as real partnership arrangements with an element of risk-sharing, a new outsourcing model involving 'a vertical cut of business process rather than the horizontal cut of information technology' (partner of Andersen Consulting in the *Financial Times* 21 October 1992). By the 1990s the company EDS was signing contacts under which it took on systems development at no cost, in return taking a percentage of the business gains by the customer.

This type of outsourcing or 'total sourcing' as it is sometimes known was influenced by writers in the fields of management and business such as James Quinn (1992), who argued that organizations of all kinds should focus on their 'core competency'. Every manufacturer, for example, should evaluate every service activity in its value chain, determine if it was 'best in world' at that activity, and if not, consider outsourcing the activity to the best-in-world supplier (Quinn 1992: 208–9). To do anything less was to forego a competitive advantage, unless there was some strategic need to retain the service in-house (e.g. to support or join up other areas where a company was indeed 'best in world' or to prevent information about such key areas leaking to competitors). Quinn did not specifically identify IT as a key area for contracting out. Indeed, many of his examples were of private sector companies developing as core competencies the technological infrastructure that they had found necessary to set up to enhance their previously core activities. But arguments like his certainly influenced the strategies of companies that were in any case beginning to realize the problems in managing this complex, technical, and crucial part of their operations, for which they lacked internal skills or resources.

As outsourcing in the private sector continued apace throughout the 1990s, markets of potential contract providers grew up in each of our case study countries. These markets were dominated by two types of company. First, IT services companies, mostly of US origin, such as EDS, CSC, and Unisys, grew rapidly through a series of mergers and acquisitions. Some of these firms were spin-offs from large accountancy or management consultancy firms, such as Accenture and Ernst and Young. Second, as the market for IT services grew and the price of IT equipment fell, so companies that originally specialized in hardware realized that they must diversify in order to succeed. The most notable example is IBM. Between 1992 and 2002, IBM's total revenue increased from US$64.5 billion to US$81.2 billion (a 26 per cent growth), but during the same period IBM services revenue increased from US$7.4 billion to US$36.4 billion (a 392 per cent growth) (OECD 2004*a*: 311).

Public sector trends

Owing to a mixture of factors, outsourcing also became popular among government agencies. Governments too were beginning to realize the difficulties involved in IT development and looked to the private sector for solutions, while these new markets of computer services providers were clearly going to see government as a major source of business, given the size of their operations. The extent to which governments embraced the trend however, varied strongly across our case study countries, with some starting our period with a high level of contracting and others changing greatly over this time. Some of this variation can be put down to another driver towards outsourcing—the extent to which the country embraced public management changes that implied more contracting out and privatization.

In the USA, the federal government computer services market developed early, as with other services to government, due to the predominance of contracting out as a management tool for most of the twentieth century. From the 1970s onwards computer companies clustered around the federal government agencies in Washington forming part of the 'Beltway Bandits' (see Garvey 1993). By 1990, the federal government accounted for 38 per cent of the worldwide facilities management revenue of US-based vendors, compared with 35 per cent for US commercial operations and 7 per cent for state and local governments (International Digital Communications 1993: 3.8). Later many of the companies raised on this market became prominent in one or more of our case study countries. Various contract requirements (see Chapter 5) meant that small players have a favourable environment in the USA, with legislation specifically geared at preserving their role. By the end of the century, the market was large and diffuse, consisting mainly of US-based but global players. IBM, the original computer giant was still prominent, with about 44 per cent of its $86 billion worldwide revenue coming from the USA and very large federal contracts with the Federal Aviation Administration, US Customs, and the US Postal Service. By 2001 even larger than IBM was EDS, with headquarters in Texas but with half of its worldwide markets coming from outside the USA and its 143,000 staff in around 40 countries and 210 cities worldwide. By 2001, EDS held contracts totalling over US$10.3 billion spread over their contracts with the Department of Transport, the Immigration and Naturalization service, the Department of Veterans Affairs,

Department of Justice, the US Census, and the US Postal Service. Both these companies emerge as major players in many of our other case study countries.

Other big players in the US market include CSC, with 68,000 staff worldwide and 10 per cent of its US$6 billion revenue (half of its global total) coming from government contracts. Its largest was the Internal Revenue Service (IRS), worth up to US$15 billion over the contract period and signed in 1998 (see Chapter 6), with other contracts in the Departments of Education, Transport and Immigration and Naturalization. Unisys is a smaller but significant player, with US$1 billion in large contracts with the Social Security Administration (SSA) (a five-year deal worth US$500 million), NASA, the GSA, the Census Office and the Treasury. In the USA, the civilian market is influenced by the budgetary state of defence, with cuts during the 1990s causing defence companies to flood the civilian IT market. By 2003, Lockheed Martin and Dyn Corp were particularly successful, although some federal officials spoke of the latter rather dismissively, questioning why 'emptying the trash cans at army depots' should qualify them to develop government IT systems. In 2001, 30 per cent of Lockheed Martin's US$23 billion sales came from US government systems integration contracts, including large contracts with the US Postal Service, the Environment Protection Agency, the FBI, the Census Bureau, SSA and the Immigration and Naturalization Bureau.

Although situated next door to the USA, and necessarily influenced by the structure of the government IT market there, Canada had a significantly different trajectory in our period. By 2003, the federal government in Ottawa still played a big role in the market, spending around one third of its IT expenditure on its own IT divisions. More than one interviewee from business spoke of the 'insourcing threat' of contracts being actively taken back in-house and several of the major vendors explained ruefully to us that the federal government was their 'greatest competitor'. Canada's new public management (NPM) push was always of a rather moderate kind, with strong cross-currents, such as a concern to not just become beholden to major American IT companies.

Consequently Canada's market remained steadfastly a mixed economy, consisting of both domestic and global companies and fiercely competitive, with no dominant player. The largest domestic player is the company CGI, with 24,000 staff globally and 17,000 in Canada, with 20 per cent of their business in the government sector. By 2003 they had the firearms registry contract and were playing a major part as systems integrator in the Secure Channel consortium, in a contract worth C$1.2 billion over seven years. As in our other case study countries, IBM was viewed by other players as an 'honorary' Canadian company. Two key global companies that might be expected to be successful in the Canadian market suffered major reputational disasters during the last twenty years: EDS, with Income Security, and Accenture. In the 'small world' government city of Ottawa, the success or failure of a government IT contract will be big news, and will 'run and run' in the *Ottawa Citizen*, affecting a company's reputation far into the future. US companies such as Lockheed Martin do well in some fields, winning the Census with IBM, for example. Partnering is important, particularly for domestic companies and IBM, although a couple of larger players took the stance that they would not partner with EDS, who they perceived not to have the partnering mentality and viewed as lacking autonomy—they 'have to go to Texas for approval'. In contrast, small companies are valued and even courted by the larger players in this market, who will self-confessedly 'do anything to win', including inviting a small company to join a contract if they have had some experience with the contracting department.

By contrast, the UK was a relatively late but also a relatively complete convert to contractorization, chiefly reflecting its role as an NPM pioneer. IT was right at the forefront of the NPM trend. For instance, the 'Next Steps' agencies created out of the IT operations of the Department of Transport and of the Inland Revenue were both privatized in their entirety. For other departments, right from 1991 IT was identified as a 'promising area' for contracting out, in an early white paper on market testing (Office of Public Service and Science 1991). The IT activities of thirteen major departments were also earmarked for market testing at that time (Margetts 1999: 150). Indeed, by the mid-1990s the relevant Minster specified IT as one of the areas 'where the Government could not maintain the investment and expertise necessary to compete effectively within the private sector and from which it was best for the Government to withdraw' (Treasury and Civil Service Select Committee 1994: xvii). In the mid-1990s, the Conservative administration introduced the Private Finance Initiative (PFI), under which contract providers were supposed to share capital involvement and associated risk in large-scale public projects, including IT systems. The initiative was continued and extended under the incoming Labour administration in 1997, so that capital funding for many such projects was not available through any other route.

The UK government IT market rapidly developed as one dominated by global players. The most successful by far by 2003 was the US-based corporation EDS, with massive contracts for the Inland Revenue (£2,500 million), Department of Work and Pensions (£2,000 million), and smaller but still significant ones for the Employment Service (£500 million), Child Support Agency and the Prison Service. The British born ICL, later taken over by Fujitsu, held big contracts for HM Customs and Excise, the Home Office, and the Department of Trade and Industry. Much smaller market shares were held by Capita (for the Criminal Records Bureau), Siemens Business Services (the Passport Agency), Logica and Accenture, while Cap Gemini made a surprise breakthrough to the leaders by winning the massive Inland Revenue contract from EDS in 2004. Smaller niche players only really come into play for specialist services, such as Web-based developments, which are 'below the radar' in expenditure terms.

In other NPM countries the impacts on the government IT market were somewhat different for various reasons. In Australia, the 'humanized' NPM wave of reforms under Labour governments at first left government IT little affected, with very conventional procurements and still substantial in-house IT staffs. However, the market was consolidated through a major central government outsourcing initiative in 1997 launched by a new Liberal-National government in a bid to decisively improve private sector involvement in government (see Chapters 3 and 5). The key winners were EDS and IBM, although CSC won a AU$200 million contract for immigration and visa systems.

In New Zealand, contracting out and privatization were a major trend throughout government from the 1980s onwards, but the impact on the government IT market was rather variable, reflecting the fact that New Zealand is a small economy quite a long way from anywhere else. Although the major IT companies cluster their offices just along the same street in Wellington as the government departments, their presence reflects as much the role of New Zealand's stock market and banking sector as it does government involvements. There has tended to be a pattern of dominance by one major company at a time. IBM's early success in the market for computer services provision to government was followed by a disastrous contract for immigration and naturalization services in the 1990s, whose problems were never forgotten. By 2001 EDS had reached a position of clear dominance.

In Europe in general, outsourcing has not reached anything like the levels in the UK or the other countries covered here. Privatization and outsourcing were not key themes in Dutch government. NPM is widely perceived as something that was tried at local levels (e.g. the 'Tilburg model') during the 1980s but is all over now. A positive attitude to the very notion of government IT might be surmized from the continuing existence of the

Ministry for General Affairs, which includes the Netherlands Government Information Service. Government agencies use consultancy firms, but in general employ individuals for management roles or outsource specific projects. Departments still maintain large-scale systems divisions which own and develop government information systems.

In the Netherlands, the government IT market is also largely domestic. Interviewees spoke of how the Dutch approach to contracting follows what is known as the 'Rhineland' model, seeking a 'good relationship', based on 'consensus and talking and mutual support', in contrast to the Anglo-Saxon model of the UK, the US, Australia, and New Zealand where financial control is more important. The Rhineland model is more typical of other European countries such as Germany, Scandinavia, the Netherlands, and France—although commentators have suggested that the Netherlands is an extreme version of this approach to the point of standing alone as 'the Polder model', that is, typically Dutch. In this market, therefore, client knowledge and experience is as important as professional expertise. Companies looking for contracts need to 'work their way up from the work floor' and deal with small contracts. Thus, while Cap Gemini in the UK goes for big outsourcing deals, Cap Gemini in the Netherlands has started with small IT assignments tendered by personnel faced with problems and deals are small. There is some change in the market (as companies raised on the Anglo-Saxon model become more global) but the most aggressive of these companies, unwilling to go through the painful process of gaining experience of the Dutch culture, find it hard to gain a foothold. The key providers in the Netherlands are Cap Gemini and CMG and three companies of Dutch origin: Pink Roccade (the former government data centre) Ordina and Getronics, who in 2005 acquired Pink Roccade after a prolonged bidding war with Ordina. Originally Dutch based, Getronics had by 2001 grown to be one of the largest European systems integration firms, with around 28,500 employees and total worldwide revenues of €4 billion, €1 billion of which comes from the USA and a quarter of which is government work. The big US players have a tiny market share. Cap Gemini has around 8,000 staff in the Netherlands out of 9,000 in Benelux countries altogether and 40,000 in Europe. EDS has been tackling the Dutch market for the last twenty years. In the early days of outsourcing, EDS took over a five-year systems integration contract with Unilever in the Netherlands, but at the end of the contract the business units moved back to Unilever 'at the speed of lightning', as one official put it. The smaller IT companies employ strategies to avoid takeover bids from outsiders such as EDS. Ordina, for example, takes care not to release too many of its shares on to the market at once.

In Japan, the NPM movement had no impact on the government IT market, which was dominated throughout the post–War period by the big Japanese computer corporations. NPM did begin to have some minor effects at the turn of the century, primarily in terms of some output-based contracts at local level. The government IT market has always been concentrated with a few big contenders. Fujitsu, Toshiba, Hitachi, NEC, and the former government data centre NTT Data (and, latterly, NTT Communications) hold most of the major government contracts. In 2000, NTT had 44 per cent of the large contract market in price terms, although spread across only thirty-seven contracts (around 8 per cent). Second was Fujitsu, with 9 per cent of contract value and 15 per cent of contracts then Hitachi with 7 per cent of contract value and NEC with 5 per cent. The top ten companies held around 77 per cent of contract value and 61 per cent of contracts. Apart from IBM Japan, famous worldwide for its success in 'going native', global companies find it very hard to penetrate the Japanese market: most of these domestic companies have held contracts renewed on an annual basis for decades. The distinctiveness of the Japanese market is further demonstrated by the failure of these same companies to really penetrate overseas markets in terms of providing outsourcing services to government. The one exception has been Fujitsu, which purchased the UK company ICL in 2001, with the aim of entering global systems integration markets, although interviewees suggested ruefully that this aim has not been fully realized.

Conclusions

All our case study countries started the twenty-first century with a plethora of plans and strategies to develop an 'electronic' or 'digital' government. In most cases the e-commerce boom meant that there was involvement and support from the highest level of government, although in some cases it was late arriving. This change added weight to the trend back from decentralizing government IT to multiple departments and agencies, which held sway from the 1980s to the commercial launch of the Internet. As a result central departments gained extra capabilities to try and promote government agencies at large to capitalize (at last) on the promised benefits of IT, particularly the Internet. But to fulfil these expectations, all our countries were, to varying extents and in different ways, reliant on a market of computer services providers, some more concentrated and some more diffuse, some dominated by domestic players, others by international companies. We turn in the next three chapters to trying to explain both the variations in country strategies and in the levels of performance they achieved. The baseline for this explanation is a systematic effort to assess the comparative performance of government IT, to which we turn in the next chapter.

3

The Comparative Performance of Government IT

In 2002, the whole main board of the Fujitsu Corporation flew into London. They were headed for a special meeting with the directors of their recently acquired UK subsidiary, ICL Fujitsu, formed two years earlier by the acquisition of a previously independent English IT company ICL with a portfolio of government contracts. On the meeting agenda was a single proposal—that the company should withdraw from its £1 billion contract with the UK government and the Post Office to build a system (called Post Offices Counter Link or POCL for short), designed to administer social security benefits using a smart card accepted at post offices. The Japanese directors found this move very difficult to contemplate because only one central government IT contract in Japan had been cancelled in this manner over the previous four decades, bringing great shame on the company involved. It took many hours of discussion for their UK counterparts to convince the Japanese directors that no similar or long-run reputational damage would follow for ICL Fujitsu in the UK if it now backed out of its obligations by agreeing with the other parties to scrap the contract. For British central government the cancellation would prove no more than par for the course. Certainly the UK directors assured their perplexed Japanese colleagues, it would be an embarrassment, but a strictly temporary one. An abortive failure on this scale was not something that would preclude ICL Fujitsu from maintaining its current portfolio of government work, nor indeed from winning new government contracts.

As they flew back to Tokyo with the painful decision finally agreed, the Japanese board members no doubt reflected that there are sharp variations in the ways in which governments handle their relations with the IT industry. Perhaps they also puzzled for a bit over the rationale for the apparently lax British government approach. But they would probably also have reflected that the public record of Japanese government IT projects working successfully only disguised a more complex picture. It was and still is (they knew) a convenient fiction behind which the central departments massed in the high rise office blocks of Tokyo's governmental district and the country's giant IT corporations (with whom the civil servants did exclusive business) could both hide a much more mixed record of achievement.

The clash of cultures captured in the 2002 incident has complex roots whose origins we trace in three distinct parts. In this chapter we begin by looking first at the sheer scale of the variations across countries in the way that government IT systems perform, focusing on seven advanced countries. Chapter 4 looks at one set of plausible causal influences upon countries' varying performance, analysing the political and managerial influences which together set the demand side of the government contractual processes for acquiring and developing large-scale IT systems. Chapter 5 then completes the explanation by examining how the IT industry's power, contracting systems, and corporate organizational cultures all condition the supply side influences on the differentiated performance of government IT systems.

Many past analysts of cross-national policy have lamented the extreme difficulty of making meaningful or effective comparisons. The conventional dilemma has been choosing between two polar approaches. The first is to opt for a 'broad but shallow' study, usually focusing on quantitative measures but with a great deal of variation between countries (making causal explanations trickier) and without necessarily capturing the most relevant dimensions of the phenomena under study—especially where the dependent variable is a complex one. The alternative approach is to focus on just two or three 'case study' countries whose experience is examined in specific detail, using qualitative research methods. This approach engages well with countries' distinctive features and histories, but it can be tricky to extract effective comparative lessons. And the different case study narratives can often 'talk past one another', or stand as isolated interesting illustrations, rather than engaging in a cumulative fashion. However, modern social science has made important progress in rendering this conventional dilemma more easily managed and fine-tuned for different kinds of intellectual tasks. So we start this chapter by explaining a different methodological approach used in this and the next two chapters, which its author (Ragin 2000) calls 'fuzzy set' methods.

The first part of the chapter also introduces the three key indicators that allow us to build up an effective picture of government IT performance, which are: the scrap rate for government IT projects; the costs of government IT; and the modernity of government systems and equipment, compared with other similar countries and with the private sector domestically.

3.1 Introducing Fuzzy Set Methods and Some Key Performance Metrics

Until recently there have been long-standing and well-understood limitations in using a small number of case studies to derive insights into wider relationships and patterns of association. Most case study work has understandably been construed as shedding light primarily on the unique situational and interactional characteristics of individual instances, primarily in terms of illuminating the detailed pathways of causation. But looking effectively across cases has not been easy, since each country's history and experience differs from its neighbours in multiple ways. Any one difference (or any unique combination of differences) may be enough to set that case off from its counterparts. Hence until the 1990s pattern-seeking was generally thought of as solely pursued via systematic quantitative work with large N data sets. In this perspective the role of case studies shrank to one of generating infilling insights into broad patterns discovered elsewhere, highlighting the distinctive features and causal mechanisms which account for unexplained variance in quantitatively based studies and make each case in some respects unique.

Our approach here follows instead Ragin's 'fuzzy set social science' approach (Ragin 2000), which in turn develops from work undertaken over the last decade on 'qualitative comparative analysis' (Ragin 1987, 1994). The aim of the method is to allow for a more systematic comparison and interpretation of rich qualitative case data. On the one hand the approach respects the distinctive value and insights achieved (only) from the in-depth study of a relatively small number of instances. But on the other hand it seeks to provide well-founded and well-codified rules for considering how cases may be sorted into sets, and how these sets may be combined and characterized. The approach emphasizes the sympathetic but highly organized study of diversity within small or smallish data-sets, where the characteristics of the case population are understood in great detail and the specification of relevant sets for analysis can be informed by deep empirical and theoretical understanding.

This approach has two main components, the first covering how to categorize cases in simplifying ways so as reduce the diversity between them to manageable levels, and the second specifying rules for looking for connections between cases and trying to determine causal influences. In this chapter we are only concerned with describing the dependent variable in our analysis, the variations in government performance. So we leave to Chapter 5 the consideration of Ragin's rules for finding causality and focus instead on the classification and categorization of cases along dimensions. With rich qualitative data covering multiple cases, the simplest way of organizing it is to specify a set whose members share a theoretically or practically important feature and then determine whether a particular case can count as being a member of that set, in Yes/No fashion. Ragin argues that it makes sense to develop this logic of qualitative categorization to deal with more graduated or differentiated data. His five-category scheme uses the codings set out below:

- *fully included in the set*, scored as 1;
- *more in the set than out*, scored as 0.75;
- *neither in nor out of the set*, the crossover point, scored as 0.5;
- *more out of the set than in*, scored as 0.25;
- *fully out of the set*, scored as 0.

Here the first operation to consider is whether on a particular criterion or dimension a country can be considered as either fully included in a set or as fully excluded from the set: very clear-cut cases of variation will be classifiable in these straightforward (Yes/No) ways. But where the case is more multi-textured than this, the remaining intermediate categories are used. The 0.5 category is used for cases that are genuinely ambiguous, where it is hard to determine whether a country is predominantly in or predominantly out of a set. If a case is neither 1, nor 0, nor 0.5, then it must lie either in the 0.75 score (where it shares a majority of features of the full members of the set, but not all features) or in the 0.25 score (where the case mostly has the same features as the non-members of the set, but also has a minority of features associated with set membership).

The scorings used in Ragin's approach are not quite arbitrary but they are obviously constructed. Ragin has a whole range of other schema that allow more fine-grain categorization of cases on similar lines and the scorings we assign would be different in a more complex ranking. But given the small number of our country cases (seven) and the inherently complex task of classifying them on even a few fundamental dimensions, we restrict our attention to the five score schema. We see in the next two chapters that scores for the intermediate cases play an important role in the handling of aggregate judgements about country cases' involvement in combined sets. But here the essential point for readers to assess is whether the information that we present is adequate for us to robustly make the qualitative judgements about set membership or non-membership described above. Using these set categories to locate and characterize cases, reduces the information needs required for consistent classification. It also deliberately coarsens and simplifies the implications of these judgements that are carried over into the comparative analysis of countries. We still aim to express different cases' fundamental diversity but also to screen out a potentially confusing mass of obscuring detail.

The next question, of course, is how this approach can work in practice when paired with particular substantive dimensions or criteria that form the focus for analysis, in this chapter assessing comparatively how successfully governments manage and develop their portfolio of investments in IT systems. This is an undeniably difficult area to operate in, because the fuzzy set method requires us to focus on the most salient and meaningful dimensions of variations across cases. We also want to look at only a few dimensions, and in this analysis with seven cases we have focused on just three dimensions in order to try and keep a manageable level of diversity. Thus the criteria we have chosen are necessarily broad ones. Formally stated they are that government IT performance improves when:

1. Government IT schemes succeed and are rarely cancelled;
2. Government IT provision is competitively costed; and
3. Government IT provision is comparably modern to private sector provision.

Note that the criteria are set based, so that they are substantively phrased and each of them is favourably aligned. In each case a country will qualify for full membership of the set if we can clearly answer Yes on that criterion, and for full non-membership of the set if we can clearly answer No for that criterion.

These criteria are manageable ones but they call for different kinds of evidence to place our seven countries against them. In some cases it is feasible to come up with quantitative variable proxies which are reasonably close to the things that interest us in each of these cases, for example, looking at published contract prices in relation to dimension 2 (although even here there are many difficulties, notably the wide gaps between the costs initially associated with contracts and their eventual out-turn costs in practice and the lack of data in some countries). However, our interest is chiefly in establishing how country cases considered at an aggregate level can be classified as fully members or non-members of a given theoretically and empirically relevant set, or as having an intermediate position between complete membership and complete non-membership of the set. In this perspective, some ranges of variation may not be relevant for us to consider. For instance, in looking at the level of modernization criterion, there may be large differences within the set of countries where government IT is judged comparable with domestic private sector provision. Conceivably in some countries government provision may be well ahead of the private sector, whereas in others it is only just narrowly comparable. But this additional (within-set) variation will not be captured in our classification approach here, because we do not judge it theoretically or empirically relevant for assessing the way in which government IT is contracted. But by contrast we judge that categorizing government IT that is unmodernized or is lagging behind domestic private sector provision is very important and we need to use finer-grain distinctions amongst the 'mixed' cases here.

Assessing countries against any of the three criteria is difficult, requiring us to put together many different pieces of information. However, there are substantial if imperfect materials available. A wide range of reports are regularly published which contain cross-national evaluations of e-government, usually focusing on a single aspect of performance, such as government websites or comparative investment levels. Few studies seem to have methods that sustain close inspection and most reflect judgements by small juries of experts or are based on the subjective views of a wider range of expert respondents. Where more objective studies are conducted they seem to reveal sharply different behaviours across countries, as with the wide variations in the spending undertaken around 1998–2000 to prepare for possible Y2K problems. Countries such as the USA or UK apparently spent tens or even hundreds of times more than other advanced industrial countries, such as Italy. But even here, extensive interpretation of data is needed. For instance, a great deal of new IT investment was reprogrammed and re-badged as Y2K spending in the USA and UK, even though it in fact had much more general impacts on systems' renewal and performance. But given the limits of most available information, we would argue that there are advantages to using data chiefly to inform and support qualitative categorizations instead of inputting relatively dubious scores directly into a quantitative analysis. Rather, we have 'triangulated' across these scores as well as the subjective views of our interviewees in each of the seven countries and also in key multinational firms. And we could also determine whether respondents' views were backed up by a wide range of available objective indicators, in-depth reports, and other information. We turn now to setting out the three criteria above in more detail and showing how countries can be categorized using them.

3.2 The Scrap Rate of Government IT Projects

There are sharp variations across our seven countries in the extent to which government IT projects were publicly scrapped in the period from 1990 to 2004, which forms our focus here. A project counts as scrapped if it is cancelled at an intermediate stage before being rolled out, but after significant levels of public spending have been incurred, or where projects are rolled out but are acknowledged as wholly or partly non-working or non-productive systems. Table 3.1 shows that we would rate the Netherlands and Japan as fully meeting this criterion (in different ways), while Australia and the UK we rate as clearly not members of this set (again in very different ways).

Starting at the bottom of this table, the UK is apparently a world leader in ineffective IT schemes for government. A large number of projects have been scrapped in the last decade, with significant losses of complete investments or with partial write-offs of investment. This record is closely associated with a pattern of price rises in contracts over implementation periods and of significantly less functionality for implemented systems than initially expected. The scrap rate accelerated (it was hoped, temporarily) after the introduction of the Office of Government Commerce's new 'Gateway' system for rigorously and externally assessing major capital projects at successive 'gates' in 1999.

Table 3.1 Membership of the set 'Government IT schemes succeed and are rarely cancelled'

Country	IT projects succeed and are rarely cancelled
Netherlands	1
Japan	1
Canada	0.75
USA	0.75
New Zealand	0.5
Australia	0
UK	0

The Australian record is also poor in the recent period, but not because of the UK's pattern of a high level of individual project failures across a wide range of agencies. Instead the problem here was the failure of a post-1997 whole-of-government initiative to outsource IT to major private companies in clusters. This ambitious programme ran into parallel difficulties across all contractors and many of the clusters, as different departmental and agency customers struggled to establish clear client–contractor relationships (see Chapter 5). In 2001, following critical reports by the Australian Auditor-General, the clustering initiative was scrapped at an estimated costs of A\$4 billion, and replaced by more conventional individual contracts between agencies and substantially the same contractors.

In New Zealand, the record of government IT contracts has been more successful than in the UK, with only one major IT system failure in the last two decades. This was a new IT system for the police force, where IBM won the contract. It was subsequently cancelled when costs spiralled and the system's effectiveness was called in question. Since then public sector project sizes have been kept small and tied to proven technologies or intermediate improvements. But given the conservatism with which projects have been set up it seems difficult to place New Zealand on more than the cusp between successful and unsuccessful performance.

Flipping to the top slot in the Table above, the Netherlands has a particularly low rate of scrapped government IT projects. The characteristic contracting approach of the Dutch civil service is to parcel out to the private sector only small-scale and specific pieces of work, or to bring individual consultants into the government. In addition, the internal public sector techniques for IT project planning in the Netherlands are well-developed and sophisticated, and there is strong political backing for proceeding in well-defined stages. For instance, new tax or welfare schemes presented to parliament must by law be accompanied by certified evidence that appropriate IT systems exist to implement them. Unless this certification exists the legislative changes cannot be passed.

In Japan, government IT projects are virtually never cancelled (although there has been one such incident where this occurred in the last four decades). It is rare even for ministries or contractors to publicly admit problems with the functionality of systems. If problems emerge in contracts, the major IT companies with big civil service contracts all respond by devoting enough extra resources to them to ensure that they are fixed, even if this makes the project involved a loss-making one for them. Reputationally it would be much more serious for them to admit a large-scale failure, since they could then lose their established position with the ministry concerned. They would also jeopardize their standing in the eyes of other ministries where they had work or prospects of work, as well as with prospective agency and corporate customers generally. So whereas in the UK there is a high level of public acceptance of government IT failures, and a weary recognition that any one case does not rule out the same company implementing other projects very well, in Japan companies fear that large public failures could create a spiral of declining reputation. Central government ministries also rarely wish to admit publicly that projects have failed, which would be bad for the department's public standing and ability to negotiate with the Finance ministry. Hence Japanese departments will often assist compliant contractors who rectify problems by drafting in more staff and resources by allowing them to recoup the costs involved, spreading extra benefits across a series of future contract negotiations. Departments and contractors will also seek to hide functionality deficits, where they occur. So long as systems are in being on time they will generally be represented as successes. These practices have adverse implications for the costs of government IT systems (see below), but on this index they mean that Japan has an abnormally low scrap rate for projects.

In most countries one might hope that the realistic norm will be for a majority of government IT projects to work successfully most of the time. The countries closest to this pattern here are the USA and Canada, which achieve relatively high but not complete levels of successful delivery. Their rate is comparable to that achieved in the private sector, which informed observers estimate at three-quarters to four-fifths of projects working within an acceptable range of their intended major target aims. Canadian projects generally perform reasonably well because major departments and agencies have retained substantial IT expertise to assess project development, and because control by the Treasury Board (effectively Canada's finance ministry) is also relatively close and detailed. There have been episodic major project cancellations, such as a major EDS project with the Human Resources Development Canada (i.e. the social security department) in 1997. But, as in this case, cancellations, non-delivery or radical underperformance are not accepted in a fatalist way, as they are in the UK. Instead they represent major reputational blows for the corporations concerned, which may then suffer a prolonged contract drought as other agencies seek to avoid any similar recurrence. For instance, Canadian federal departments reacted to the EDS problems by demanding in future contracts the specified commitment of particular individuals deemed to be the crucial managers or technologists for their new projects.

In the USA, extensive project vulnerabilities in the IT sphere are acknowledged, but strong controls are built into the contractor-selection stage which make it counterproductive for major corporations to default completely on deals. For instance, information-sharing amongst federal departments and agencies has increased in response to Congressional criticisms of a previous willingness to separate out performance by major firms across different policy sectors. Functionality downgrades have remained more common. Expectations are often managed downwards in terms of systems capabilities, extended timelines for the automation of processes, and some projects written off or scheduled for replacement more speedily than originally envisaged. All these problems occurred with tax-raising systems during the mega-scaled and deeply troubled IRS tax modernization project from the 1980s onwards (see Chapter 6). The extraordinary number and scale of tax subprojects that were scrapped during the 1990s led to Congress directly controlling disbursements for future tax system modernization work, which also had to be organized by the IRS in a more modularized way, focusing on specific deliverables. The American IT industry also learnt long-running lessons from the IRS affair, recognizing both that future success with larger projects would inevitably be tied to progress on bottom-line deliverables and that the reputational costs of large failures had considerably increased. In 2001–2, for instance, the major EDS 'Navy-Marine Corps Intranet' contract ran into severe difficulties, as the company grappled with the considerable diversity of systems across navy and marine corps shore bases which it was seeking to replace with an integrated systems architecture. The onset of hostilities in Iraq in early 2003 saw an extraordinary effort by the contractor to be seen to be committed to delivering flexibly on the contract, helped by extra war-related credits and renegotiation elements.

3.3 The Costs of Government IT

In designing, procuring, and operating IT systems a successful government is one that regularly and consistently achieves pricing levels comparable to those attained in the private sector or in other countries. But this apparently straightforward criterion is never easy to operationalize because government systems are often larger than those in the private sector and they are also differently structured. Comparisons across countries are also difficult because there has been little by way of convergence amongst governmental IT systems, which remain stubbornly differentiated in response to country-specific policy influences and administrative procedures. However, from interviews with government administrators and industry respondents across our seven countries, and scrutiny of the publicly available information about major government IT contracts, it is possible to group countries into three categories. Table 3.2 shows our assessment of how this criterion applies in the period 1990–2004. In two of our case countries, the Netherlands and New Zealand, government IT prices seem on a par with those in the private sector. In two other countries, the USA and Canada, there are indications of limited government sector disadvantagement, with contract price levels perhaps somewhat higher than those achieved by major corporations. And in the three remaining countries, Japan, Australia, and the UK, there are considerable grounds for believing that contract prices for government IT are relatively high.

The Netherlands and New Zealand have been successful in paring prices to market levels for very different reasons. In New Zealand the government's intensive contracts scrutiny regime, and strong incentives for chief executives to secure fully defensible prices and conditions for contracts, placed some acute pressures on the major IT industry players who have traditionally dominated the government market. The relative decline in major project work from government and the depressed condition of the New Zealand economy for much of the late 1980s and 1990s squeezed industry profit margins. In the Netherlands, by contrast, government agencies have been successful in becoming just another set of medium-sized customers, each dealing fluidly with a diversity of corporations on well-specified and sensibly scaled contracts for tractable and easily monitorable projects.

Canada and the USA fall in the second division on the pricing of government IT, coming somewhat below full comparability in pricing with the private sector for different reasons. In Canada, the specificity of

Table 3.2 Membership of the set 'Government IT provision is competitively costed'

Country	Government IT provision is competitively costed
Netherlands	1
New Zealand	1
Canada	0.75
USA	0.75
Japan	0.25
Australia	0.25
UK	0.25

government systems compared with those in the US federal government means that adaptation is always needed for Canadian implementations, whereas in business the same (mainly US-dominated) corporations can deliver the same applications as in the much larger US market. In the US, government work was for a long time more rule-bound and relatively expensive for large- and medium-sized firms to compete for. Before the early 1990s there were very formal, open-ended and time-consuming government tendering procedures, long lead times, inflexible contract terms, no opportunities for joint returns or profits, and a public scrutiny regime orientated towards preventing any firm from making super-normal profits, for whatever reason. These legacy problems were made worse by the possibility of formal contract challenges by losing firms, which were often activated in the 1980s, further slowing down the delivery of products until dispute resolution procedures ground slowly to a conclusion. This background helps explain the early 1990s phenomenon of government 'buying a 286 [PC] at a 386 price'—that is, securing delivery of last-generation IT at current-generation prices. President Clinton's National Performance Review (NPR) marked a major catch-up effort by the US federal administration to modernize its procurement processes and break the tradition of uncompetitive prices. By introducing call-off contracts, electronic marketplaces and open-market purchases using agency credit cards for smaller amounts of equipment, many of the earlier problems were relatively quickly addressed by the later 1990s. The federal government also made intensive efforts to professionalize its procurement executives, upgrading their skills, and pooling expertise across agencies and even tiers of government within the American federation. But there remain indications that governmental procedural costs, and a certain level of risk associated with undertaking high-profile government contracts, contribute to major contract prices in the US public sector still being somewhat above those in the private sector.

In the remaining three countries, Australia, Japan, and the UK, governments all seem to perform worse than the private sector for different reasons. In Australia, the price competitiveness of government contracts was relatively high but unsurprisingly took a lurch downwards during the forced outsourcing of government services. This strongly ideological cross-government initiative effectively created a closed market for the country's largest IT companies, in the end largely peacefully partitioned amongst them.

In Japan, close, managed relationships between ministries and major IT companies have apparently persisted, with little evident competition despite annual maintenance contracts. Accordingly informed observers believe that Japanese IT contractors are charging relatively high prices, especially for maintenance work on contracts already installed with proprietary systems. Although changes of contractor do take place, Japanese firms are reluctant to take on maintenance work for systems they have not themselves installed. And companies seem to invest quite a lot in specifying their systems in ways that insulate them from later challenges. The tradition of contractors picking up the tab for unexpected problems in rolling out new systems also means that maintenance costs can be increased for a run of years, so as to let firms recoup earlier losses incurred.

In the UK, civil servants take great pride in insisting that competed contracts let under long terms achieve market-comparable or better prices. They point to scrutiny by the UK's strong supreme audit institution (the NAO) to support their contention. And initial contracts let by departments and major agencies to contractors have indeed often been competitively priced. However, the UK also became unique amongst the countries we analysed in the extent to which government departments effectively acknowledged that when policy changes or other new developments made alterations to existing IT systems essential, then often only the incumbent IT supplier could plausibly deliver these mid-contract changes. Large IT firms dealing with government grew expert in estimating the likely scale of policy-induced changes, often effectively driving a coach and horses through the carefully specified initial contracts. It became expected practice to pitch prices for initially competed tranches of work relatively low, in the confident expectation that later revisions and extensions would create negotiated contracts of between four and six times the initial competed contract price (NAO 2000). Assessing negotiated contracts for price competitiveness is sometimes attempted, suggesting that initial prices are rarely matched in later contract additions and extensions. For instance, the initial decision to outsource the Inland Revenue's IT services in 1994 to EDS was costed by the civil service at £250 million for a ten year contract (see Chapter 6). Within six years government auditors established that the likely contract cost had risen to over £1 billion (NAO 2000). The government later faced major problems in re-contracting at the end of the decade-long contract, but responding to perceived failures and rigidities in EDS's performance eventually did reallocate the next ten year's work to a rival, Cap Gemini–Ernst Young—but at a new (initial) contract price of £4,500 million, a cost escalation of eighteen times the original price a decade earlier.

3.4 The Modernity of Government IT

The final dimension on which we seek to position countries is the up-to-dateness of government sector IT systems and networks compared with private sector provision. A within-country focus is necessary here because of the differences in per capita GDP between, say, the USA and Japan on the one hand at the rich country end of the spectrum and New Zealand on the other. These per capita GDP variations feed into different IT levels via varying tax receipt levels. Raising 1 per cent of GDP in taxes in the USA or Japan produces a great deal more resources than accomplishing the same operation in New Zealand.

Our focus here is both on fundamental back-office systems and large databases, and on front-office software, network speeds and capabilities. It also encompasses the level of development of e-government services compared with e-tailing, electronic banking and other Web-orientated sectors in each country. Table 3.3 shows that the Netherlands clearly meets the criterion and a further three countries (Canada, Japan, and Australia) come close, reflecting high-investment levels there. The UK and New Zealand seem to be the areas with the worst provision on this criterion.

Again we score Netherlands narrowly top here, with public sector agencies having fully modern IT, on a par with that in larger private firms. The fundamental Dutch IT systems are modernized and well-structured, with less of a backlog of legacy problems than comparable countries and many large private sector corporations involved, but each in small parts of the overall systems. Public sector offices also transitioned to fully Web enabled networks by an earlier date than other countries. E-government progress was perhaps less in the Netherlands for some years,

Table 3.3 Membership of the set 'Government IT provision is comparably modern to private sector provision'

Country	Government IT is comparably modern to private sector provision
Netherlands	1
Canada	0.75
Japan	0.75
Australia	0.75
USA	0.5
UK	0.25
New Zealand	0.25

but then private sector take-up of the Internet has also lagged behind other leading European nations. And Dutch citizens seem to have adapted rapidly to the provision of government services online, with the Netherlands coming ahead of our other case study countries in a cross-national study of e-government usage in 2003.

Three countries, Canada, Australia, and Japan, we would rate as one rung lower on the modernization ladder. In each there has been a good level of investment in updating fundamental systems, and public sector offices mostly have Web-compatible networks and desktop systems of recent vintage, especially in Japan (where ministries by 2003 universally used laptops, relatively rare at this time in other governments, as noted in Chapter 2). However, Japan's e-government progress has to date been restricted, highlighted by the low levels of usage shown in Table 3.4 below, although a recent initiative seeks broader inter-connectedness across government systems. Canada and Australia, by contrast, topped most e-government rankings from 2000 onwards, overtaking an initial US lead by dint of well joined-up policies. Both countries achieved a more concerted buy-in from their better integrated civil services, which perhaps also have somewhat more progress-orientated organizational cultures. However, all three countries have some substantial legacy problems in major systems, placing them somewhat behind the Netherlands.

The USA, we would rate as on the cusp between being modernized and lagging behind the private sector. Some aspects of US processes show fast adoption, especially in terms of generating government websites and adopting new technical standards (such as XML). The competitive US IT market, especially after the NPR, means that there is a relatively rapid diffusion of technical innovations within the government sector, especially in terms of front-office systems and lower cost innovations, like

Table 3.4 Usage of e-government—the percentage of total population claiming to have accessed government online in the last year (including information seeking)

	2003	2002	2001
Netherlands	52	41	31
Canada	51	48	46
Australia	47	46	31
New Zealand	45	40	NA
USA	44	43	34
UK	18	13	11
Japan	15	13	17

Source: Taylor Nelson Sofres 2003.

starting basic websites. However, the US federal government also shows some persistent weaknesses. Some very large legacy systems have only been partially modernized, of which the massive IRS systems are perhaps the most long-running and best known example. US departments and agencies also still have remarkably siloed systems, with inter-agency communication limited even in apparently high saliency areas, such as national security. While the USA originated more government websites far faster than any other nation (up to 3,000 in the Pentagon alone by 1999), it also took until late 2000 to provide any effective central finder site for the federal government as a whole and longer still to create fledgling integrated e-government systems. Many superficially impressive US e-government achievements (such as 45 million Americans filing their taxes online) also turn out on inspection to rest on very long-lived electronic data interchange (EDI) systems, some dating back to the 1980s. Far fewer transactions use Internet protocols. Set against the background of a very large and dynamic private sector, there is a small but still clear gradient between the modernity of the public and corporate sectors' IT.

The two countries lagging behind in the modernity stakes are New Zealand and the UK. New Zealand's problem is twofold. First, it slipped dramatically down the OECD's rankings of countries in terms of GDP per head in the 1980s and 1990s, only starting a modest clawback in 2001. So resources for running the public sector have been strained in many dimensions, with renewals of major government IT systems often put off. Second, the NPM system of chief executives on short-term contracts being constantly assessed for cost savings and administrative paring back has strongly militated against IT modernization. Chief executives have strong 'bureau-shaping' incentives to avoid major IT system renewals taking place on their watch, with all the attendant risks of cost overruns and new system shortfalls. It was far better, in their view, to restrict new contracts to essential 'patch-and-mend' operations to keep legacy systems in being and pass the problem along to the next in line for the agency top job. As a result, three crucial but unmodernized legacy systems underpin essential New Zealand government operations (tax, social security, and policing/law and order). Industry sources regarded them as fundamentally anachronistic and fragile. In addition, the high level of fragmentation of systems across multiple agencies meant that New Zealand launched a joined-up programme only in spring 2001, years behind other comparable small countries like Singapore and Finland, whose governments responded to the mid-1990s Internet and electronics booms far more dynamically and effectively.

The UK's government IT systems also score badly, despite a superficially more centralized and better-funded effort at modernization post-1997, including an internationally well-publicized e-government campaign. During the 1980s and 1990s the squeeze on public spending under Conservative governments led to a long-run underinvestment in IT modernization. By the end of the 1990s and even into 2002 this investment deficit left major government agencies struggling to get by with non-Web compatible networks and extensive front-office systems that were not even PC-based, but still using dumb terminals. Legacy IT systems in the UK also developed historically as jungles of interacting separate mainframes. For instance, in 2003 there were almost 200 systems running in social security and 100 in tax-collection. Even a smaller sized agency like Customs and Excise had a complex map of around sixty single-function systems, which is very difficult to adapt to new policy demands. From 1999 onwards, the new Labour administration loosened public spending controls and launched major IT initiatives to catch up. But the results did not match the rhetoric. For example, the UK's well-publicized e-government campaign focused for four years on getting central government departments and agencies to get their services online. This push created considerable costs in terms of dedicated extra budgets of £1 billion, but the government campaign presented the task as being about service availability and not about citizen usage of services. In areas like e-taxation the UK lagged behind the USA, Canada and even other nearby countries, such as Ireland. In the early 2000s, the UK was on a par with Japan in terms of e-government usage, as shown at the bottom of Table 3.4. In other areas, such as the development of joined-up IT systems in health care and law and order, it will be many years before performance improves even if implementation goes very well. Meanwhile the contrast between public and private sector IT systems is strong in the UK.

Conclusions

In the fuzzy set social science approach how you put together information gathered under different criteria is as important as how you code it in the first place. The growth of quantitative methods and their intellectual predominance has meant that most modern social scientists rather unreflectively do the task of putting bits of information together (data aggregation) in a quantitatively shaped way. For example, in composing combined measures of different things we commonly allow shortfalls in one dimension to be compensated by strong performance in another. Suppose a university uses such an approach to admit students using overall test scores as the admissions level, then they may turn a blind eye to a literarily gifted student's poor mathematics scores if they are more than compensated by high scores elsewhere. But if we are looking at whether people or cases are members in different sets we cannot afford to take this stance. If a university wants to recruit people who are both maths competent and can be effective in literary work they need to look at the component test scores separately and admit only those who are in the intersection set with competence in both areas. Similarly, Ragin argues that when using a set-based methods approach we cannot meaningfully allow clear membership of a set on one criterion to compensate for non-membership on another. For instance, the combined set of 'tall blond people' cannot include very tall brunettes, because however tall these people are, it cannot meaningfully compensate for their not being blonde.

Using the same logic Table 3.5 pulls together the ratings for our seven countries discussed above and considers how we can compose and score their membership in an overall set for 'Government IT performance is effective'. Ragin's key rule for composing and scoring multi-criteria sets is to use the intersection set, defined here as $(S \cap C \cap M)$ and shown in the penultimate column of the table. Here we enter the minimum score achieved by each country across the columns for scrap rate, cost and modernity criteria, and we use that to order the sequence of rows. This approach puts the Netherlands and then Canada clearly as the most

Table 3.5 Summary codings for the components of the performance of government IT, 1990–2003

Country	IT projects succeed and are rarely cancelled (S)	Government IT provision is competitively costed (C)	Government IT is comparably modern to private sector provision (M)	Government IT performance is effective: the intersection set S . C . M (minimum)	Union set S + C + M (maximum)
Netherlands	1	1	1	1	1
Canada	0.75	0.75	0.75	0.75	0.75
USA	0.75	0.75	0.5	0.5	0.75
New Zealand	0.5	1	0.25	0.25	1
Japan	1	0.25	0.75	0.25	1
Australia	0	0.25	0.75	0	0.75
UK	0	0.25	0.25	0	0.25

effective government IT performers across the board. It places the UK in the bottom position with Australia in the penultimate slot. And the remaining three countries occupy intermediate positions.

The final column here shows another set-based scoring, the union of the three sets defined as (S ∪ C ∪ M). Here we take the maximum score achieved by a country across the three component criteria for effective government IT performance. Ragin suggests that comparing scores for the union set with those for the intersection set provides an important way of summarizing variation in performance across cases. Three countries (the Netherlands, Canada, and USA) show relatively little variation at high overall levels of performance, while the UK also shows little variation, but at a low level of performance. The remaining three countries (Japan, Australia, and New Zealand) show much more variation in the scores achieved across the three different dimensions of government IT's effectiveness. We turn now to the task of trying to explain both the levels in governments' performance patterns and the variations around these levels. In the next chapter we look first at how far differences in public management and public administration factors seem to shape countries' divergent experiences with government IT development.

4

Explaining Performance I:
The Impact of Governance Institutions
and Bureaucratic Cultures

Every modern bureaucracy has control of information at its core. But that does not mean that controlling information is recognized as an especially core activity by the officials in government organizations, especially top decision-makers. We noted in Chapter 1 that the systematic generation of records, along with their permanent storage in an accessible and reusable fashion and the ability of skilled operators to cross-reference and make connections between different files, remain fundamental capacities for government agencies. But in any organization many business-critical functions, once they are highly formalized and routinized, can easily appear as dull, unglamorous, samey—run-of-the-mill tasks to be avoided in favour of more interesting, less predictable kinds of work. How business and agencies manage this tension, between routinizing business-critical tasks and consigning them to middle- or low-ranked actors on the one hand and keeping in view their key contribution to organizational success on the other, can often make a considerable difference to their performance. Modern IT decisions focus this tension in an acute form, since major investments often orientate and constrain organizational strategies for long periods ahead, as well as consuming considerable resources in their own right.

In national government agencies the management of IT developments is arguably one of the most important areas where handling normally routine-but-critical functions transmutes into strategic choice-making for the duration of the decision and implementation period. This unusual strategic phase will often pose a challenge for the organization's more 'normal' modes of operating and for its regular organizational culture to handle. In some cases, top officials and their political decision-makers may be asked to think through unfamiliar issues, quite different in their time-scales, processes, and implications from their regular activities. How well organizational cultures already incorporate reference to technological de-cision-making within their regular operation, or can adapt to do so during key decision periods, may have an important influence upon the organization's success in making IT choices.

The governance, institutional and bureaucratic culture influences on which we focus attention here mostly consist of an interacting set of general and rather specific technological governance characteristics. We expect four dimensions to be linked to the varying performance of government IT across countries:

1. *The underlying governance institutions of a country provide few or weak publicly visible overview and political control mechanisms*, so that the executive is normally dominant vis-à-vis other branches of government. This effect is a general one, but the fewer public controls there are over governments, the less successful we expect them to be in managing IT investments.

2. *The bureaucratic culture of the government system does not assign a high priority to handling the development of technical policies and projects*. It provides weak institutional mechanisms for handling technology development. The more a country qualifies under this heading the less successful we expect its government IT performance to be.

3. *NPM was rapidly and extensively adopted from the 1980s onwards.* Although in its early days NPM assigned some rhetorical significance to using new technologies (including IT systems) within government, we fundamentally expect NPM countries to perform less well in handling government IT. The characteristic impetus of this 'reform' movement was towards fragmenting government organizational systems and strengthening the role of corporate sector actors (including the IT industry) in providing government services.

4. *Since the advent of the Internet in the mid-1990s there has been either no centralized e-government initiative, strongly backed by the political leadership, or the initiative has been long delayed.* Generally speaking we would expect such an initiative to help boost government IT performance, especially if it focused increased resources on improving the relative modernity of governmental systems.

In each case we have slanted the criteria so that the more that countries can be counted as fully members of each of the three sets, the worse their government IT performance should be expected to be (a negative association). Again, given the small number of country cases considered here, and the inherently complex task of classifying them on even a few fundamental dimensions, we restrict our attention to the five-category scheme developed by Ragin and discussed in Chapter 3 where the available categorizations are: *fully included in the set*, scored as 1; *more in the set than out*, scored as 0.75; *neither in nor out of the set*, the crossover point, scored as 0.5; *more out of the set than in*, scored as 0.25; *fully out of the set*, scored as 0.

4.1 The Controls on Executive Action

Underpinning everything that governments do is a dynamic of political accountability, that is both an obligation to explain major decisions convincingly before they are undertaken and a duty to answer in public for actual performance. All our case study countries are liberal democracies with strongly developed public accountability and answerability mechanisms and hence some degree of 'checks and balances' on unfettered executive action. But four of the countries—the UK, Canada, Australia, and New Zealand—are originally 'Westminster model' systems that traditionally assign far more scope to the executive and far fewer powers of scrutiny to the legislature. And one country, Japan, is a dominant party system where a single party has virtually monopolized ministerial positions since the early 1950s. We expect that the weaker the controls on government action the worse the performance of governments will be in managing IT policies, simply because they can 'get away with' more than is possible for the executive in a system where it is closely monitored (especially *ex ante*). Table 4.1 shows our summary characterization of our seven countries on this dimension of having weak controls on government decision-making. The Netherlands and the USA are the only countries excluded from the set completely and Japan and the UK are the countries that qualify most for inclusion. Canada, Australia, and New Zealand have different 'in-between' profiles, reflecting their varied trajectories away from the Westminster model.

Japan is perhaps the clearest case of a country with weak publicly-operating controls on the executive. The same party, the Liberal Democratic Party (LDP) has been continuously in power since 1953. It has been the sole party of government for all except a few years of coalition

Table 4.1 Membership of the set 'The underlying governance system has few or weak publicly operable controls on the executive'

Country	The underlying governance system has few or weak publicly operable controls on the executive (E)
Japan	1
UK	1
Australia	0.75
Canada	0.5
New Zealand	0.5
Netherlands	0
USA	0

government (1993–9), when the LDP was still the major coalition partner. This dominant party system has only strengthened since the end of the cold war in 1989, with the electoral decline of the Japanese Socialist Party and the fragmentation of the anti-LDP vote. The main legislative control on government action is the powerful parliamentary party of the LDP, where there are long-lived factional groupings that jockey ceaselessly for power behind different ministerial figures and senior faction leaders (often not ministers). But this control focuses chiefly on the allocation of portfolios and the operation of policies that matter intensely to party factions, like World Trade Organization (WTO) negotiations or subsidy levels for rice farmers. On more routine executive decision-making the legislative controls are few and the government can operate with a high level of secrecy and not much public disclosure. The pattern of bureaucratic predominance which saw Japan through its long development boom from the 1950s to the late 1970s has subsequently been eroded on major policy issues. The central bureaucracy is no longer the planning centre for economic development, and private sector influence has grown greatly. But the bureaucracy remains largely dominant on all issues of its own operations and government secrecy remains intense. For instance, key documents, such as government budgets, are still published with many specialized bureaucratic characters that can only be read by those with many years of bureaucratic training and induction.

The UK is the only other political system to score a perfect 1 on this criterion. Until the late 1990s it was the least changed Westminster system country, with perhaps the weakest legislature of any mature liberal democracy. This may seem an odd statement, because the constitutional concept of 'parliamentary sovereignty' is a central dictum, arguing that the legislature has scope to pass new laws as it wants, without being restricted by constitutional or judicial constraints. Yet within Parliament itself, control rests with the government of the day, so long as that party has a secure majority in the lower chamber (the House of Commons). In all but three post-war election years the plurality rule electoral system has delivered a strong, artificial majority of seats to whichever of the top two parties has most votes (the so-called 'leader's bias' effect). Strong party discipline then means that the government will be able to pass 97 per cent of its laws through the Commons unchanged, while the ability of the upper chamber (the House of Lords) to make changes is small and confined to few issues. The Commons select committees exercise a degree of bipartisan scrutiny over individual Whitehall departments. And the powerful Public Accounts Committee backed by the NAO is the main *ex post* control on how departments implement government policy. For many years, particularly prior to 1992, public and media scrutiny of government were constrained by a highly restrictive Official Secrets Act. The UK civil service is also long-established and relatively prestigious and the weak level of scrutiny feasible has historically given them strong informational advantages in controlling policy processes in a relatively insulated way. But it was not until the start of 2005 that a Freedom of Information Act finally came into operation. The post 1997 Labour government responsible for this change also introduced a range of constitutional measures (including devolution to Scotland, Wales, and London, and the introduction of new proportional representation voting systems for these new institutions) which marked an extensive move away from the Westminster model. But these changes left executive predominance within central government almost completely untouched.

Amongst the other originally Westminster model countries, Australia is the closest to the UK situation at the national (Commonwealth) level of its federal system. Australia uses a modified form of plurality rule voting (called the Alternative Vote system) for electing its lower chamber of the legislature (the House of Representatives), but two main party blocs (the Liberal-National and Labour parties) have controlled most representation here and alternated control of government between them. However, at the upper chamber (Senate) level the constituent states of the federation are equally represented and elections are held using proportional representation, producing greater representation of other parties and a considerably enhanced degree of scrutiny of legislation. The Senate's Public Administration committee has also been able to develop expertise on how the public service system operates and the general information regime has been more open than in the UK for far longer. Add in the strong influence of the state governments in many aspects of public policy delivery, and a strong constitutional framework policed by a powerful High Court, and the Commonwealth government is considerably more constrained than its British counterpart. But a government with a secure legislative majority and elite civil servants at national level still exercise the predominant influence within the system.

Australia's neighbour, New Zealand, was for a long time an archetypal Westminster system. A small country (with only 4 million people), New Zealand has only ever had a unicameral legislature with 120 (mostly part-time) MPs. When the electoral system was plurality rule the party system showed two blocs (the Liberal-Country party and the Labour party) gaining most votes and seats, with strong artificial majorities and with the government ministers dominating in the small Parliament. Critics argued at this time that the country had 'the fastest law in the West' with the fewest controls on the executive. The civil service was well-developed and respected and there was little external expertise to challenge its decisions. In 1996, however, New Zealand changed its electoral system radically following a big growth of third and fourth party voting and two referenda calling for reform. The new system uses proportional representation elections and has produced a more diverse parliament with four or five main parties (fluctuating somewhat). The former top two parties remain most important but the new party system ensures that coalition governments are often necessary. Along with coalitions has come more pre-legislative bargaining and hence greater scrutiny of executive decisions.

Canada is the final Westminster system and again federalism has been a main source of difference pushing the country further from its British-influenced origins over time. The party system is complex with rather different federal and provincial-level systems, especially in Quebec where linguistic nationalism has been strong, and in western Canada where different provinces at different times have cycled through new right-wing parties. The centrist Liberal party has been most commonly in government and still has some aspects of a dominant party. The Canadian legislature has a very weak upper chamber (the all-appointed Senate) and a lower chamber with strong party discipline. But the majority party's 'caucus' of MPs has generally been a more powerful influence on both leadership succession and detailed policymaking than the UK parliamentary parties. And there has been a considerable 'churn' of party fortunes at federal and provincial level, with the Liberals challenged by a succession of different conservative parties and a left-liberal New Democratic Party being represented federally and even winning control of the largest province (Ontario) for a time. The Canadian federal civil service has also developed on different lines, retaining the British generalist civil service tradition in some aspects but also strongly influenced by the closely proximate US model, with its greater professionalism orientation and more open system of making policy. The Canadian policy style has also tended to be more consensual and effectively inter-departmental. Freedom of information legislation was introduced in 1991.

The USA is one of the two countries with the strongest systems of checks and balances. Plurality rule elections have ensured a Democrat and Republican duopoly for control of the Presidency (although third candidates regularly stand here) and also maintained the world's most perfect two-party system in Congress. Yet because third parties get so little support, the lower chamber (House of Representatives) elections in fact operate very proportionately. In Senate elections, with only two members per state the seats distribution is of course badly malapportioned, but contingently elections operate generally competitively, with a reasonably close balance of the two parties. The complete separation of the executive and the bicameral legislature means that 'divided government' situations often occur, where the party controlling the executive does not control at least one house of Congress. In addition, party discipline is low (with cohesion scores of around 65 per cent compared to 95 per cent in Westminster system countries). And the 'corporate' sentiment of Congress is strong, with legislators taking a firm collective stance in favour of close accountability of the executive. These factors add up to perhaps the strongest legislature in any political system anywhere in the world, for instance with far and away the strongest legislative budget-making powers. Add in a powerful Supreme Court policing a closely written constitution and an independent-minded judiciary, plus a strong federal system with 50 states that take on most domestic responsibilities, and the USA clearly has a most elaborate system of checks and balances. There are various offsetting factors which recreate substantial areas of Presidential 'privilege' and less controlled executive action in specific fields—especially in defence and intelligence areas. Here the US, as the world's leading military superpower, has inherited some of the divided (almost schizoid) features that characterized the British and French empires at their peak, and a substantial secret zone where Congressional controls and public overview are much less. But even here problems and issues often emerge more over time than in equivalent areas in other countries.

The Netherlands represents another pole of strong control over the executive within a parliamentary system. Proportional elections and a complex party system mean that coalition governments are the norm. Although the coalitions (once formed) are relatively enduring and cohesive, the main elected chamber of the legislature (confusingly called the second chamber in Netherlands) exercises close supervision over the government. Inside cabinets there is also a lot of discussion and cross-supervision of ministers from one party by their coalition partners, producing stronger collective responsibility mechanisms with internal checks and balances. There is also a more expertise-based lower chamber with considerable detailed policy grip. Finally, the Dutch political and administrative culture is an open one, with close media scrutiny and long-standing freedom of information provisions.

4.2 Bureaucratic Culture and Mechanisms for Handling Technology Projects

The character and extent of institutional and bureaucratic influences upon current policymaking is the subject of a vast literature covering much of political science. But looking just at technical decisions such as those involving IT restricts the focus considerably. Table 4.2 shows our summary characterization of our seven countries on the dimension of having weak systems for technical decisions, with Netherlands the only country excluded from the set completely and New Zealand and the UK the countries that qualify most for inclusion. The USA, Canada, and Australia, have relatively strong systems and Japan is classified here as an ambivalent case.

Table 4.2 Membership of the set 'Weak cultural and institutional systems for handling technology decisions and projects'

Country	Weak cultural and institutional systems for handling technology decisions and projects (C)
New Zealand	0.75
UK	0.75
Japan	0.5
USA	0.25
Canada	0.25
Australia	0.25
Netherlands	0

The Netherlands' strong arrangements for handling technological decisions reflect the country's great dependence upon technical expertise to keep the sea out of more than a third of the country's current land area. Even in the modern period a large amount of public sector expenditure, US$2.2 billion in 2001, is spent on environmental protection such as water management, not only on sea defences but also on the management of the major rivers flowing through the country to the sea. The so-called 'polder culture' captures the extraordinary importance of these factors in the Dutch state's development. It has translated into well-developed procedures for making systematic evaluations of technical projects and requiring careful certification that project expectations will be met. Within the Netherlands civil service the predominant culture places a high value on technical professionalism, which is also respected by politicians and public opinion. Civil service culture is therefore strongly supportive of IT professionalism and chimes with wider societal attitudes. Dutch agencies place a premium on recruiting and promoting technical personnel, who can rise directly into the higher civil service. Agency management teams and boards regularly include all relevant professionals and in IT-intensive agencies an information director is common. Central controls on IT projects' effectiveness are strongly institutionalized, notably in the legislative requirement that IT systems' preparedness has to be certified to Parliament. Finally, coalition governments help strengthen parliamentary scrutiny of technical decisions and facilitate holding officials to account for performance.

Next in our ranking are the USA, Canada, and Australia—all three large, federal countries spanning enormous areas and scoring high on having technologically orientated bureaucratic cultures and governmental systems. In each case, maintaining a governmental and public service presence across large territories gave the federal government apparatus a strong interest in new technological solutions from their earliest days. And the need to interlink federal and state government services created an additional impetus to adopting IT. In all three countries the mix of services and spending at the federal level always included a higher proportion of scientifically based or technical services than with unitary states. This effect made their civil services more open to high-technology professions, a trend especially accentuated in the USA with its massive defence, space, and nuclear energy establishments. The USA has strong common public service norms, but it is essentially a department- or agency-based civil service system, with more technical agencies dominated by senior staffs with professional backgrounds. Australia and Canada both inherited a generalist civil service organized on UK lines, but they have operated their systems in distinctive ways. Canadian practice has been influenced by lessons learnt from the neighbouring USA, while Australia's commonwealth tier has always assigned more role and influence to scientifically trained officials than in the UK.

In the modern period all three countries have also taken IT functions seriously in terms of departmental management. In the USA, as noted in Chapter 2, the OMB in the Executive Office of the President plays an important oversight role and departmental CIOs mandated under the Clinger-Cohen Act of 1996 were intended to form a key part of the senior management team in departments. CIOs' roles in practice have varied, with some playing a strategic role and others being more technical/advisory in their approach. But given their statutory role and the influence of close Congressional scrutiny, their advice has by law to be taken note of in making IT decisions. The Council of Chief Information Officers (CCIO) established at the same time has its own central staff to monitor and advise the President and Executive Office on government-wide IT issues and trends. It meets regularly and has achieved a considerable concertation of government policy. From 1998 onwards some US departments and agencies appointed senior figures also as Chief Knowledge Officers, with a brief to cover departmental knowledge management processes more widely than the use of ICTs. In 1999 OMB and CCIO developed the concept of a Federal Enterprise Architecture Framework (FEAF), which sought greater concertation between IT developments across the federal government as a whole. Under the Bush presidency from 2000 onwards the FEAF was more closely linked to budgetary allocations, with funding refused for developments duplicating work already done somewhere else in government and a stronger 'do it once, not multiple times' approach to IT development.

Both Canada and Australia followed the US pattern by appointing CIOs in the mid-1990s with very similar briefs. In fact CIO roles were more consistently implemented at departmental level in both countries than in the USA. And in Canada the government-wide pooling of CIOs' influence was also very significant, especially in being integrated with Treasury Board overviews of financial matters and in the country's strikingly successful e-government initiatives (see Section 4.3). In Australia CIOs' concertation was less influential and in the late 1990s the impetus for joining-up agencies and departments often came from a separate agency, the National Office of the Information Economy (NOIE), established to promote e-government changes.

At the other end of the spectrum, the country closest to having weak technical decision systems is the UK, for a wide range of reasons. The UK is a small land area and had a strikingly unitary government system with closely regimented local governments, until the implementation of devolution in 1999, near the end of our period—so that there has been little push for technical linking across governments. As detailed in Chapter 1, the British civil service system strongly emphasized the recruitment of 'generalists' without specific professional training, and technical staffs were traditionally exiled into separate hierarchies until the 1980s, where they were 'on tap, not on top'. Inward movement to the civil service by outside technical experts was severely restricted by an emphasis on life-long career paths. Departmental management systems were modernized in the late 1980s when an extensive process of agencification was undertaken (see next section), which 'hived off' most large blocs of technical work into discrete agencies. By the 1990s departments had established management boards on which sat representatives of the remaining divisions and sections, overwhelmingly policy divisions run by generalists. Systematic measures began only in the late 1990s to develop better professionalism within the civil service in fields like IT, financial accounting, and procurement management, along with efforts to attract more 'late' entrants to the service from other sectors.

In addition UK government IT functions were so extensively contracted out throughout our period (see Chapter 5) that most departments and many major executive agencies no longer retained any senior level IT official within their ranks. It was common for departmental management boards to include no one with any IT expertise. When Labour ministers mounted a push to promote e-government in the late 1990s they were forced to appoint generalist officials (whose normal briefs were often nothing to do with IT) as completely artificial 'e-government champions' to try and get management boards to give the issue at least some serious attention. Few departments appointed a CIO and the post of 'chief knowledge officer' is either unknown or where it does exist it is assigned to a low-level member of the departmental library staff rather than to a knowledge transfer specialist. It was not until around 2002 that the CIO role generally became a serious, top-level appointment, with the appointment of Richard Granger to run the National Health Service's new IT system at a reputed salary of £250,000 a year—far more than the salaries paid to top civil servants in departments (Permanent Secretaries), or even to the Prime Minister. A council of CIOs was eventually set up in Whitehall in 2005, and the head of e-Government Unit (in the Cabinet Office) was appointed to both chair the Council and to serve as the head of profession for IT managers and professionals across central government as a whole. At this time too, measures were taken to improve professional education and development. But these came too late in our core study period (1999–2005) to have any significant effect on how we rate the UK's technical policy preparedness here.

All these features leave the UK rating as more inside the set of countries weakly organized for IT decision-making. The cultural limitations of the bureaucracy were in general shared with, and compounded by, similar limitations of the political elite grounded in professions like law or public relations. Their attitudes in our period were well captured by Alastair Campbell, the director of government communications for new Labour's first six years in power:

I worked for Tony Blair for almost a decade [1994–2003], but did not use a computer. I should add that the Prime Minister is not much better. He, too, is at heart a pen and paper man.

So it is with some humility that the Prime Minister leads Britain towards technological progress. And it was without the faintest knowledge of how such progress was delivered that I oversaw a revamp of Government processes to take account of the internet's growing significance in communication with the public. (*The Independent* 11 January 2006: 39)

But the UK is not by any means a completely clear-cut or unambiguous member of the set of countries weakly organized for IT policymaking. However poorly informed political elites may have been, and however amateurish their understanding of informatization processes, British governments have certainly developed a large number of big IT systems. And in our period they have spent large amounts of money on IT modernization, supporting the view of them as 'hyper-modernist' in some particular respects (Moran 2003). Within the European Union some 2004 estimates suggested that the UK was undertaking up to a quarter of all IT capital spending in the government sector across the continent. And the UK's more general public management systems undoubtedly have considerable capacity for handling such big decisions and issues, however poorly government IT systems have performed in particular. For example, in the UK it is very rare for legislation to be left unimplemented and the administrative system has a fundamental capability for speedy, nationwide, and reliable implementation that is widely admired internationally. These countervailing considerations mean that we have scored the UK at 0.75 here rather than at 1.

New Zealand shares the same slot as the UK, partly because for a long period it had similar 'Westminster system' characteristics with an executive-dominated Parliament and a generalist civil service. The implementation of electoral reform in 1996 has subsequently moved New Zealand away from the Westminster paradigm, but executive predominance on administrative issues has changed less than other areas. The initial UK-generalist pattern of bureaucratic culture altered significantly as a result of strong NPM changes from the mid-1980s onwards (see Section 4.2), but not towards incorporating more technical expertise. New Zealand civil society has been an enthusiastic adopter of new technologies, especially any new communication technologies—partly because the country is so far away from anywhere else. But this pro-technology cultural stance found no real echo in the New Zealand public sector throughout this period. In particular, New Zealand, unlike the UK, has not had a big programme of IT improvements.

Japan is classified here as the most ambivalent case for a number of reasons. Japanese civil society and the governance system generally both place a strong emphasis on scientific and technological development, reflecting both the country's rapid industrialization experience from the late nineteenth century and its more recent post-1946 economic recovery. Japanese business is additionally strongly industrially orientated and the educational system assigns high priority to these issues. Yet the policy-making ranks of the Japanese higher civil service have also been dominated by university graduates from the law schools of a few major universities. This pattern is especially strong outside the main technical ministries (notably construction, which is run by engineers) and the trade and industry ministry (where technologists have historically played a more central role). There is a strong socialization of top civil servants within each ministry, with lateral movements between departments being very rare. So departmental cultures are remarkably distinct and persistent over time.

Most Japanese departments coped with the need to develop IT systems by hiving off responsibilities extensively to large private corporations, retaining little internal capacity even to act as an intelligent customer. There are no CIOs in Japanese departments and no government-wide network of IT professionals. The Ministry of Finance plays the key scrutiny role but has not developed specific expertise in IT systems. Political scrutiny of departments' and agencies' plans has also been muted in the modern period, with the LDP occupying a dominant position and continuously in office, with a secure parliamentary majority for all but a brief period of coalition government. While the LDP committees play a key policy role in some issues (like privatization and trade), this is not true not in internal administrative organization matters. Thus, Japan is an interesting hybrid case, combining a strong societal pro-technology orientation with a conservative and non-technically orientated civil service culture.

4.3 New Public Management Changes

Beginning in the early 1980s in the UK and Australia, and subsequently developed strongly in New Zealand and the UK, a movement known as New Public Management (NPM) dominated the agenda for changing or reforming public sector organization for two decades thereafter. In its early days NPM was often represented as introducing modern business management methods into public administration, which was usually to include more use of technology. In the mid-1980s this component included using more IT to displace previous paper-based operations, along with a shift to more PC-based systems instead of relying on mainframes. But this pro-IT theme was a distinctive feature of NPM only very briefly. It soon petered out and ceased to be discussed, because all public sector organizations increased their use of IT and changed the character of the IT they were using. So from the mid-1980s onwards, the NPM movement focused essentially on organizational restructuring changes that we argue below have been inimical to government IT performance. Before characterizing our countries in detail in terms of their NPM exposure, we first need to briefly review the movement's key features.

There is now a substantial branch industry in defining how NPM should be conceptualized and how NPM has changed, in particular as it has evolved through the New Zealand, Australian, UK and latterly European public administration systems. The result is that 'NPM is a slippery label' (Manning 2000). Different conceptualizations of NPM all stress different things. For Barzelay (2000: 156) it 'is primarily concerned with the systematic analysis and management of public management policy. This policy-domain relates to all government-wide, centrally managed institutional rules and routines affecting the public management process'. Rival conceptions characterize NPM in terms of specific policy principles, or 'trait' policy interventions seen as typical, or as an overall 'paradigm' for reforming government institutions. But even amongst these accounts NPM is variously characterized. Sometimes it is represented as copying business managerialism (of a now older kind) and in terms of unusually strong customer service orientation. But at other times NPM is defined in terms of internal organizational cultures and the use of a repertoire of more individualist, less hierarchist organizational control mechanisms (Hood 1998). Some conceptions additionally seem to assimilate NPM into strongly normative concepts, as in Aucoin's (1996) discussion of 'the well performing organisation'.

Our approach here recognizes NPM as a two-level phenomena (Dunleavy and Hood 1994). It has been, first, a strongly developed and coherent theory of managerial change based on importing into the public sector central concepts from (relatively) modern business practices and public choice-influenced theory. The three chief integrating themes in NPM have focused on:

- *Disaggregation.* Splitting up large public sector hierarchies in the same way that large private corporations earlier moved from U-form to M-form (multi-firm) structures; achieving wider, flatter hierarchies internally; and re-specifying their information and managerial systems to facilitate this different pattern of control. In the public sector this theme implied a strong flexibilization of previous government-wide practices in personnel, IT, procurement and other functions (Barzelay 2000).
- *Competition.* Introducing purchaser/provider separation into public structures so as to allow multiple forms of provision to be developed and to create (more) competition amongst potential providers. Increasing internal use was made of competition processes to allocate resources (in place of hierarchical decision-making). The 'core' areas of state administration and public provision were shrunk and suppliers were diversified.
- *Incentivization.* Shifting away from involving managers and staffs and rewarding performance in terms of diffuse public service or professional ethoses, and moving instead towards a greater emphasis on pecuniary-based, specific performance incentives. In the public sector this shift implied a movement 'down grid and down group' in Douglas's cultural theory terms (Dunleavy and Hood 1994). Its impact has been particularly marked for professional groups (Kirkpatrick et al. 2004).

But underpinning each of these three overarching ideas there was a prolific second tier of NPM-badged or NPM-incorporated ideas, a string of specific inventions and extensions of policy technologies that continuously expanded the NPM wave and kept it moving and changing configuration. Changes at this level were mostly driven in the first instance by the application of economic, business, and public choice ideas to pragmatic problems in public sector provision. But they were only implemented in practice as they were successfully adapted (or managerially and legally 'domesticated') to seem feasible in a public context. Yet a key part of the appeal of these second-level changes has also been that they fit into a wider reform movement and gain intellectual coherence from their link with the higher-order ideas above. We list these practices within each of the three NPM themes below.

The disaggregation components include:

- Purchaser–provider separation
- Agencification
- Decoupling policy systems
- Growth of quasi-government agencies
- Separation out of micro-local agencies (MLAs)
- Chunking up privatized industries
- Corporatization and strong single organization management
- De-professionalization
- Competition by comparison
- Improved performance measurement
- League tables of agency performance

There are signs that several of these strategies are being reversed or stalled in most places where they have been tried, but the enthusiasm with which they were pursued in the 1980s and 1990s in the UK and New Zealand in particular has left important organizational legacies. In the UK, the 'Next Steps' agencification programme once expected to include five-sixths of the central civil service, in fact stabilized at somewhat over half the total, and its claimed improvements in services provision have been closely questioned (James 2003; Talbot 2004). In New Zealand, the country's pioneering NPM structural changes have left a country with 4 million people with over 300 separate central agencies and 40 tiny ministries, in addition to local and health service authorities. Since New Zealand NPM was lauded by Alan Schick (1996) as the future for advanced industrial countries (but not developing countries), this luxuriant administrative fragmentation has in fact proved ineffective in helping the country make the most of its economic prospects. By 2000, New Zealand languished with the second lowest level of GDP per head amongst the OECD countries, although from 1999 a new Labour government embarked on more successful non-NPM policies. Unsurprisingly, combating the vertical siloing of agencies came to be identified by the country's top civil servants as a key priority for change (Bhatta 2003). The fragmentation of quasi-government agencies in the UK has similarly raised issues of duplicating costly separate management hierarchies for very similar functions. Little wonder then that a 2004 OECD paper cautions against agencification: 'Creating new organisations is a blunt instrument best used to build important new capacities, rather than as a stimulus for management improvement. The proliferation of more or less autonomous arm's-length public bodies makes collective action difficult' (OECD 2004: 4).

Decoupling policy systems and developing strong corporate management in agencies has clearly been seen in the UK as problematic, engendering management attitudes obsessed with intermediate organizational objectives rather than service delivery or effectiveness. Pushing independent institutions and the chunking-up of privatized industry regulation and ownership spectacularly came to grief in the UK with the effective bankruptcy of Railtrack and continuing controversy over rail governance arrangements (House of Commons Transport Select Committee 2004). MLAs first took off and then survived in the UK health and education sectors (Pollitt, Birchall, and Pearson, 1998). But both schools and hospitals were subsequently considerably restructured to foster a more integrated 'community' focus, with relatively high levels of continued central direction. Customer-seeking MLAs in the UK, the Netherlands, and Scandinavia have also stimulated some continuing use of league tables and improved performance measurement, which are the main continuing legacies of the NPM disaggregation theme.

The competition components include:

- Quasi-markets
- Voucher schemes
- Outsourcing
- Compulsory market testing
- Intra-government contracting
- Public/private sectoral polarization
- Product market liberalization
- Deregulation
- Consumer-tagged financing
- User control

Many of these components have stalled in recent years, but again they leave problematic legacies with particular relevance to government IT strategies. The most important is the almost complete outsourcing of government IT functions to private sector systems integrator firms in Australia, the UK, and New Zealand (described in Chapters 2, 3, and 5). Marketization of government services is still extending in some sectors in some advanced industrial countries, but few serious voices now believe that this is or should be anything more than a pragmatic response to immediate problems or opportunities for improvement. The large-scale cost reductions and quality enhancements of the planning and management functions anticipated by privatization enthusiasts in the 1980s and 1990s are no longer looked for. Some of these components have proved unworkable, notably the concept of full-scale quasi-markets which was phased out in health services in both Italy and the UK. Schemes for vouchers have also been little implemented and one UK pioneer (the Individual Learning Account) was quickly scrapped after falling prey to very high levels of provider fraud (NAO 2002*b*). Almost the only genuinely growing component of the competition theme has been consumer-tagged financing, so that public sector budget flows follow consumers instead of flowing in as-of-right fashion to governmental providers. User control of facilities has become established in schools systems in the UK, (Pollitt, Birchall, and Pearson 1998, Chapter 6) and some Scandinavian countries, but generally in a more politically regulated, close cooperation framework than anticipated by early enthusiasts in the early 1990s.

The incentivization components include:

- Re-specifying property rights
- 'Light touch' regulation
- Capital market involvement in projects
- Privatizing asset ownership
- Anti-rent-seeking measures
- De-privileging professions
- Performance-related pay
- PFI—the private finance initiative
- Public–private partnerships
- Unified rate of return and discounting
- Development of charging technologies
- Valuing public sector equity
- Mandatory efficiency dividends

This theme shows the highest proportion of still-developing NPM trends, some of which are relatively detailed rationalization changes with relevance for digital era public management as well as to NPM narrowly conceived. The unification of rates of return and discount rates, resource accounting, the valuation of public sector equity, and even mandatory efficiency dividends for public sector organizations all fit into this category. Critics also argue, however, that under NPM a flawed but still working and powerful public sector ethos was broken up by the piecemeal implementation of pecuniary and performance-based systems, with inherently lesser organizational capacity. Once traditional modes of handling organizational issues were eroded and could not easily be rebuilt (especially at a single-agency level), public sector managers often have had little chance but to continue looking for new forms of incentivization mechanisms to supplement their dwindling apparatus of control.

Increased pay differentiation inside public agencies is evident in the USA, UK, and Australia. But expectations that performance-related pay would significantly improve the performance of agency staffs have been greatly down-rated. These approaches claimed to produce streamlined and focused, business-like public organizations. But empirical research in Sweden suggests that there 'NPM creates heterogeneous, conflicting and fluid organisational identities, rather than the uniform and stable business identity it is supposed to' (Skålén 2004: 251). And some significant aspects of the incentivization theme (focusing on increasing private sector involvement in public sector provision) have either been reversed or proved far more consistently controversial than exponents anticipated.

Capital market involvement has proceeded furthest in the UK, with PFI, from the mid-1990s, under which contract providers were supposed to undertake a share of the risk in large-scale projects. Yet it also created new risks of catastrophic failure and potential losses of refinancing gains. The progress of PFI projects in construction has been disputed, with critics citing repeated underscaling and rising service charges for hospital projects, but defenders pointing to better timeliness and cost control in the build phase of PFI construction projects (NAO 2003b). A recent study commissioned by an accountancy professional body of 'design, build, finance, and operate' (DBFO) road schemes concluded: 'in just three years [of service payments] the Highways Agency paid £618 million, more than the initial capital cost of £590 million. . . . This means that the remaining payments on the 30-year contracts (worth about £6 billion) are for risk transfer, operation and maintenance' (Edwards et al. 2004). (Normally annual roads maintenance costs should be a small fraction of their initial capital costs.) In late 2003, after more than a decade of experimentation, the UK Treasury banned PFI and public–private partnership deals altogether for government IT, reflecting the chequered history of ineffective risk-transfer to contractors and high scrap rates for IT projects noted in

Chapter 3. Few PFI advocates now anticipate large-scale cost savings compared with (well-run) conventional procurements, and criticisms continue that the UK government is already overpaying for PFI projects on a heroic scale.

Given this analysis of the themes and components that constitute NPM, Table 4.3 shows how we score our seven countries in terms of their openness to NPM ideas and changes. It should be clear from the account above that the UK and New Zealand must count as core NPM countries, with each generating large numbers of distinctive NPM initiatives. The differences between their NPM trajectories were also substantial, however, for several reasons. Because there was no regional or devolved government in the UK until 1999, central policymaking involved many decisions and systems covering 60 million people. So the UK's NPM became distinctively 'corporate' in its approach, strongly orientated to handling major projects and systems using new NPM techniques, including involving private finance and large corporations in public service delivery. And because the UK government in this period was a relatively big entity on a global scale of public sector customers, it attracted strong amounts of corporate lobbying and buy-in on a wide range of NPM issues.

These features did not apply in New Zealand, whose whole national government is not much above the scale of a large metropolitan local authority in the UK. So here, although the ideological commitment to NPM in Wellington was just as intense from 1985 to 1996, especially within the Treasury, the movement became a kind of cult of close corporate management of small government agencies. Here the 'running government as a business' theme of early NPM endured far more. But instead of developing rapidly towards PFI and private sector involvement, as in the UK, it petered out instead in radical changes of accounting practices

Table 4.3 Membership of the set 'High openness to NPM changes'

Country	High openness to NPM changes (M)
New Zealand	1
UK	1
Australia	0.75
USA	0.5
Canada	0.25
Japan	0.25
Netherlands	0.25

(such as full-on accruals accounting) and tight specification of 'contracts' for chief executives of the very small, policy-only ministries and larger executive agencies. And whereas NPM in the UK became an approach wedded to incessant reorganizations and large public management reform projects, in New Zealand the NPM incentives acting strongly on senior managers favoured attention to detail, cost paring, and avoiding major risk factors during their terms of office.

The other three English-speaking countries in our cases have different degrees of ambivalence in their stance to NPM. Australia was an early NPM leader, pioneering some distinctive NPM reforms. But under Labour governments the initially radical impetus for change here faded into a more humanist style by the mid-1990s, which foreshadowed the approach adopted in the USA during the Clinton-Gore NPR period. The switch of government created a strong take-up of outsourcing and some later incentivization elements of NPM were imported from the UK. But Liberal ministers in the late 1990s were otherwise fairly pragmatic and conservative in their changes of major administrative systems. Thus, Australia is a clear NPM country, but in a less intense way than the UK or New Zealand.

Both the USA and Canada also implemented parts of the NPM agenda but resisted other parts. The USA made some concerted NPM-style changes during the NPR period. But it never embraced the whole agenda proactively, mainly interspersing periods of cutbacks with periods of administrative stasis. Federal officials and American public management or public administration academics only began to recognize the NPM term itself very late on, many arguing that the ideas involved were already long in play across the USA's federal, state and highly fragmented local governments. Once the NPR period passed, it is hard to see any self-conscious or concerted NPM effort, despite some large NPM-like projects or experiments. Thus, we have classed the USA as neither within nor outside NPM, and scored it as 0.5.

Canada undertook some NPM-like reforms in the late 1980s and early 1990s, but in a much more humanist and less technocratic way than the UK or New Zealand. During the ascendancy of Liberal governments NPM innovations were recognized and discussed widely in Ottawa, but there was no coherent political push behind them, beyond a certain penchant for using 'off budget' agencies and organizations, a strategy which had other political origins. Nor did the Canadian civil service culture ever develop along the UK 'business process' or New Zealand 'accountability' lines, instead retaining its historically well-entrenched and consensual public service ethos and traditions. Hence we categorize Canada as 0.25, almost out of the NPM set but with some complicating features.

Two of our countries, Japan and the Netherlands, are classed here as predominantly resistant to NPM. Japan pioneered some big-scale privatization initiatives (notably on its railway system and in telecoms). But core central government administration remained organized on very orthodox public administration lines throughout our period. For instance, the Japanese Post Office resisted any form of corporatization for many years and changes only began to commercialize it after 2004. Not until the very end of our period did Japanese ministries and local governments begin to discuss NPM changes in self-conscious terms. Some observers predict extensive changes away from the traditional strong bureaucratic style towards more flexible and faster-changing Anglo-American public management approaches (see Furukawa 2001). But in our period these shifts remained small scale.

The Netherlands also implemented some detailed NPM ideas at a technical level or in individual projects, for instance, in outsourcing state unemployment services to private providers and in using voluntary sector bodies to deliver public services at local levels. But these changes were made for very specific reasons, and without a strong or concerted political push for NPM as such from the Netherlands' coalition governments. The civil service also maintained a pretty strongly corporatist set of public sector arrangements throughout our period.

The impact of a country being heavily exposed to NPM we expect to be adverse for government IT performance for two different groups of reasons. There is a dimension of especially the UK's 'corporate NPM' approach that had major implications for the contractual relations between government and the IT industry that we review in detail in the next chapter. The distinctively institutional aspects of NPM (on which we concentrate here) impacted on government IT performance primarily in three ways:

- strengthening the fragmentation of public sector organizations, via disaggregation, agencification, and stronger corporate management of each separate agency;
- reducing the size of some agencies in ways that made it harder to retain in-house IT expertise, which anyway NPM advocates should not be retained (see next chapter);
- weakening or destroying the previous machinery for central provision or coordination of government IT, so that IT changes could only be

undertaken in heavily siloed ways and at a tempo that meshed with the interested of de-concentrated agencies.

These institutional impacts damaged government IT performance by increasing the gulf in understanding between politicians and top civil servants engaged in policy-making and the public agencies delivering IT-intensive services. And the strong new government siloing pressures within NPM countries and loss of central policy capacity both slowed down and fractured the coherent and joined-up re-envisioning necessary for effective e-government strategies, to which we now turn.

4.4 The Role of E-Government Initiatives

The final element in the institutional and bureaucratic context for government IT policymaking is the absence of a strong centralized or early e-government initiative. The salient empirical features of these commitments have been surveyed above (in Section 2.1) and we shall not repeat them in detail here. It is useful to make clear what the criteria here mean and then to show how the countries have been scored in the Table 4.4. A strong commitment is indicated in one of at least two ways:

- either significant extra or earmarked e-government expenditures;
- or the public identification of a specific target for e-government provision or growth by the leading figure in government, the Prime Minister in a parliamentary system or the President elsewhere.

Table 4.4 Membership of the set 'No strong, centralized, and early e-government initiative'

Country	No strong, centralized, and early e-government initiative (I)
Japan	1
New Zealand	1
USA	0.5
Netherlands	0.25
Australia	0.25
Canada	0
UK	0

A centralized commitment is one where a central department or agency within the national government controls significant resources that can be distributed in a discretionary way so as to:

- encourage e-government projects and promote acceptance of Web and digital technologies; or to
- set clear transgovernmental targets for e-services provision or the take-up of electronic access by citizens or businesses; and to
- foster favourable private sector trends—such as e-commerce growth, increasing computer and Internet literacy and access, and the reduction of 'digital divide' problems.

Early adoption is defined as a case where major developments occurred before 1998–9, that is, in the first four or five years following the first widely available Web browser (the Mosaic browser launched in 1994, which subsequently became Netscape). Any country where substantial initiatives occurred only after 1999 is defined as a latecomer. Note that all the criteria here concern decisional processes and sequences. They focus on the strength and impetus of the institutional push for e-government change, and not on the outcomes achieved, which will often reflect multi-causal processes. The table above shows our classification of countries against these criteria.

Two countries are clear-cut cases without strong, centralized, or early e-government initiatives, albeit for radically different reasons. In New Zealand, the dominance of NPM influences carried through into a high level of departmental and agency fragmentation that was clearly inimical both for the development of e-services and for the coordination of the provision that was put in place, hesitantly and piecemeal. NPM also meant that there was a hollow centre in Wellington, with a long lag in the development of coordination infrastructures, portal sites, and coherent strategies until the 2001 initiative by the State Services Commission. Even this slow government reaction was not backed by much central funding and lacked strong Prime Ministerial endorsement.

Japan's feeble and delayed e-government efforts in the 1990s are harder to explain. The key influences seem to have been the remoteness of the top administrative class from understanding the potentially radical implications of the Internet and the Web for government sector organization, strongly compounded by the long-standing outsourcing of government IT provision to computer companies, themselves somewhat removed from participating in the cutting edge of technology and more broadly in software development. There were suggestions of a concerted approach to e-government and e-commerce around 1999, and the Japanese government throughout this period was investing heavily in anti-deflationary public spending in efforts to restart the faltering economy. But it was not until 2001 that a properly resourced and coordinated programme (the eJapan Strategy) was launched, with targets for 'one-stop' online service delivery, by which time the country was lagging well behind not just the USA but most other advanced industrial competitors.

At the other end of the spectrum, two countries (Canada and the UK) score zero on this criterion. They are clearly not members of the set, because they had strong, relatively early, well-resourced, and long-sustained e-government initiatives. In the UK e-government goals were backed by a strong Prime Ministerial commitment quite early on (in autumn 1997). And the initially unambitious strategy was substantially tightened up in 1999, backed by £1 billion of dedicated funding over seven years, and centrally coordinated by a central unit (the Office of e-Envoy) reporting to the PM. The UK's effort reflects both the strong centralization of power in the Westminster system and the 'high modernism' orientation of the new Labour government and the top-level civil service (by this stage). The UK is an unusual case because, despite these indications of strong commitment, its concerted e-government campaign for a long time had relatively weak and long-lagged impacts, as we saw above. But decisionally the UK was clearly in a different camp from its fellow NPM pioneer, New Zealand.

Canada made a similarly timed commitment as the UK, although for a while its resource boost for e-government seemed rather moderate and its Access Canada programme attracted less attention than the showier starts made in the USA or Australia. However, unlike these cases the Canadians stuck with their e-government ambitions in a long-term way. And unlike the UK, they compensated for relatively fewer dedicated financial resources available for allocation by central agencies by pushing along a more collegial and cooperative effort. Their programme pooled resources more effectively across the big spending departments, created a Federal Enterprise Architecture Plan (FEAP) that predated the US efforts, and even bridged across to (some of) the provincial governments in the Canadian federation.

The Netherlands and Australia both had appreciable e-government initiatives. But they are categorized here as less clear-cut non-members of the set of countries with such programmes, again for several reasons—but all basically reflecting less prominent back-up in terms of resourcing or less strong commitments of political capital. Australia took an early lead under a Labour government, with one of the first and initially most demanding pledges on making services available in electronic form, plus strongish central backing from two agencies. The early momentum generated was sustained by strong and imaginative Web and Internet commitments by big-spending departments, such as the Australian Tax Office and Centre-link. But after the switch of government control in 1996, the edge fell off the e-government programme, with relatively slower development of government portals and integrated services, and a more stale feel to central coordination efforts. In the later 1990s much administrative and IT industry attention was diverted to the mandated privatization of government IT services instead. And even when this effort was de-emphasized there was no return to the previous e-government impetus in terms of financial or political commitments. (This effect may also reflect the interesting pattern in the Australian private sector, where rapid productivity gains were being made from the late 1990s despite the country's very small IT sector, unlike (say) the USA, where ICTs were critical for the upswing in private sector productivity growth.)

The Netherlands in some ways seems the opposite case to the UK, achieving what seem like considerable results and growth in e-government usage (see below) but with a much more diffused, unpolitical, and cheaper set of interlocking initiatives. Partly this effect reflected the established presence of 'informatization' as a theme of Dutch public management, long before the Web became a key motor for change. The Netherlands had never scrapped its apparatus for central coordination of a less directive and more collegial kind, and it was adapted relatively easily to the needs of the new era. The strong development of computer literacy in schools, widespread PC access, and the later public appetite for Internet use all meant that some relatively early but low-cost interventions seemed to work through the governmental system at national and local level in effective ways, without an apparatus of mandatory targets (beyond an early, unambitious 25 per cent e-services target for 2002, that soon became redundant). Hence the Netherlands too is categorized as 0.25, almost in the set of countries with major e-government initiatives, but with some room for doubt.

Finally, the USA is perhaps the hardest case to classify on this criterion. President Clinton's NPR in 1994 included a very early and in retrospect far-sighted set of Internet-era goals. It was also a strong political commitment, albeit in practice the follow-through came mainly from his unusually activist Vice President, Al Gore. But there was then little real impact in terms of specific e-government resourcing or central provision. Thousands of federal websites blossomed and grew quickly, reflecting US agencies 'can do' approach to technology innovations and stronger household and enterprise take-up of the Internet. But within the government sector

Internet information was provided in poorly coordinated and unindexed ways, federal versus state government barriers were poorly bridged, and 'digital divide' issues were not much addressed. For instance, there were four or five abortive attempts to establish a government-wide portal at federal level, before one very low-cost initiative (*www.first.gov*) finally succeeded in becoming established from 2000. The NPR had more or less run its course before the end of the Clinton presidency and the Bush White House had other priorities and modes of operating. Bush's low-key messages of support for continuing e-government efforts were emphatically not linked to dedicated funding or much creative thinking. The Bush OMB team's efforts stressed preventing agencies duplicating each others' IT investments or efforts, and the reduction of competitive agency efforts by integrating them with the relatively conservative FEAF. Partly displaced by later initiatives, for instance around homeland security, these switches of policy make the USA a relatively ambiguous case as a centralized e-government initiative.

4.5 Putting Together Governance and Bureaucratic Influences on the Performance of Government IT

Each of the four dimensions of governance and bureaucratic arrangements reviewed here we expect to be unfavourable for government IT performance. Yet Table 4.5 shows that for most countries the scoring picture on these dimensions is pretty mixed. There is only one country, New Zealand, that has middle to high scores (expected to be adverse for government IT performance) on all our criteria and even then, the minimum is 0.5. Japan has a minimum of 0.25. Five countries achieve zero scores on at least one criteria (shown in the minimum column)—the USA, the Netherlands, and the three Westminster systems, Canada, Australia, and the UK. Yet only the Netherlands uniformly achieves a low score on all criteria, followed at a little distance by the USA and Canada with a couple of 'in the middle' scores. As well as New Zealand, both the UK and Japan have two or three completely adverse scores—shown by the maximum column in Table 4.5. The table shows strongly varied scores assigned to the UK (spanning the full range), and to Japan and Australia (both with a range of 0.75). In these countries then the pattern of influences on government IT performance from governance and bureaucratic factors was rather mixed, compared with the favourable set-ups in the Netherlands, USA, and Canada, and the adverse patterning in New Zealand.

Table 4.5 Summary codings for the components of the influence of bureaucratic and governance institutions, 1990–2005

Country	Governance system has few checks and balances on the executive (G)	Weak cultural and institutional systems for handling technology decisions and projects (C)	High openness to new public management changes (M)	No strong or central-ized e-government initiative (E)	G . C . M . E (minimum)	G + C + M + E (maximum)
New Zealand	0.5	0.75	1	1	0.5	1
Japan	1	0.5	0.25	1	0.25	1
UK	1	0.75	1	0	0	1
Australia	0.75	0.25	0.75	0	0	0.75
Canada	0.5	0.25	0.25	0	0	0.5
USA	0	0.25	0.5	0.5	0	0.5
Netherlands	0	0	0.25	0.25	0	0.25

To try and work out the influence which these rankings have on government IT performance, we set them against the scorings for government IT performance given in Table 3.2 (page 74 in the previous chapter). Again we closely follow the suggestions made by Ragin (2000), focusing most attention on the intersection set shown in the penultimate column of the two tables. Our primary concern in both chapters has been to assign cases to sets, or to intermediate scaling points. The horizontal axis in Figure 4.1 measures the scorings we have assigned for the governance and bureaucratic influences upon government policymaking (the independent or causing variable here). The vertical axis shows the scorings for the level of performance of government IT (the dependent or caused variable) assigned in Chapter 3. The key coordinates in each case according to Ragin are the minima on the two dimensions.

These combined scorings for the intersection sets in both dimensions are marked as black dots in Figure 4.1. There is a broadly negative relationship between the independent and dependent variables here. That is, the more that governance and bureaucratic structures were rated as likely to worsen IT performance on the lines argued above, the less effective the

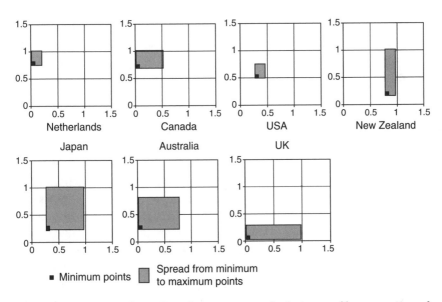

Figure 4.1. Mapping the codings for seven countries in terms of bureaucratic and institutional features (horizontal axis) and the performance of government IT (vertical axis)

performance of government IT has indeed turned out to be. This relationship is not hugely strong, however. It works well for the four countries shown in the top row of Figure 4.1, but poorly for the three countries in the bottom row. When just looking at the minimum score on the horizontal axis, Japan, Australia, and the UK all rank at 0 or 0.25 on the governance and bureaucratic influences dimension, not dissimilar from the Netherlands, Canada, or the USA.

We also need to look at the impact of the variations in countries' scorings across the two sets of criteria, shown by the union set, which Ragin argues can be captured by looking at the maximum scores in Tables 3.2 and 4.1. Three countries, the Netherlands, the USA, and New Zealand, show a minimal level of variation in their governance and bureaucratic structures, while Canada is only a little more broad brush. However, the variation from minimum to maximum scores is much higher for the Japan, Australia, and the UK.

Looking at the rectangular space of variation from the joint minima points to the joint maxima points is useful. It provides a kind of visual sensitivity test, graphically illustrating the extent to which each country's scores on the six component aspects examined here are similar or more divergent. The range of shapes shown also visually captures the many differences that exist across the seven countries examined here. Overall Figure 4.1 suggests that there is a causal association between the governance and bureaucratic criteria considered here with the performance of government IT, but with a good deal of variation and uncertainty about the coding of the bottom three countries shown.

One possible objection here is that the last variable we have considered in this chapter, whether countries launched concerted e-government initiatives, is too closely related to the dependent variable, the performance of government IT, one of whose components relates to the modernity of government IT, including an e-government element. To see what difference it makes to leave out the e-government element, Figure 4.2 shows just the long-run bureaucratic and institutional influences on the horizontal axis. Only three countries' shapes are affected by this change, all of them Westminster systems with strong e-government initiatives. For Canada and Australia the change is minor, moving their minima from 0 to 0.25. But for the UK the impact is considerable, shifting its minimum from 0 to 0.75. The overall effect is to strengthen the view that for the Netherlands, Canada, the USA, and the UK there is a relatively clear negative relationship between the criteria considered here and government IT performance.

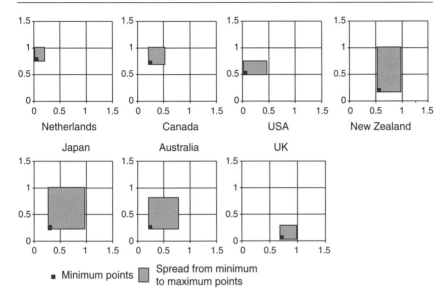

Figure 4.2. Mapping the codings for seven countries in terms of long-run bureaucratic and institutional features (horizontal axis), excluding the e-government initiatives variable, and the performance of government IT (vertical axis)

This effect is less clear-cut in Australia, New Zealand, and Japan, where (in different ways) societal culture influences the political culture to be somewhat more supportive of technological initiatives.

Conclusions

At first sight it might seem axiomatic that the political and institutional influences on government IT will be decisive factors on how government IT performance maps out. After all, the variables considered here condition the situations within which policy decisions are made and act directly upon decision-makers. But our analysis shows that although there are certainly interesting associations, the links here are not as strong or as straightforward as might have been expected. A moment's reflection will also suggest why this might be the case, namely that governments are not directly producing their own IT performance, but instead turning to the IT industry to deliver much of the systems and management needed to sustain modern ITs. We need, therefore, to consider the impact of these industry influences in more detail, which forms the focus of the next chapter.

5

Explaining Performance II: Competitive Tension and the Power of the IT Industry

Corporate power is an easy thing to discuss in general terms, but a hard thing to calibrate. Reviewing the possible differentia of the IT industry's position in relation to government agencies on public sector IT contracts suggests that three dimensions are particularly salient:

1. *The extent to which the formal, legal requirements surrounding government IT contracts emphasize the maintenance of 'spot' market contracting and vigorous and unfettered competition.* Closely related to this stance is the maintenance of 'orthodox' procurement practices, essentially the supply of services to government agencies in small packets that are and can be easily openly competed in the marketplace, if not by 'all comers' then at the least by (almost) all qualified corporations operating in the market.

2. *The market and technical dominance of large firms in the government IT market,* which is specific to the sector and can often be radically different from that in other IT markets. Our key focus here is on civilian or general purpose IT systems, excluding weapons-related IT systems in the military agencies.

3. *The extent to which government agencies retain the capacity to maintain or re-establish their own in-house IT service, and to design, coordinate, and implement substantial IT projects.* A key question here is whether an in-house unit can at a minimum still take the systems integrator role or act as the procurement manager in an orthodox contracting set-up for meeting the agency's IT needs.

These dimensions are manageable ones but they call for different kinds of evidence to place our seven countries against them. In some cases it is feasible to come up with quantitative variable proxies that are reasonably close to the things that interest us in each of these cases, as for example, looking at market concentration data in relation to dimension 2. However, our interest is chiefly in establishing how country cases considered at an aggregate level can be classified as fully members or non-members of a given theoretically and empirically relevant set, or as having an intermediate position between complete membership and complete non-membership of the set.

In this perspective, it is worth mentioning again that some ranges of variation may not be relevant for us to consider. For instance, in continuous variable terms there may be large differences within the set of countries with government IT markets dominated by large firms—some countries may have 60 per cent of the market going to the top five firms and others have 90 per cent. Yet we may have many grounds for believing that any 'extra' level of variation above (say) 50 per cent of the market going to the top five is not relevant for the way in which government IT is contracted or for the influence which the largest corporations can wield in the contracting process. Similarly, knowing market concentration ratios is a useful indication of possible large firm influence. But we need to supplement it with other kinds of information before allocating countries to the polar 'large firms dominant' or 'not dominant' sets, or alternatively trying to decide whether they are 'mixed' cases and closer to one pole or the other.

Again, given the small number of country cases considered here, and the inherently complex task of classifying them on even a few fundamental dimensions, we restrict our attention to the five-category scheme developed by Ragin and discussed in Chapter 3 where the available categorizations are: *fully included in the set*, scored as 1; *more in the set than out*, scored as 0.75; *neither in nor out of the set*, the crossover point, scored as 0.5; *more out of the set than in*, scored as 0.25; *fully out of the set*, scored as 0.

5.1 De-Emphasis on Open Competition for Contracts

The nineteenth century model of contracting developed with the rise of public companies to regulate spot contracting in the market. Its key elements are secret competitive bidding against a publicly available 'request for proposals' issued by the government agency and publicized in open advertisements. Normally the lowest price bids for standard products are accepted, unless there are exceptional and well-established grounds for doubting the credentials or capabilities of the firm with the lowest priced bid. With more complex products, where it is harder to fully include all key quality differences in the product specification, greater attention needs to be paid to establishing a final bidders list consisting only of qualified companies with the right expertise and assurance systems to deliver a satisfactory product. But within this group price competitiveness should still be decisive in open competition.

Table 5.1 shows our summary view of how far countries have gone in their government IT contracting towards formally renouncing the open competition model. The most explicit government tending to set aside open competition in the 1990–2005 period was the UK. Australia and New Zealand have broadly followed this lead but not gone as far. The Netherlands and the USA still place most reliance upon maintaining vigorous market competition. In different ways, Canada and Japan have adopted a more ambivalent stance.

The UK moved into its distinctive position of de-emphasizing open competition in IT procurement very early in the 1980s, following a lead taken from construction industry projects, where a long-run movement to selective tendering and then to negotiated contracts took place as early as the late 1960s and early 1970s (Turpin 1972). The thrust of central government advice on large IT procurements moved to progressively de-emphasize formal open competition by a large number of different routes, beginning with a strong emphasis on selective tendering with only the most qualified companies. From 1985 to the early 1990s the NPM emphasis on agencies and departments taking direct responsibility for their own internal management meant that a range of government-wide internal checks

Table 5.1 Membership of the set 'De-emphasis on open competition'

Country	De-emphasis on open competition (N)
UK	1
Australia	0.75
New Zealand	0.75
Canada	0.5
Japan	0.5
Netherlands	0
USA	0

and controls on IT contracts were progressively dismantled. The new arrangements created a much more de-concentrated system than previously, where large departments could run their own policies in their own way and where the expert Treasury capacity to scrutinize IT contracts (admittedly via the ineffectual CCTA) was first run down and then abolished altogether. Partly in response to experience of large IT projects failing, government advice also put more and more stress on carefully controlled selective tendering, with an intensive pre-qualification stage leading to the selection of no more than two or three prospective bidders, between whom competitive tension was none the less supposed to be maintained.

The growth of very large and very long-term outsourcing contracts was a key element of NPM contractual innovation in the UK, and it proceeded further and faster in government IT than anywhere else in the world. For instance, the IT aspects of all central government income tax and other tax collection IT operations have twice been contracted out as whole (in 1994 and 2004), in each case for a decade. Central government IT deals in the UK regularly involved huge contract prices and contained few if any safeguards against 'information impactedness' problems. Here an incumbent contractor working for an agency acquires a near-insuperable information advantage about the agency's systems and operations over rivals hoping to supplant it, which translates into substantial protection against effective competition.

Australian contracting policy was similar to the UK's in the pre-NPM era. However, from the late 1980s under a Labour administration the government moved to remove curbs on contracting that sought to provide safeguards on the involvement of smaller, Australian-based companies in the government IT sector. Instead emphasis was placed upon a more strictly 'liberal' interpretation that prioritized price competitiveness, however obtained, and encouraged departments and agencies to involve large external corporations more in the design and development of their major business systems. The advent of a Liberal/National administration committed to downsizing the state led to a prime ministerial initiative to force all commonwealth departments and agencies to outsource their entire IT operations to the private sector. The vehicle chosen to achieve this objective was a centrally decided 'clustering' of departments into groups, each of which would transfer its IT operations lock, stock, and barrel to one of the largest international and Australian-based IT corporations. After four years this cluster scheme fell apart amidst acrimonious disputes between departments, and strong criticisms from the Australian National Audit Office and a government-appointed special inquiry team. Only a few small fig leaf clauses mandated that large firms provide a degree of support for Australian small firms and IT sector development via partnering and mentoring schemes. On the other hand, Australian processes did retain elements of real competition at the stage of the initial cluster contract allocation. And once clustering failed department and agency officials did their best to reduce their dependence on single contractors and to encourage relatively rapid recontracting and preservation of core 'intelligent customer' capabilities.

By contrast to these two cases of competition requirements being marginalized or sidelined, some countries still place open competition at the centre of their contractual regimes. They have developed a number of approaches for coping with or mitigating the advent of oligopolies or the possible loss of expertise to large contractors. In the first place, contractual law is still very much based upon open, all-comers competition, rather than restricting access to firms on a pre-qualified list. Contracts are deliberately configured so as to preserve a capability for mid- and small-sized firms to bid as plausible main contractors, so that giant, all-encompassing projects are rarer. Governmental staff may do more of the 'systems integration' role, letting out discrete packages of work to different corporations and managing their joint working. Rules favouring small businesses' involvement, or those advancing participation by home-country-, ethnic-minority- or female-owned firms alongside 'majors', can have the effect of broadening and enhancing competition. And in the more competitive policy regimes government ministers, agencies, and officials all see the maintenance of requisite diversity in the government IT market as an important policy goal. For them it is a key background condition that needs to be maintained by active steering and appropriate inducements.

In these terms the USA and the Netherlands are clearly the most wedded to competitive contracting, although their approaches are radically different ones. US departments' policy is to encourage and develop the government IT market by keeping it very vigorously competitive and encouraging the emergence and development of small technology companies. US government IT operations show tremendous scale and variations, with both civilian office systems specialists and large defence sector–based contractors having significant market shares. So maintaining a diversity of major contractors has been relatively easy at federal level. US contracts were for a long time configured in ways which also fostered frequent competition, with terms limited to three years, large-scale projects modularized into discretely contractable pieces, and considerable Congressional and OMB resistance to more innovative contractual vehicles. Although multi-year and multi-task contracting vehicles developed in the NPR era and have been used increasingly since the end of the 1990s, the pre-qualification criteria here were relatively easily met and the 'A' list contractors in each vehicle are still numerous and must compete in only a slightly reduced way for specific task orders. New contract vehicles also have restrictive thresholds (sometimes evaded or expanded by serially letting contracts) and are subject to periodic review. There is a vigorous culture of contract surveillance and contractors are prone to contesting any awards that seem to them unfair, facilitated through a Board of Contract Appeals. But the history of close industry surveillance and litigious contestation of any dubious contract awards by agencies have contributed to maintaining the salience of rigorously abiding by formal competitive rules. Most government officials are keenly aware of the dangers of becoming overdependent on one or a few suppliers, and departments and agencies take active steps to ensure that they retain options and can solicit genuinely competitive bids for all contracts.

In the Netherlands, the maintenance of a competitive government IT market is achieved by radically different, corporatist means. Agencies and government departments split contracts up into what are by international standards very small packages of work—single contracts exceeding US$1 million, for example, are relatively rare events. Each agency likes to develop and keep up relations with a plurality of suppliers and a conscious effort is made to ensure that this diversity does not reduce over time—if one contractor seems in danger of dropping out of the race, the agency may bring forward appropriate packages of work to keep it engaged. Agencies also have large in-house IT capabilities (see below), so that they have the option of carrying out contracts themselves if competitive bids cannot be found in the private market. Large projects are always envisaged from the outset as multi-contractor and designed so that the agency maintains options for tenderers.

The New Zealand case is close to the fully competitive levels found in the USA and the Netherlands, but not quite wholly in the same set. Historically New Zealand's dominant central government developed close relationships with a small number of multinational IT industry majors, with their office blocks crowding around the civil service district of Wellington. Like other Westminster systems such as the UK and Australia, New Zealand in the early 1980s looked as if it could develop away from the open competition model of IT procurement. In fact the country's distinctively strong NPM developments took it on a radically different route to the UK and Australia, one which pushed it back towards a greater emphasis on open competitive tendering, accepting lowest cost bids, and avoiding newer contract forms and vehicles.

The centrepiece of the New Zealand NPM changes was that the chief executives of government departments and agencies all became contracted employees, appointed for short terms of around three-years, and tasked to implement for their client ministers detailed contracts on behalf of their department and agency. Chief executives became personally answerable for all aspects of their agency's performance and central to most of their contracts for around a decade and half were demanding cost reduction and cost efficiency targets. The NPM arrangements strongly encouraged risk-averse behaviour by chief executives, including the break-up of IT projects into modularized smaller-scale changes where the agency's potential exposure to losses was minimized, and improvements were fitted as far as possible within chief executives' three-year terms. This stance led to a scrupulous insistence on operating all competition processes rigorously and impartially, and a strong move away from negotiated contracts. These considerations lead to our categorization of the New Zealand case as not a fully competitive one, but clearly more competitive than not, even though the key mechanisms producing competition are the NPM changes rather than the overt contract regime itself.

The Canadian federal government's trajectory is a second intermediate case. It combines aspects of the other Westminster systems' willingness to tolerate deviations away from market competition requirements, with the USA's strong pro-competition emphasis. Canadian departments and agencies have easy access to much the same large and relatively diversified IT industry as operates in the USA. US corporations' culture of exercising vigilance over contracts, and their litigousness over any apparent deviations from open competitive tendering have had a powerful effect on Canadian policies too, along with the formal provisions of the North American Free Trade Area (NAFTA) on open competition for government services. The impact of these practices has been dulled somewhat, however, by a Canadian corporatist style of negotiating contractors' involvement in large projects, while placing a premium on avoiding undue government dependency and maintaining a larger government capacity to take back the direct management of failing IT projects and systems. The conservatism of many US corporations in handling a different public administration system has combined with some Canadian defensiveness, seeking to protect the remnants of a separate IT industry (such as

WordPerfect Corporation) from being swallowed up by bigger rivals over the border to mean that the government IT market in Canada does not show the same diversity as in the USA. These considerations all suggest categorizing Canada as on the cusp between the two sets, sharing aspects of each.

The final intermediate case is Japan, perhaps the most complex de facto policy situation, and the country whose modus operandi in government procurement is most resistant to easy classification by outside observers. On the surface Japan is apparently strongly committed to the open competition model. All government IT contracts are officially short term, usually lasting no more than one to three years, with the vast bulk of them being annual procurements. Longer-term contracts are virtually unknown, and no formal acknowledgement is made of negotiated contracts, nor are any innovative contract vehicles in use. Open tendering is practised, so that any firm can in principle enter the race for any particular contract, with new companies bidding 'out of the blue' or established contractors elsewhere deciding to challenge an incumbent. In its dealings with the WTO Japan strongly insists on the complete openness of all government contracts to bids by multinational or non-Japanese companies and on the absence of any pro-Japanese rules or biases of any kind.

But in practice, as noted in Chapter 2, the Japanese government IT market is highly oligopolistic and closely structured. Virtually all available systems work is distributed across the main Japanese contractors, especially NEC, Hitachi, and Fujitsu (each of which began as essentially hardware firms but have subsequently developed software and systems integration capabilities), NTTD (the former government data centre) and IBM Japan, the only foreign player that over time has been able to establish itself in the Japanese government market. IBM is involved in domestic business community activities and the current president is a major player. The company has developed a reputation for trustworthiness with the Japanese government from the 1970s and can 'claim to be part of Japan', as one official put it. The firms generally have very long-lived relationships with individual ministries, and the annual contracting round is in most years purely formalistic, since it would not be practicable for any firm except the incumbent to take over the running or maintenance of ongoing proprietary systems put in place by a rival. Very occasionally, at the end of one integrated project and the launch of another by a department, one of the Japanese majors will challenge an incumbent rival for work from a department or agency with which it has not previously had a relationship. Occasionally also another Japanese company may win a role within a consortium fronted by a Japanese major. But most annual competitions produce only one credible bid, and Japanese companies have relationships lasting at least fifteen to twenty years with the departments where they have established links.

5.2 The Market and Technology Dominance of Large Firms

Large firms can acquire an oligopolistic dominance in two main ways—by cornering the market, so that as a group they can mop up so many available resources for designing and managing large and complex IT systems that new entrants are more or less precluded; and by acquiring a technological expertise that new competitors find hard to match. Over the entire period that we studied, the largest government IT systems were almost invariably supplied in an a la carte design mode, with little modularization and each system having strong *sui generis* characteristics, features which both intrinsically favoured large contractors and which they worked hard to sustain.

Table 5.2 shows our overall judgements of the degree of large firms' market and technical predominance, with the Netherlands standing out as a country with little such influence. The two countries with the largest and the smallest government IT markets, the USA and New Zealand respectively, were the nearest cases where large firms' predominance was constrained, again as we see for divergent reasons. By contrast, three countries (the UK, Japan, and Australia) all show virtually complete predominance for a few large IT companies. Canada occupies a more ambiguous position for a number of detailed reasons.

Table 5.2 Membership of the set 'Large firms' market and technical predominance'

Country	Large firms' market and technical predominance
Australia	1
Japan	1
UK	1
Canada	0.5
New Zealand	0.25
USA	0.25
Netherlands	0

A key set of data underpinning our scores above are the estimated market shares of the largest firms. There are considerable differences here in our ability to surface objective data, so our scores are derived from a mix of firmly based market estimates published in IT industry or government statistics, and more subjective estimates derived from our interviews and surveys of qualitative indicators. Despite the data difficulties it is clear that the market share of the top five firms in 2000 ranged from below a fifth in the Netherlands to over 90 per cent in the UK and Australia. The middle countries show around a third to two-fifths of the government IT market in the hands of the top five firms, a relatively highly concentrated market by any private sector standards. In the US, where there is more data available than any of our other countries, we estimate that the market share of the top five is around 20 per cent. The UK is quite unusual in the extent to which a single very large systems integrator corporation, EDS, was on its own in a near-dominant position within the government IT market throughout much of the 1990–2005 period covered here. Officials in many other countries that we visited consistently remarked that this must be an unbalanced situation and believed that their governments would not allow such a configuration to arise there.

Looking briefly at each of the countries we can note some other indications of large corporations' market and technical influence, many of them specific to one country. In the USA rules mandating small business participation (and to a much lesser degree participation by ethnic minority-owned and women-owned businesses) have fostered the development of small- to mid-sized companies, some of which deliberately restrict the scale of their operations so as to qualify for government consideration. Consortia arrangements are also flexible and more balanced than in most other countries, with small- or mid-sized firms sometimes operating as the main contractors and IT majors or even systems integrators acting as subcontractors to them.

New Zealand shows an interesting pattern of large firms dominating the government IT market in terms of market share, but without the IT industry as a whole being in a strong position. With a population of only 4 million people New Zealand is a tiny market in world terms, and the presence of major companies (such as IBM, EDS, and others) at all partly reflects the country's active banking majors and a stock market that works when other world markets are shut, plus a tradition of having a well-educated, English-speaking but relatively cheap workforce. The large companies have long had oligopolistic control of the government IT market but since the early 1990s there has been a virtual cessation of large or long-term IT projects, helped along by a major fiasco with a police IT modernization programme. The personal answerability of chief executives in government ministries and agencies and their desire to minimize costs has led to relatively bleak conditions for all industry actors, with old systems kept in being without major replacements and with small contracts that are rigorously tendered. New contract vehicles (such as multi-task contracts, output-remunerated contracts, and PFIs) have all been lobbied for energetically by the major firms and IT industry bodies, but to date have been conspicuously absent in New Zealand.

At the other end of the range shown in Table 5.2, the countries with dominant IT firms, there are also a range of patterns. In Australia the lasting legacy of the Liberal National government's outsourcing initiative was a wholesale transfer of commonwealth government IT functions to the four or five largest Australian-located IT corporations. These large blocs of work were let by negotiated contracts that effectively excluded any competition from small- or mid-sized companies. The Liberal-National government's experiment left the large companies occupying stranglehold positions as main contractors with whom the rest of the industry had to deal in order to have any access at all to the government IT market. The subsequent crises of the clustered contracts, and their eventual unravelling in 2003, came too late to open up any substantial scope for new competition to enter the market. The lengthy contractual uncertainty and turmoil involved also meant that at national level there was much less use of NPM-inspired new contractual vehicles in Australia. However, some radical innovations occurred elsewhere, such as a move to a single IT supplier across all government departments in South Australia—but again the contract went to a large international systems integration firm.

In the UK Conservative government policies of favouring outsourcing (via compulsory competitive tendering for all IT services) placed a premium on securing the involvement of large IT companies, especially systems integrators. EU rules governing the transfer of civil service or other public agency staffs to private contractors required that their existing terms of employment be preserved, and effectively made it impossible for any but the largest IT companies to bid as main contractors to take over the running of established IT centres and operations. Wholesale outsourcing of complete IT functions was encouraged by the Conservative policy of 'strategic review' where very large blocks of work were reappraised every five years—with a strong presumption that unless government was 'best in world' at doing something then it should be outsourced. Successive

Conservative and Labour governments also placed a great deal of emphasis on the development first of PFI projects and later of public–private partnership arrangements, under which the ownership of key strategic government databases and computer projects could be transferred wholesale to (inherently) large IT companies.

A harder aspect to assess concerns the extent to which IT firms dealing with government agencies have strong advantages in terms of their knowledge of technology. In competitive IT markets knowledge is quite widely distributed and it is generally easier for governments to commission different sources of advice from other firms, from private practice consultants or from university experts. In concentrated IT markets, governments confront more severe problems in getting major contracts evaluated or estimating pricing levels. In small countries, such as New Zealand, private consultancy is less well developed, although system complexity may also be less. In relatively large economies, such as the UK, consultancies can be used to assess contract designs and progress by large firms. In addition, in some circumstances governments may be able to secure divergent private sector opinions or alternative ways of proceeding through lobbying by different industry contenders or coalitions bidding for major projects, or through 'countervailing powers' effects. For example, if a systems integrator is committed to using a particular technology, firms that produce rival technologies may be able to sponsor a generalized critique that expands the information base available to government. However, market concentration will tend to subvert many of these processes, as consultancies or manufacturers will not want to erode their position with established dominant or large-scale contractors.

5.3 The Potential to Run Government IT In-house

The most fundamental way in which public sector organizations can constrain their dependence on private sector contractors is by retaining the capacity to run their own IT operations if they cannot attract the right kinds of firms and bids at what they judge to be appropriate price levels. Historically, government agencies played a key role in the development of some of the largest IT systems, especially in the defence and welfare state sectors (Margetts 1999). The USA managed the creation and maintenance of its giant systems from the outset using private sector contractors, a pattern closely followed by Japan in its post-War construction. But in the other countries we studied the potential dismantling of substantial public sector IT staffs began to be discussed in the 1980s and to be put into practice extensively in strong NPM countries in the 1990s. The ability to effectively commission alternative sources of advice is also bound up with the wider capacity of government departments and agencies to act as an 'intelligent customer' in their dealings with the IT industry.

Table 5.3 shows our summary judgements of how far different governments retained an in-house capacity to manage or develop their own IT systems. In three countries, the UK, Japan, and Australia, governments more or less completely seceded any capacity to run their own IT operations in-house in this period. By contrast all the other countries retained a substantial capacity in this area, with the Netherlands particularly retaining most expertise in the governmental sector.

Looking in more detail suggests that a number of different forces were evidently at work across different types of agencies as well as across countries:

A concern to retain operational IT expertise was evident in some kinds of agencies (especially scientifically based agencies, such as patents offices) in all our countries. In some countries with competitive IT markets this stance is more generalized. In the Netherlands retaining a high level of in-house IT capabilities within public sector agencies has been integral to maintaining relations with large numbers of contractors mainly carrying out small-to-medium projects, scoped, defined, and integrated together by government personnel. In the USA, systems integrator companies have had some success in pushing into the area of defining overall systems architectures and managing large-scale projects, but most agencies still retain a high level of IT-qualified staff—although impending waves of retirements among federal personnel may reduce governmental capacity here sharply in the next decade.

Table 5.3 Membership of the set 'Little public sector in-house IT capacity'

Country	Little public sector in-house IT capacity (I)
Australia	1
Japan	1
UK	1
Canada	0.25
New Zealand	0.25
USA	0.25
Netherlands	0

How resources are allocated to contract management is a key influence upon government's capacities in countries where most IT is outsourced. In the private sector companies that outsource their IT operations to contractors will commonly dedicate between 5 and 10 per cent of the overall contract price to managing and improving their relationship, and retaining sufficient expertise available to managers. However, governments in some countries which use outsourcing a lot have often tended to assign much lower levels of resource to contract management, often as little as 0.5 or 1 per cent of the overall contract price. Where IT outsourcing reflects a political/ideological push by ministers, as in the UK under the Conservatives and Australia under the Liberal–National coalition, monitoring costs are pushed down most, as if ministers believe that so great an alignment of interests between firms and agencies can be achieved that it is unnecessary to insure against it.

The concentration or dispersion of IT and contract expertise within government is important in some countries heavily influenced by the NPM movement, such as New Zealand and UK. From the mid-1980s to late 1990s, both ran down or abolished completely previous central capabilities for monitoring or evaluating IT contracts and trends, especially following the logic of decentralizing to agencies and removing centralized hierarchic controls. In the UK, large transfers of staff to the biggest contract providers further denuded in-house IT capability. Some minimal central capacity then had to be rebuilt (painfully) from the late 1990s to cope with e-government demands, the need for 'joining-up', and to re-impose contract disciplines—as with the creation in the UK of the Office of the e-Envoy (assigned a £1 billion budget for putting government on the Web), NHS Connecting for Health (which finally grappled ten to fifteen years late with integrated IT systems for the National Health Service), and the Office of Government Commerce (which concentrated expertise in contract evaluation and from 2000 finally began to control the incidence of completely non-working government IT projects). In other countries, like Japan and Australia, IT and contract expertise remained with large departments throughout, albeit at rather minimal levels in Japan. In countries with more fragmented IT markets the need for central expertise is lessened because the competition process generates more information and agencies anyway retain more in-house IT expertise.

The pace at which governments learn from their experience is also an important influence on how they concentrate or disperse knowledge. In the UK the Treasury promoted the PFI process from the early 1990s, with in many cases contractors being invited to provide the finance for new IT investments and system developments in return for a stream of future income responding to the availability of the systems and the extent of government use of them. PFI processes were supposed to cut costs and improve the reliability of delivery by forcing contractors to internalize the risks of new IT systems development and to manage these processes more rigorously and tightly. For almost a decade a body of evidence accumulated casting doubt on this fundamental logic in relation to IT projects, where government could rarely bear the costs of catastrophic non-delivery and the asset value of non-working systems for contractors was also negligible. Only in 2003 did Treasury advice at last acknowledge that this was a doomed hope for government IT, banning PFIs in IT because agencies and departments effectively had to keep intervening to bail out PFI contractors in difficulties every bit as much as with conventional procurements.

5.4 The Overall Power of the IT Industry

Putting together the three dimensions of IT industry power covered above, Table 5.4 shows that the most clear-cut cases, at opposite ends of the spectrum, are the Netherlands and the UK. The Dutch central government retains three strong capacities constraining the power of its IT suppliers by maintaining a strongly competitive market, issuing small- to medium-sized contracts only, maintaining a diversity of suppliers, and retaining a strong capacity to manage and integrate projects via its own strong in-house staffs if needed. With identical scores across three criteria the Netherlands showed a very consistent profile. In different ways the USA and Canada approximated the Netherlands, but with more variation across criteria. At the other end of the spectrum, the UK in the 1990–2005 period had the most concentrated government IT market in the world, with a near monopolistic lead supplier, huge contract sizes, poorly understood use of PFI contracts for inappropriate IT projects and virtually no in-house capacity to manage (let alone develop) IT systems. Australia and Japan mirrored the UK on the last two criteria but with somewhat less of a downgrading of open competition rules. In the middle, New Zealand shows the most ambivalent profile, with a strong market share for the top five companies even as small contract sizes and restrictive conditions constrained the overall power of the IT industry. Japan and New Zealand show the strongest variations between the intersection set scores and the

Table 5.4 Summary codings for the components of the IT industry's influence in relation to government, 1990–2005

Country	De-emphasis on open competition (N)	Large firms' market and technical predominance (L)	Little public sector in-house IT capacity (I)	The IT industry is in a powerful position vis-à-vis government: the intersection set N . L . I (*minimum*)	Union set N + L + I (*maximum*)
UK	1	1	1	1	1
Australia	0.75	1	1	0.75	1
Japan	0.5	1	1	0.5	1
New Zealand	0.75	0.25	0.25	0.25	0.75
Canada	0.5	0.5	0.25	0.25	0.5
USA	0	0.25	0.25	0	0.25
Netherlands	0	0	0	0	0

union set scores, while the other five countries show very little variation in their scores—indeed, the Netherlands and the UK show no variation at all.

The strong bunching of these scorings for the power of the IT industry contrasts quite markedly with the more varied scores assigned to countries in Chapter 4 for the public management and public administration influences. They suggest that a more clear-cut picture can be given here and that the chances of mis-scorings are correspondingly less. Perhaps they also point up the transmutability of market power, highlighting the difficulties of constraining the influence of market dominance. Where large firm predominance is allowed to arise in one aspect it is likely that it will diffuse through the contractual system, creating cumulative predominances throughout.

5.5 How Industry Power Adversely Affects Government IT Performance

The final link in the analysis is to compare the scorings for government IT performance given in Table 3.5 in Chapter 3 with those for the power of the IT industry vis-à-vis government agencies given in Table 5.4. Again we closely follow the suggestions made by Ragin (2000), focusing most attention on the intersection set shown in the penultimate column of the two Tables. Our primary concern in both chapters has been to assign cases to sets, or to intermediate scaling points. Figure 5.1 gives a useful synoptic view of our findings in Tables 3.5 and 5.4. The horizontal axis here measures the scorings we have assigned for the power of the IT industry (the independent or causing variable here). The vertical axis shows the scorings for the level of performance of government IT (the dependent or caused variable) assigned in Chapter 3. The key coordinates in each case according to Ragin are the minima on the two dimensions, shown as the black dots in Figure 5.1, which show the combined scorings for the intersection sets in both dimensions.

There is a very clear negative relationship between the independent and dependent variables here. The greater the power of the IT industry, the less effective the performance of government IT has been. This relationship is much stronger in Figure 5.1 than that between public management influences and government IT performance shown in Figure 4.1, suggesting that industrial power for IT corporations is a more important negative

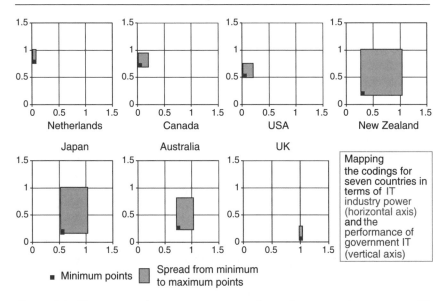

Figure 5.1. The impact of corporate power on the performance of government IT

influence on government IT performance than the public management influences.

But we also need to look at the impact of the variations in countries' scorings across the two sets of criteria, shown by the union set, which Ragin argues can be captured by looking at the maximum scores in Tables 3.5 and 5.4. Two countries, the Netherlands and the UK, at each end of the IT power spectrum show only a minimal variation in the scorings for government IT performance. And two further countries, Canada and the USA, show only a modest variation in the scorings across criteria on both dimensions. In the remaining three countries (Japan, New Zealand, and Australia) there is a much higher variation in maximum scores from minimum scores on the dependent variable and in Japan and New Zealand on the independent variable also.

Looking at the rectangular space of variation from the joint minima points to the joint maxima points is useful. It provides a kind of visual sensitivity test, graphically illustrating the extent to which each country's scores on the six component aspects examined here are similar or more divergent. The range of shapes shown also visually captures the many differences that exist across the seven countries examined here. Figure 5.1 shows a clear pattern indicating a strong causal influence from the power of the IT industry to weak performance across governmental IT projects. The association is apparently a strong one, ordering the country cases into the clear sequence shown in Figure 5.1, but also showing the diversity or consistency of country scorings documented here.

Conclusions

Telling governments that competitive markets are a better context in which to do large-scale IT procurements (or PFI projects) is hardly radical news. Many government officials in some countries and agencies made clear to us that this proposition is still axiomatic for their organizations. Yet some governments under pressure to deliver better IT performance, and perhaps unhappy with their existing in-house capabilities, have extensively departed from the older approach. Industry and public management exponents of such a shift have argued, apparently persuasively, that a more concerted style of contracting with a more heavily concentrated or oligopolistic industry is no danger at all to successful government IT operations. Alternatively, they suggest that shifting to closer and more negotiated relationships with an oligopolistic industry *does* carry some risks, but that reasonably managing the shift can also generate important compensating benefits which more than make up for the loss of a competitive context. Neither of these key propositions finds support here.

Instead it seems clear that government–IT industry relations have become dangerously unbalanced in at least one major country (the UK) and that in Japan and Australia the predominance of (more) large firms has also had significant drawbacks. In each of these cases politicians and public sector managers and top officials have responded to long- and short-run market forces, operational pressures and project contingencies, but in ways which have caused or tolerated substantial shifts in the government IT market towards oligopoly. By contrast, countries like the Netherlands and the USA, which have fostered competitive markets in innovative and well-disciplined ways, have enjoyed substantial benefits. And Canada's relative success in managing a quite-concentrated market in a balanced way also illustrates that there is no inevitability about the onset of a degenerative picture.

It is worth underlining that the essential causative feature of better government IT performance has been the ability of some liberal democratic states to maintain the existence of competitive tension in their government IT markets, however few the number of suppliers they have competing there. Despite the cumulative character of market distortions it is important to stress that there is always a huge diversity of ways in which governments can act to stop their options being constrained here and to maintain strong levels of competitive tension and effective competition. There is no necessary incompatibility between using large firms and keeping down their power to dictate terms to government agencies. Even in markets that look at first sight as if they are dominated by large firms, creative governments can act to maintain competitive tension.

Denmark is an interesting example here. A tiny market in European terms it only ever attracted the independent involvement of one of the international IT majors, IBM, which might have expected to become the dominant player. In fact, the Danish government was from the start acutely sensitive to the need to maintain competitive tension and for many years, until the 1990s, it maintained its own central in-house IT systems management and development company, Datacentralen. This governmental provider was sold by a Liberal-Conservative coalition government in 1996 to the international IT major CSC. But the relationship between IBM and the newly privately owned company did not in fact change very markedly from that which had existed hitherto. Government agencies still had more or less guaranteed strongly competitive bids from two alternate suppliers, each playing to considerable, distinctive strengths, as well as having in many cases a capability to manage or develop IT systems in house. In the local government sphere, where the central government's in-house provider did not compete with IBM, many local authorities maintained their own simpler systems. And the Danish local government association founded their own collective in-house provider, designed to more easily achieve critical mass in systems integration work. This in-house provider was also subsequently corporatized as the predominant local government IT supplier KMD, although the local authorities collectively retained ownership of the company. Hence the small Danish market has had only three relatively large providers apart from smaller in-house teams particular to one agency or authority. Yet the Danish government and local authorities between them have managed to create and sustain a market where considerable competitive tension is maintained, prices are competitive, the modernization of government IT has been high, an appropriate investment pace has been kept up, and the scrap rate for government sector IT projects has been low.

A more general sidelight can also be shed on the government IT sector and state–industry relations in this critical area. Although the tasks of government across our seven countries are remarkably similar, and the service needs, GDP levels and political contexts are certainly quite comparable, the range of variations in government–IT industry relations charted here is substantial. In our research we looked constantly for 'policy transfer' and 'policy learning', concepts triggered as significant by our research sponsors, yet found little evidence of these processes beyond a residual level. Equally our own older theoretically based speculation that government IT would prove to be fertile ground for 'the globalization of public services production' found little support, despite the presence of the same few globally sized and structured systems integrator or hardware corporations across many of the case study countries. In an allegedly globalized world, in a policy sector with some of the most standardized technologies and products, and some of the largest transnational corporations, the patterns of government–IT industry relations are still resolutely nationally defined. So the seven cases drawn on here are genuinely and importantly differentiated, not in any sense seven facets of a single globalized picture. One implication is that our conclusions must inevitably remain vulnerable to reconsideration with the production of new cases showing different patterns of state–IT industry interaction, as well as to the contestation of our detailed country codings set out here.

6

Taxation: Re-Modernizing Legacy IT and Getting Taxpayers Online

A state that cannot collect taxes, or can collect only part of its taxes, is crippled. In Schumpeter's famous dictum of 1919, the government budget is 'the skeleton of the state, stripped of all misleading ideologies'. If the analogy is apt, then tax-raising agencies are the cells that produce these bones. So, tax administration has a special centrality within public management. The bureaucracies that collect taxes are closely watched over by the Treasury or finance ministry and by legislatures or their public accounts committees. Technologies for better tax collection have been eagerly adopted by modern tax bureaucracies. But so much has this been true that these agencies' current critical problems often centre on very large, 'legacy' computer systems. Developed early on in the history of government IT, these systems are now too massive to change and too mission-critical to lose. To keep their millions of lines of old code working takes a long time and consumes vast resources in simple patching and mending. But to re-modernize legacy IT systems now poses a major challenge for Western governments. We review the basic set-up of tax bureaucracies and tax systems in our seven countries; the operation of government IT markets in the tax sector; progress in e-taxation; and the state of the art in tax administration IT at the end of our period.

6.1 Tax Bureaucracies

Tax administration is a distinctive type of bureaucracy, in some ways a world unto itself, for several reasons. Most obviously, tax agencies collect the revenue that allows all other government agencies to operate, filling the public purse as well as constituting a drain on it. As a result their resource demands are often appraised differently and their warnings and sensitivities perhaps attended to somewhat more by politicians than is true for regular departments. At the same time taxation is essentially the coercive requisitioning of resources from citizens and enterprises, and the detailed operations of tax administration relies very directly on legal and regulatory powers to ensure compliance and to punish non-compliers. So, tax departments are never popular with politicians' constituents and the detailed operation of their powers often gives rise to controversy, with close political attention paid to any expansion of staff numbers or activities.

Even the interface between tax bureaucracies and politicians is distinctive for tax agencies in most liberal democracies. Amongst our seven case study countries only the Netherlands operates national taxation as a single regular directorate within its Ministry of Finance. All the other countries have constituted their national tax agencies as distinct semi-autonomous bodies and in two countries (the USA and the UK) the agencies are run by their own boards, which are particularly able to repel inappropriate attempts by ministers or the president to influence their operations. The rationale for these protections is that the long-run health of the tax system requires that it be operated in a strongly impartial and independent way rather than possibly becoming a vehicle for governments to pursue their political enemies. Similarly, the highly sensitive information on individual and corporate incomes that tax agencies acquire should never fall into the hands of partisan politicians who might misuse it for political ends.

This closed-in character of taxing agencies goes along with a strong emphasis on a legalistic and strong-regulatory approach to their work, reflecting the primacy of the 'authority' function in these agencies' toolkits. This approach fuels the need for a strong hierarchical pattern of work organization, with close supervision of subordinates by superiors, relatively small 'spans of control', multiple layers in the hierarchy and strong internal auditing and self-policing units, alert for any hint of employee wrongdoing or misanalysis of taxpayer affairs. As a result national taxing agencies are amongst the largest and purest examples of strongly Weberian machine bureaucracies in the modern world, with still-large operating cores, a very developed middle line management, a strong strategic apex (always with either a constitutionally independent board or at least a strong management board) and an extensive technostructure of analysts tweaking the tax system to optimize performance and implementing long-run business modernization plans, mostly IT focused. Tax agencies also have strong support services, notably in IT if this function is kept in-house, or doing contractor-liaison if IT roles are outsourced.

In our seven case study countries, the 'standard' function mix for national tax agencies always includes levying national direct taxes, and in most countries covers social contributions, sales tax (such as value-added tax, VAT, or goods and services tax, GST), and the collection of excises. Other elements of the function mix in some but not most countries include levying real property taxes, wealth or inheritance taxes, and aspects of motor taxes, plus sometimes administering (rather than just collecting) social contributions and administering or enforcing customs laws. Table 6.1 shows additions to and subtractions from the 'standard' function mix for each of our case study countries, the wide range reflecting several forces. Some countries started out with a single tax agency and have simply added to its sphere of responsibilities over time. Others started out with separate administrations for different kinds of taxes (especially customs and social contributions) but then pulled them into the national direct taxes agency to achieve economies of scale. The UK was the last of our case study countries (and indeed of most countries) holding out against this trend, but even it merged the previously separated Inland Revenue and HM Customs and Excise to form Her Majesty's Revenue and Customs (HMRC) in 2005, having previously absorbed another agency collecting social contributions. In the UK, there has also been an ambitious effort towards incorporating social security functions into the tax system, with the Inland Revenue (and now HMRC) charged with paying 'tax credits' or positive income to low-income families and workers. We show below that this was in many ways a step too far, requiring procedural and cultural change that neither the tax agency nor its IT contractors was well adapted to deliver.

The overall consequence of these various structural pressures can be charted in the second column of Table 6.1, which shows that the tax agencies in our case study countries are very large organizations in terms of their staff numbers. In big countries like the USA, the UK, and Japan, they rival the personnel numbers of the largest multinational companies. Despite years of 'automation' in tax administration, in all our case study countries except tiny New Zealand, managing a tax bureaucracy still involves superintending tens of thousands of staff. The table also shows that there are significant variations around the 'standard functions' of running national direct taxes, national VAT and excise taxes, and collecting social contributions. New Zealand and Canada do the least functions, while the IRS in the USA has no VAT roles. The UK has gone furthest in

Table 6.1 The staff size of national tax agencies in our case study countries, and their range of functions, in 2004

Country (and department name)	Staff numbers	Differences from 'standard functions'
United States (Internal Revenue Service: IRS)	100,200	*Functions not handled:* VAT *Extra functions:* wealth and inheritance taxes and administers social contributions *Employee taxpayers:* must generally file annual returns
United Kingdom (Her Majesty's Revenue and Customs: HMRC)	81,900	*Extra functions:* wealth and inheritance taxes, real property taxes, motor vehicle taxes; administers social contributions and customs laws; makes some transfer payments as 'tax credits'
Japan (National Tax Agency: NTA)	56,300	*Functions not handled:* Social contributions *Extra functions:* wealth and inheritance taxes and motor vehicle taxes
Canada (Canada Revenue Agency: CRA)	38,400	*Extra functions:* administers social contributions *Employee taxpayers:* must generally file annual returns
Netherlands (Tax and Customs Administration: TCA)	25,400	*Extra functions:* wealth and inheritance taxes, motor vehicle taxes and administers both social contributions and customs laws
Australia (Australian Tax Office: ATO)	19,200	*Functions not handled:* social contributions *Employee taxpayers:* must generally file annual returns
New Zealand (Inland Revenue Department: IRD)	4,500	*Functions not handled:* social contributions or excise taxes *Extra functions:* pays family assistance (transfer payments)

Source: OECD (2004: Tables 1, 2, and 18).

Notes: Staff numbers are rounded to the nearest hundred. 'Standard functions' are defined here as national direct taxes, social contributions, national VAT, and excise taxes. The default setting is that employee taxpayers do not generally file individual tax returns, so we note exceptions from this pattern.

cramming many different assessing, form-handling, and financial payment functions into its tax bureaucracy. A further key influence on the administrative loads associated with income taxation is the use of 'pay as you earn' (PAYE) provisions where employers deduct income tax at source before paying their staff, as compared with the requirement that individuals should generally file tax returns as in the USA, Canada, and Australia.

The tax structure of our case study countries also varies markedly, with between 40 and 27 per cent of GDP being collected as taxes across all government levels. In most of our case study countries, taxes on personal incomes accounted for 12 to 13 per cent of GDP, but slightly more in New

Zealand, half this level in the Netherlands, and less than half in Japan. VAT takes 5 to 9 per cent of GDP, except in the USA where it is missing at the national level. Taxes on corporate profits account for around 4 per cent of GDP in most countries, but are half this level in the USA—a pattern that is also followed in excise taxes. Social contributions account for a massive 14 per cent of GDP in the Netherlands and over 10 per cent in Japan, but are much lower in other countries and missing altogether from the workload of the national tax agency in Australia and New Zealand. Looking at the share of total taxes taken by the main components raised nationally, direct taxes on incomes are close to four-fifths for four of the English-speaking countries and somewhat lower in the UK. These taxes are much less important in Japan and the Netherlands, both of which have very high social contribution levels. The USA has the third highest share of social contributions.

Finally, it is worth noting the importance of taxpayers' composition and scale as factors affecting the organizational structures of taxing agencies. The main forces of change are partly demographic, with old taxpayers leaving the workforce and new workers joining it; partly economic, with booms or recessions causing increases or declines in own-account workers and small businesses; and partly policy changes, with large numbers of individuals or small businesses entering income tax or VAT brackets when minimum thresholds are lowered or eroded with inflation, but moving out again if minimum tax thresholds are raised. There is also wide variation in the scale of the task faced by the tax agencies in different countries. At one end of the scale, in the USA, the IRS has nearly 140 million individual and business taxpayers to keep track of, whereas in New Zealand the number of all taxpayers combined is less than 3 million. Countries also have quite different ratios of taxpayers to the labour force, varying from at or just below 1.0 in Australia, the UK, the USA, and to a lesser degree the Netherlands, through to ratios of 1.4 and 2.4 in Canada and New Zealand, where there are more taxpayers than people in the labour force. In Japan, only a third of the labour force are individual taxpayers.

Looking briefly across the organizations involved, the US IRS is amongst the biggest civil service organizations in the world: it generated more than US$2 trillion in gross annual revenue by 2003. Its staff costs account for 70 per cent of its operating budget and IT resource costs for much of the rest (18 per cent). IRS' organizational culture has been identified as distinctive, insular with military-type career paths extending over very long periods of time and involving rotating assignments. The agency is regionally decentralized, which has at times caused coordination problems and means that personnel tend to be generalist without technical skills (Bozeman 2002).

By the late 1990s, however, IT management was recognized as needing more specialist treatment.

In the UK, for most of our period there were still two major tax agencies (Inland Revenue and Customs and Excise) until the 2004 O'Donnell review proposed that they merge in the new 'super-tax' agency, HMRC. The larger Inland Revenue (with running costs of around £3 billion annually, around half spent on staff) was responsible for the administration of income tax, corporation tax, capital gains tax, inheritance tax, and stamp duties. Customs and Excise was responsible for VAT and all import and export duties. Both agencies were non-departmental ministries, run by boards and with complex 'legacy' constitutional structures requiring multiple internal clearances before tax changes were made. They reported to HM Treasury and from the late 1980s were run on 'Next Steps' principles. Both came under pressure in the 1990s to contract out IT operations in line with the Market Testing initiative and both embarked on substantial PFI contracts in the early twenty-first century.

In Canada, the tax authority is the Canada Revenue Agency (formerly called the Canada Customs and Revenue Agency until 2004). Like the British agency it was formed out of the previously separated Tax and Customs and Excise agencies, but at a much earlier date, in 1996. Altogether, the whole process of fully converging the two components took around ten years to accomplish. But effective integration occurred within seven years and the merger was widely regarded as a success (World Bank Group 2003). In 2003, the agency had around 55,000 staff in total, 30,000 working on tax and 15,000 on customs, and numbers increased slightly in 2004 as Table 6.1 shows.

In the Netherlands, the Tax and Customs Administration of the Ministry of Finance is responsible for all revenue collection. It was also formed in 1987 from previously separated tax and customs administrations so that it was effectively merged by the beginning of our study period.

In Australia, the Australian Tax Office (ATO) is responsible for collecting all Australian government revenue, including personal and business taxation and excise duty, with receipts totaling around A$146 billion in 1998–9. The ATO had an operating budget in 2003 of around A$2.2 billion and its administrative costs were mainly on labour (60 per cent), technology (10 per cent), office operations (9 per cent), accommodation (9 per cent), and consultants–contractors (6 per cent) (ATO 2003: 114). In mid-1999, the Australian government introduced a new GST, a 10 per cent levy on the supply of goods and services which replaced the wholesale sales tax and some state and territory taxes.

In Japan, the tax system is managed by the National Tax Agency, within the Ministry of Finance. Its operating culture is strongly legalistic, and it has a presence throughout the country organized at the prefectural level. Despite Japan's large size, with a population of 127 million people, the NTA must handle relations with only a sixth of this number (21 million citizens, less than a third of the labour force) who are registered as individual taxpayers. Although the minimum level for paying VAT is high in Japan, a relatively large number of businesses (3 million) complete a tax form every year. This is one-seventh of the number of individual taxpayers, compared with around a twentieth in the USA or the UK.

Finally, in New Zealand, the Inland Revenue Department has responsibility for tax collection, and operates at a much smaller scale than comparable agencies in other countries, which makes its problems somewhat more tractable. IRD collects 80 per cent of the government's revenue, and also collects student loan repayments and pays family assistance.

6.2 Contracting IT for Tax Administration

By the time our study period starts in the early-1990s, virtually all our case study countries had 'over-mature' tax information systems, built to run on mainframe computers twenty to thirty years earlier, using relatively early programmes and procedures. The challenge that tax bureaucracies faced was to re-modernize their tax systems on a better set of foundations and equipment, and at the same time to cope with the changed ability of civilian government to attract the expertise needed to operate their systems, in competition with the burgeoning computer services industry, especially the largest 'system integrator' IT firms. Different countries took different courses of action, with the UK, New Zealand, and Japan, all plumping in varying ways for a near-complete transfer of responsibility to contractors. The USA and Australia also made extensive use of contractors, but retained considerable in-house expertise. By contrast, Canada and the Netherlands grappled with their re-modernization problems using predominantly in-house expertise.

In the UK, the Inland Revenue was an early if modest pioneer in IT, first establishing a computer system to handle straightforward data processing tasks in the 1960s. The department completed a relatively successful computerization of individual PAYE income tax in the late 1980s, leading to a system which commentators and officials then labelled the 'Rolls Royce' of government computer systems (see Margetts 1999)—meaning that it was reliable but expensive. The project was reliant on a close relationship (similar to 'relational contracting' more common in the private sector) with the British company ICL, which was treated as a 'national champion' in the IT field and favoured in the 1980s relative to often better qualified US competitors, like IBM (Margetts 1996: 275). In 1981, ICL nearly collapsed and brought in Fujitsu as a partner, subsequently blurring its privileged position, which anyway was an anathema to the Thatcher government. By the early 1990s, the Inland Revenue's reputation for IT was comparatively impressive for a UK government department, with the Treasury observing '...the Inland Revenue have got a track record on IT. They have huge complicated systems but on the whole they seem to have produced them on time and to budget. And they seem to run budgets well' (Margetts 1996: 279).

In 1994, the Inland Revenue took the decision to outsource all its IT operations, tendering for a single large company to run the entire Inland Revenue IT department (ITO) in what was then the biggest outsourcing contract ever awarded. The market-testing requirements of the Major government pushed the Revenue into a contract model very different from that developed under Compensation of PAYE (COP)—a project to automate personal income tax in the 1980s. The contract was based on the specification of a constant volume of work with a fixed price going down 50 per cent over the 10-year period of the contract, originally estimated to cost £250 million. EDS won the tender in a final run-off from CSC and took over the systems and 1,900 staff in 1994. The contract was plagued with high profile problems, particularly the spiralling costs of self-assessment, introduced in 1996. Price increases, changing contract requirements, and policy changes made by ministers meant that variations and additions to the contracts had to be negotiated with EDS, so that the total bill increased to £1.2 billion by 1998 and then was estimated at around £2.4 billion by 2000. Yet throughout the period of the EDS contract, the IR computer systems were also plagued with operational problems. Officials in tax offices around the country said that downtime, lock-outs, and delays fixing problems were compromising the service, lowering staff morale and hitting productivity (*Accountancy Age* 5 November 1999). In 2000, reports suggested that the IR was unable to make end-of-year tax checks on the records of many millions of taxpayers due to problems with incompatible computer systems (*Kabledirect* 26 July 2000).

Yet ministers remained so impressed with Inland Revenue's general capabilities that in 1999 it was asked to set up tax credits for childcare— an approach subsequently expanded into a much more ambitious system for paying income supplements to people in work with low incomes. The tax credit system was a huge challenge for IR, because the department had little experience of the problems of assessing people's incomes so as to reliably pay transfer payments on a regular short-run basis, as opposed to coercively demanding payments once a year. In the event there were also severe problems with the software that EDS put in place, so that from 2003 to 2005, there were repeated problems in the information given to families, many of whom were overpaid and then hit with large bills from IR demanding repayments of money sent to them. IR and EDS fell out in a major way, with IR threatening to sue the company through the courts for around £300 million of lost overpayments which IR blamed on faulty EDS software. In late 2005, EDS finally settled this dispute out of court, paying around £80 million to the department.

With this background the UK government was clearly keen to ensure that a competitive tender took place when the Inland Revenue contract came up for renewal in 2004, incentivizing other companies to compete against EDS for the tender. In December 2004, the new £4.3 billion contract was awarded to the much smaller firm of Cap Gemini–Ernst and Young (CGEY, with around 50,000 staff worldwide to EDS's 120,000) and with Fujitsu as the main subcontractor. The deal was for an initial period of ten years, with an option to extend it for up to eight additional years and a six-month transition period from EDS starting in January 2005. CGEY executives gloated, while EDS admitted to being 'extremely disappointed' in the decision: 'The Company continues to believe that it offered the best solution at the best value' (EDS press release).

Some of the risks inherent in megadeals of this kind was evidenced by the fact that while EDS's shares stayed the same when its lost contract was announced, CGEY's shares dropped on news of the award. As an industry news bulletin put it after the announcement, 'Huge deals bring huge risks . . . As we have said many times before, "megadeal" contests are like a game of chicken. The last vendor to say "no" to a deal gets stuck with it' (see, e.g. *Annex Bulletin* 99–04, 2 April 1999). What follows is often meagre profit margins, if not ' "mega losses", such as the one EDS is experiencing in 2003 over its $7 billion US Navy contract' (*Annex Bulletin* 03–13, 11 December 2003). Around 3,000 staff were transferred from EDS to Cap Gemini as part of the deal, but some key personnel did not move. EDS estimated the cost of handover at £60 million.

The UK's Customs and Excise department was also an early user of IT. In particular, it was a pioneer in the use of electronic data interchange (EDI), with almost all import–export transactions undertaken electronically on the Department's CHIEF system by the 1990s. During the 1990s, the number of the agency's 22,000 staff working on IT services stabilized at around 950. This number dropped significantly to 660 in 1999 when Customs and Excise signed a £500 million PFI contract with ICL/Fujitsu to provide managed infrastructure services (excluding mainframes) to offices throughout the UK, involving the transfer of assets and 328 staff under EU 'transfer of undertakings' rules (TUPE). The new infrastructure was to provide all HMCE staff with a desktop system. The contract was held up due to concerns of the Japanese banks providing financial backing (*Government Computing* February 2000), which explained in part why by 2002 the agency's desktop system already appeared outdated. The system was based on conventional ITs rather than web-based technologies, and even by 2002, a significant proportion of staff in the department using PCs rolled out since the signing of the contract did not have access to the Internet (see Dunleavy and Margetts. 2002: 70). These factors mean that the UK's newly merged tax department HMRC set up in 2004 will have the daunting task of bringing together two distinct systems, with different contractors, different identifiers, and different customer segmentation strategies.

In New Zealand, the IRD traditionally outsourced virtually all its work, relying on EDS as its main supplier. Through the 1990s its main systems became more aged but were not replaced, coping reasonably with the small numbers of taxpayers (despite the over-registration in New Zealand compared with other countries, considered above). In December 2002, IRD announced the launch of a new IT strategy, the result of a benchmarking exercise which bravely compared its IT environment with twenty-three similar organizations, including ten international tax authorities, five US state tax authorities, and five international banks. The study showed that the Inland Revenue's technology environment was equal to or better than the other organizations, with lower than average IT costs and fewer than average IT staff. The strategy fed into the department's overarching mainframe system, FIRST (Future Inland Revenue Systems and Technology), the aim of which was to completely remove paper from the New Zealand tax system. Accenture, the main contractor for the system, claims that it will produce NZ$500 million savings annually.

In Japan, computing and IT for taxation has always been outsourced, following the practice in the rest of central government. Even when the first computer was introduced to the NTA in 1966, private companies were responsible for recording data input into the host computer. In 1988, automatic data processing (ADP) and batch processing was introduced to local offices. The core of the NTA's current system for all types of taxation is called KSK. It started to be developed in January 1995, and was intro-duced to two local tax offices that December. By August 1996, it was in nineteen tax offices and sixty-three by September 1997, including all those in the Tokyo region. By November 2001, all NTA's tax offices were covered. But there was no Internet connection for tax offices and no availability of online tax declaration, although it was planned for the future. The KSK is still the 'backbone' of Japan's online tax system. The original aim of the system was to make the clerical work of tax administration more efficient, and officials considered that this aim has been achieved. The number of taxpayers has increased, the regime of taxpayers is more complex, the amount of clerical work has increased, but the number of staff employed by the tax department has reduced.

The importance of the tax system and the long-standing practice of outsourcing means that the Ministry of Finance held the fourth largest contract in the Japanese government in 2003, for an Integrated Tax Man-agement System. The contract was worth around £300 million annually and was held by the main contractors Bunshodo, but with IBM, NEC, and Hitachi doing most of the work, plus Toshiba carrying out optical charac-ter recognition work (OCR) and IBM managing the client servers. NTTD has some involvement in software development. Each company develops software in relation to a specific piece of equipment, in true Japanese style. Strangely, the company that has been responsible for joining these sys-tems up is Bunshodo, having won the bidding long ago for a task which really amounts to systems integration. The Bunshodo corporation is a small Japanese company with around 320 employees. It started as a com-mercial printer in 1912 and is still principally an office stationary and supplies company, selling some information processing equipment. Bun-shodo's website proclaims proudly that it undertakes 'configuration and operation of the general management system of the National Tax Admin-istration Agency', but the description of the company and its core mis-sions of 'designing and constructing office space for the base of information receiving/sending' seems far away from conventional systems integration tasks. NTA officials admitted in interview that they have few staff with any particular systems expertise or knowledge of the private sector. Altogether, only 200 staff deal with the tax system as a whole. Both the operation of the system and all development work is carried out by the vendors.

In the United States, the IRS has quite a different scale of operations from most tax organizations, which may explain why it both uses con-tractors very extensively and yet retains a considerable in-house capacity.

IRS is probably the single largest civilian organizational IT user in the world (Bozeman 2002). It was an early user of IT, opening its National Computer Centre in 1961: the Centre is now the home of the IRS Master-file that includes information on all taxpayers. In the 1960s, these systems were state of the art: by the mid-1990s, they were 'antiquated and would be more at home in the Smithsonian [the famous Washington museum] than in one of the most complex information-processing organizations in the world' (Bozeman 2002: 5). IRS tried to grapple with its problems of obsolescence with the Tax Service Modernization project (TSM), whose key years were 1990–6, although planning started years before. Many TSM components were eventually cancelled before being fully implemented, but after substantial costs had already been incurred. For example, Cyberfile (an abortive experiment to allow e-filing) cost US$17.1 million, and SCRIPS, an image-processing system designed to cope with scanning paper forms cost US$285 million before being scrapped. In addition, an integrated database of taxpayer account information was cancelled at a cost of US$179 million and a case-processing system at a cost of US$45 million. Worst of all, a document-processing system to digitize paper tax returns was scrapped after US$284 million of the originally planned US$1.3 billion had been spent. This was 'by some accounts one of the most striking failures in the public management of information technology' with critics of TSM differing 'only in the degree of severity of their criticism' (Bozeman 2002: 6). These serious problems meant that IRS was subject to special scrutiny, required to split work into modules and report effective progress on each milestone to Congress before further tranches of funds were released.

The largest and most thoughtful study of TSM concluded that one of the most important lessons was that 'contracting out requires management within' (Bozeman 2002: 8). The emphasis of TSM was always on trans-formation and long-term planning, with Congress told (and perhaps sur-prisingly, accepting) even in 1989 that TSM would cost US$4 billion and would not be operational until 2000. Originally, the idea was that it would be carried out internally rather than by outside contractors who would need to learn about the IRS and its business. An eight-year US$1.4 billion contract with AT&T was signed in 1991 to provide around 50,000 elec-tronically linked machines. But apart from this, there were no mega-contracts in the early years of the TSM project. During the key years, the project was managed from the top by people with business-line expertise rather than technical expertise, to an extent where some commentators suggested that lack of technical expertise was one of the reasons for the project's failure. As the scale of failed projects became clearer, Congress became insistent that more of the IT development and implementation should be outsourced. In December 1998, the IRS awarded the fifteen-year US$5 to US$15 billion Prime Systems Integration Service Contract to CSC in what IRS called the single biggest systems integration project ever undertaken (*Government Computer News* 7 February 2000). CSC's work involved full-scale programme management, coordination and systems integration for overall systems modernization. Subcontractors included IBM, KPMG, SAIC, Unisys, and a number of small consulting firms. Yet 'almost no one seems to feel the IRS has a history of effective use of contractors', Bozeman argued in 2002 (p. 32) so that the then current strategy cast a shadow over the future of the project. In fact in the fiscal year 2004, IRS expenditure on IT fell dramatically to US$1.2 billion from the previous year's level of US$1.9 billion, reflecting the fact that the prime contract was largely completed and that at least some of its objectives were realized, keeping the enormous US tax system on the road.

In Australia, the ATO also has a firm grip on IT issues, although it also has well-established and large-scale contracting arrangements. These long pre-dated the Liberal-National government's failed IT clustering and mandatory outsourcing initiative of the mid-1990s, which ATO managed to stay out of. But like all Australian government departments, ATO remained under pressure from ministers to increase outsourcing of its IT operations, with ever increasing opposition from the Commonwealth and Public Sector Union (CPSU). In mid-1999, the agency let a major contract to EDS to upgrade its entire IT infrastructure. Some 380 staff left ATO, 130 of them joining EDS. The project was scheduled to deliver savings in the order of AU$100 million over a five-year term. Later, civil service unions claimed that the ATO secretly started outsourcing application development work to EDS, causing 'scope-creep' to 'blow out EDS's original five-year, AU$500 million contract to nearly AU$1 billion' (*The Australian* 16 March 2004). In 2003, the ATO was receiving adverse publicity for 'spending tens of millions of dollars annually' employing large numbers of IT contractors to conduct in-house development and maintenance 'in addition to the AU$1.33 billion it will have spent with EDS by the time its outsourcing contract ends in 2006' (*The Australian* 25 November 2003). ATO appointed a new Chief Information Officer, who aimed to replace the single giant contract with a selective sourcing strategy from 2006 but said that the office would continue to use large numbers of external contractors to fill skills gaps and provide relief during peak work loads.

The ATO does use other suppliers, relying on IBM mainframes, and using Accenture for the Business Register and e-government sites like the taxpayer portal and business portal. In late 2003, the agency extended its voice management contract with NEC, a ten-year deal worth A$107 million by the time it ends in mid-2008. ATO has long had a big base of servers and desktops and middleware running on Microsoft plus it disallowed the use of UNIX or Linux, a dependence that became increasingly controversial when it adopted earlier releases of bug-ridden Microsoft technologies. In March 2004, the ATO announced that it would outsource application development work for the first time as part of its Change Program, putting out tenders worth up to A$700 million. However, the office retains in-house capability and officials said that the work would be done by joint ATO-contractor teams in facilities set up by ATO. Finally in 2004, the ATO responded to criticism and moved away from a Web services architecture based entirely on Microsoft's .NEW framework, signing a AU$14 million contract with IBM as a key subcontractor under Accenture, a move which grew IBM's Canberra workforce by 10 per cent in its first year (*The Australian* 2 November 2004).

In Canada, the Canadian Customs and Revenue Agency (the previous name of the CRA) had a strong record on prioritizing the importance of IT, which has meant handling many issues in-house. Officials pointed to the fact that three consecutive CEOs have confirmed that 'IT is a core competency of the agency'. Forty years ago, CCRA started to build up a strong core of IT expertise which never became unmanageably expensive, so 'why change it?' For this reason, even for Canada where levels of government outsourcing are generally lower than most of the other countries covered in this study, CCRA had distinctively low levels of outsourcing. Indeed, the agency never outsourced a large-scale systems integration project in or before our study period. Staff consider that any systems integration projects they have been involved with have been problematic—the most notable being a collaboration with health and benefits agencies and Accenture to enable the security for allowing citizens to provide change of address details online, which staff were 'not happy with'. In fact, when asked what proportion of IT activities were outsourced, the IT manager asked 'how do you round below 1 per cent?' For such outsourcing as they do, Bell Nexxia and CGI are their main contractors.

In 2003, the agency had around 3,000 IT staff, with about 350–400 contractors. The IT budget of C$400 million was around 10 per cent of the overall budget of CCRA, which was about C$4 billion. CCRA have what staff labelled an 'incremental change model' (like the US Social Security Administration, see Chapter 7). The IT organization does not operate independently from the rest of the agency: business and technical groups have a 'rich tradition of each feeding the other', with IT people brought right to the top of the business. Thirteen years ago, the head of IT was moved to a more senior level with all the other assistant commissioners, reporting directly to the CEO rather than reporting through business services as before. Throughout the 1990s, there was an incremental service transformation agenda, with common systems across tax lines introducing economies of scale for specific tasks common to all taxes, such as identification, assessment, accounting, and case management.

In common with tax agencies in the other countries (such as the UK and Australia), the CCRA have remained relatively autonomous of (in fact resistant to) central control and coordination. The agency has never really used the central procurement services of the Public Works Board, and by 2003, had not signed up for the forthcoming Secure Channel project, with officials voicing some scepticism about the project and feeling that the procurement process works against 'agileness', because the Treasury Board was imposing rules on what agencies may and may not do. CCRA have a multi-year agreement with IBM and Hewlett-Packard for desktops, servers, and laptops. For now, the main IT divisions seem to be successful in their resistance to any central pressures to outsource, even stonewalling some units within CRA who are in favour of outsourcing desktop support, for example. For them, pressure may come from Treasury Board, but if it does not, the agency will continue along its current path.

Finally, in the Netherlands, the Tax and Customs Administration (TCA) within the Ministry of Finance also has a long history of expertise in ICT development. It was described to us as 'the best operated tax department in the world' by the CEO of one private sector provider. In common with the rest of the Dutch government, contracting by TCA is characterized by small contracts and low levels of outsourcing. The department uses the 'preferred supplier' agreements set up by the Audit Office in the 1990s (and favoured by many departments after the strengthening of EU procurement legislation for IT tenders in 2000). In 2001, TCA had nine operational agreements. The department uses the preferred supplier agreements to maintain competition between its suppliers, working out every half year how much business each of its 'preferred' suppliers has and then awarding them more or less business during the next six months to adjust for any discrepancies. Ordina is probably the longest-running supplier to the TCA, providing IT architecture, infrastructure development and management, and some aspects of application development and management.

6.3 Moving Taxpayers off Paper

Tax might seem to be a natural e-government service. First, most personal and corporate tax payments are actually made by businesses. In most countries (except the USA) PAYE systems mean that many individual taxpayers file no individual tax returns, because taxes due are deducted from their wage packets by employers before the individual ever receives them. Second, even where personal taxpayers must file tax forms in large numbers, the people involved are generally wealthier than other citizens and more concentrated in the working age groups. They more often have PCs and Internet connections and knowledge, in many cases with access provided via their workplace. Finally, even taxpayers who lack such facilities can use intermediaries such as tax accountants or tax software packages, both of which can help reduce the apparent complexity of the tax systems appreciably. In countries like the US and Australia, the tax agency has worked proactively with intermediaries to develop cheaper, standardized services and to get software out to individual taxpayers. So it is no surprise that revenue agencies tend to lead the way in the provision of e-government services (Accenture 2003). However, there are differences across the countries, and in only one of our case study countries (Canada) is the tax administration consistently cited in Accenture's international surveys as an e-government innovator.

This variation reflects the fact that there are also some substantial barriers to the spread of e-taxation (Margetts and Yared 2004). Small businesses' opposition to increased workloads is often matched by citizens' conservatism about how they meet their tax obligations to report their affairs. Individuals doing their own returns often prefer to work things through on paper so as to make corrections or 'tweak' their returns without this being visible to tax officials, as corrections on an online form may be. And they may perhaps be fearful that returning complete data electronically will enhance the capacity of the tax agency to make more sophisticated or fine-detail checks on their situations. Above all, for small businesses and citizens alike, embracing e-filing for tax purposes entails incurring some transaction and transition costs (the costs of learning a new procedure). A mass of evidence now suggests that both groups may postpone making this investment in learning new methods for long periods, unless and until they are specifically incentivized to bite the bullet and change from paper to e-filing, or are mandated to do so (Margetts and Yared 2004).

From the supply side, a country's success in developing online filing of taxes across countries can also be inhibited by the extent to which tax agencies innovated in the 1980s and early 1990s with EDI systems. These are *sui generis* methods of companies with the right kind of (fairly expensive) computer equipment filling in forms electronically and communicating information and payments to the tax authorities. They were particularly picked up by the customs authorities in many countries, especially in Britain, the USA, and Australia for use in import and export notifications, and by the IRS and ATO to encourage individual income tax submissions via tax intermediaries. But, ironically, moving from tailor-made EDI systems (which cannot be meshed easily into integrated business software and may not run on modern IT equipment) to Internet-based systems is still a considerable investment and technology challenge, and one that increases the more widely EDI systems have been used.

The combination of these different influences has nonetheless left the majority of tax agencies across our case study countries standing out as islands of e-government advance compared with other central government agencies. In five countries e-filing of taxes moved ahead swiftly—the USA, New Zealand, Australia, Canada, and the Netherlands—with more lagged or mixed achievements in the UK and Japan.

In the USA, the IRS has long been the world leader in the electronic filing of income tax returns, because it luckily implemented a quick fix solution in the mid-1990s, at the same time as the agency was mired in its mushrooming TSM problems. IRS officials interviewed suggested to us that the software developed to facilitate electronic filing was really a massive piece of 'middleware', which translated the data input by users via the Internet into the antiquated IRS legacy systems. Such a strategy may sound messy, but it is similar to that used by many leading private companies during the 1990s to kick start e-commerce. It worked with (rather than against) the 'build-and-learn' nature of web-based technologies (see Dunleavy and Margetts 1999). Even by January 1999, the proportion of US citizens filing their taxes electronically was about 24 per cent, increasing to 29 per cent by the end of that year. In 2000, 24.7 million clients filed their taxes online and one-third of these did not submit any paper when submitting their returns. According to the IRS's 2000 Strategic Plan, the approximate administrative cost of an electronic return was US$0.56, while the equivalent for a paper return was US$2.71. The IRS hired Booz Allen and Hamilton to research innovative ways of projecting filing costs, assessing that paper returns averaged US$1.50 in direct costs, while e-costs averaged around 74 cents. The objective was set to reach 80 per cent by 2007 (*Government Computer News* January 1999).

Part of the IRS's success also reflected the nature of the American tax system, where individuals have to file returns estimating their tax liabilities and making payments to meet them upfront. This produces a huge inflow of excess funds into IRS as citizens overestimate their liabilities or just play it safe to avoid interest charges or penalties, necessitating millions of often substantial repayments by IRS. Online payers were offered extra time to file their return and quicker repayments. By 2004, 60 million tax returns had been 'e-filed'—over half of returns made. Over two-thirds of these, 43 million, were e-filed by tax professionals using the IRS service but a growing number of those filing individually without tax professionals were using the new 'Free File' website, where users could obtain tax filing software for free.

In New Zealand, the Inland Revenue Department (IRD) became innovative in terms of offering services electronically in comparison with other government agencies, but only after a shaky start. In April 1999, the agency launched an e-filing system called Ir-File, which immediately ran into problems with its security system, which relied on digital certificates. The system used Windows cryptography to process the certificate and users with non-Microsoft browsers had to download plug-ins. IRD was overwhelmed with calls to its help desk from users who could not log in, requiring the hiring of extra help-desk staff. In 2000, IRD scrapped the system after sixteen months of operation, with an unsuccessful attempt to brand the move to the media as an 'enhancement' (*idg.net* 31 July 2000). The new system worked in a similar method to online banking, with 128-bit encryption provided by the browser and a user name/password log-in.

In 2000, the department published a five-year plan entitled *The Way Forward—2001 Onwards*, aimed at achieving the streamlining and simplification of tax processes (especially for small business), creating an environment promoting compliance, enhancing human resources, and enhancing the administration of social policy business (NZIR 2001). By 2000–1, IRD received 49 per cent of returns electronically and processed 140,000 electronic employer schedules (involving 1.4 million individual tax payer details, 65 per cent of all salaried wage earners). In 2004, Net-Guide magazine described the IRD website as one of the best in the country and the 'first port of call for personal and business taxation'. The site was the most visited of all government websites, receiving around 70,000 page views per day. In 2002, the IRD launched an online service for businesses filing GST returns over the Internet, and received more than

3,000 GST returns electronically in the first two months. In 2004, the IRD offered citizens a chance to participate in a redesign of the website, aimed at giving 'customers a better experience' and ensuring that the agency could adapt to future demand. The aim was to involve citizens in both the design (the new look site was available for preview through a link on the current website's homepage for two months) and in improving content, with extensive usability testing.

In Australia, the ATO was an early leader in electronic services, ahead of other Australian government departments even when Australia was viewed as the world leader in e-government at the end of the 1990s (see Dunleavy and Margetts 1999). Officials interviewed at the time were extremely optimistic about the extent to which the work of the ATO could be carried out on the Internet, claiming that 'Eventually, the ATO will become its web site' (quoted in Dunleavy and Margetts 1999). The ATO introduced an e-tax pilot in 1997, which went national in 1999. By 2002, 25 per cent of the 2.2 million Australians who do their own tax were submitting e-tax forms. Another 7 per cent used Australia Post's Tax Pack Express service, which manually entered data from Tax Packs for a faster return. The ATO was targeting its efforts on converting younger and older age groups to e-taxation: in 2003, the 24–34-year-old bracket accounted for more than 40 per cent of e-tax users. Apart from convenience, the biggest selling point of e-tax was the shortened processing time: a paper submission takes six weeks to process, whereas e-tax takes fourteen days. Parts of the press applauded the ease of use of the application:

Despite colour-coded manuals and step-by-step instructions, the task of filling out a tax form is almost universally approached with fear and loathing. The computerised version removes much of the pain and confusion with an interview-based process in which information is entered in a series of windows similar to help wizards. At the end of the process the program presents an on-the-spot estimate of your tax rebate or debt. (*The Australian* 1 July 2003)

In addition, ATO has worked to encourage most personal taxpayers to use tax accountants and used its regulatory muscle to ensure that these intermediaries too file online.

For business taxation, ATO became a leader in international tax modernization when it used the introduction of the GST in 2000 to create the Australian Business Number (ABN), assigning a unique identification number to every Australian business used to manage businesses' interactions with the ATO and other agencies. All companies had to obtain an ABN and electronic sign up was made compulsory for tax consultants when it was introduced. Businesses with yearly revenue of A$20 million or more were required to file GST electronically from the start. The ATO was also part of the development of a successful portal for businesses, the Business Entry Point which by May 2000, shortly after its introduction, was attracting 4 per cent of total Australian Internet traffic (ATO 2000). By 2004, 50 per cent of business registrations were done online and small business could lodge their Business Activity Statements online and view their accounts on the ATO website, using free digital certificates. To incentivize them to do so, businesses lodging and paying electronically via the Business Portal received a two-week deferral on their lodgement deadline for three-quarters of the year.

However, these successful initiatives and ATO's reputation as a world leader suffered from setbacks in the early 2000s. In July 2003, the Australian National Audit Office delivered a 'scathing' report on the ATO's administration of the Australian Business Register. The report claimed that the A$128 million project to develop central collection, storage, and verification of business data had huge problems with data integrity, with insufficiently robust procedures for migration of ABN data from other ATO systems and limited upfront checking of information provided by applicants. PKI services were not made publicly available until December 2002, six months after the other functions had been delivered and well after the introduction of GST, when it was necessary to issue 2.9 million ABNs. By 2004, ATO had also come under fire from the business community who claimed that its phone services, online services, and general advice were inadequate. The launch of a business website in 2003 was followed by a wave of complaints from businesses: 'the ATO wants us to do everything online because it's cheaper for them, but at the moment it is not the best mechanism for keeping businesses up to date' (*The Australian* 3 February 2004). It remains to be seen whether a 'Tax Agent Portal' launched in 2004, offering access to an online self-service library of tax office products, services, tools and information concerning the tax system will overcome these problems: usage figures in 2004 were 16,600 registrants conducting 20,000 log-ins and 745,000 page hits every week (Accenture 2004: 63). Meanwhile, early in 2004, the ANAO produced another report claiming that federal government departments' monitoring and evaluation of Internet services was poor, based on analysis of websites and services of five agencies, one of which was the ATO.

Overall, however, the ATO performs well against some of the other tax administrations covered here. In 2003, the ATO published a Channel Strategy which used primary and secondary research to determine customers' needs and desires in terms of electronic versus other channels, something we did not find in any other country. And the agency estimates average transaction costs, something recommended but not achieved in the UK (Dunleavy and Margetts 2002).

In Canada, the CCRA was early with the Internet. With a leap of 'technological luck' the agency eschewed client servers and moved straight to web-based technologies. The agency started thinking about e-filing in 1986. And in 1991 (three years before the first web browser), the first people filed taxes 'electronically', with some measure of security over private lines, uploaded to the mainframe. The take-up of electronic filing has grown steadily since then and is relatively high compared with the other countries in our study. For example, 43 per cent of individuals filed tax online in 2003, which was up 15 per cent on the previous year (*London Free Press* 28 April 2004). Of the 23 million returns in 2003, 645,000 were via telefile, 6.7 million via agents filing electronically, and 2.4 million filing online. However, all electronic filing took place via custom built tax calculation software, which had to be bought, at around C$20–40. From 2003 the government required software vendors to make free software available for low-income Canadians (those with annual income of below C$20,000). Of 13.2 million paper returns, 6 million were printed via the software.

The agency gives a refund 10 days faster to online filers, having calculated a cost of C$1.47 to process a paper return. The CCRA claims that the high take-up of electronic filing has allowed them to close one of its tax data centres and redeploy about 1,350 people who had previously processed paper returns (*Financial Times* 23 June 2004). Information is transferred directly into CCRA's systems, with no re-keying of data. The clear economic benefits to the tax administration of electronic filing caused some media commentators to criticize bitterly the CCRA's continuing policy of expecting taxpayers to purchase tax software, in contrast to the USA (*Ottawa Citizen* 26 April 2003; CanWest Interactive 13 April 2003).

The CCRA was included as a best-practice example in the 2002 Accenture international trends survey and listed as having improved further in 2003. The agency find that their customers are using the website more and more to find tax information. They have hired usability experts to improve their information provision for specific groups, such as students, seniors, and tax professionals. They analyse usage statistics regularly—their website receives 25 million hits every month. However, they do not accept e-mails or online queries. During 2004, CCRA targeted e-services more at businesses, improving information provision, offering more channels for filing returns and paying taxes and introducing a new Internet-based filing service allowing certain business to electronically file returns for GST, in addition to a direct payment option using electronic banking.

In the Netherlands, the Ministry of Finance was also quite an innovator in thinking about e-taxation issues. Its 1999 report entitled *Taxation in a World without Distance*, explored issues arising from e-commerce and widespread use of the Internet. As in many countries, the TCA was innovative in developing IT-based services compared with other Dutch departments and agencies. Early on it launched a website under the name the Digital Tax Department, a website for younger people and a business website in addition to downloadable tax return software being also available on disk. From the beginning, user requirements were used to provide tailor-made information in response to questions about age and circumstances. The agency is good at taking initiatives to coordinate data in an active way, using information from employers to send out a 'pre-populated' form, with much of the information already completed, so that taxpayers need only fill in the still-missing information. The authority were also early to introduce some incentives to increase take-up of e-services, for example, an initiative in 2000 whereby users could get their tax rebate before the 1 July if they filed online. TCA also experimented with using the web to encourage more widespread involvement in policymaking. In January 2001, there was a change in the tax law and the first draft of the legislation was put on the web, before it went to the parliament. The taxation authority found themselves deluged with advice from tax consultants as to how to improve the draft law. Those who wrote the law were impressed— the advice was good and the legislation much improved.

Consequently, the Netherlands was an early leader in take-up of electronic filing. The number of digital tax returns submitted to the TCA rose to 16 per cent of all IB/VB returns for 1997, from 7 per cent in 1996. The site had 2.5 million hits in January 1998 compared to 1 million in January 1997. In 1997 there were 80,000 downloads of the T-form (for tax refund) and 15,000 downloads of the J-form (for tax refunds for youth). By 2001, 2 million citizens were filing online, with further progress just waiting for electronic signatures. By 2004, there was a fully functional online submission and assessment system, and the processing of returns for citizens was highly automated, although e-services for businesses were not so advanced. The time taken to deal with tax returns has been reduced by five months in recent years, at a time when the number of returns has increased by 20 per cent, and the tax authorities have seen staff reductions of more than 10 per cent. The TCA has been involved since the 1990s with other departments (particularly the Central Bureau for Statistics, CBS, and the Branch Organisation for Social Security, LISV) in an attempt to reduce the burden of delivering information by means of electronic services. In this context it is currently investigating the possibility of locating the output side of corporate administrations on a single website.

Turning to countries where the e-taxation experience has been more mixed, in the UK figures for electronic filing of taxes lagged behind most of our other case study countries up to 2004. In line with the government's overall targets for e-government, the Inland Revenue and Customs and Excise both had initial targets for 100 per cent online availability of their services by 2005. Uniquely among UK government agencies at the time, they both also had a take-up target for e-tax usage (50 per cent) written into their Service Delivery Agreements with the Treasury from 2001. But by 2004, both departments seemed far from achieving that target.

For the Inland Revenue its problems dated back to August 2000, when the department's online self-assessment site had to temporarily shut down, and the launch of its self-assessment page was delayed from April to June due to security concerns. In 2002, another major security problem forced the Revenue to shut down the online tax return facility for five weeks and 'the future of Internet filing seemed bleak. Fewer than 1 per cent of taxpayers—about 75,000 people—used the service to file their forms for the previous tax year' (*Times* 6 September 2003). For the 2001–2 tax year, there was a fourfold increase with 325,000 people sending in returns via the Internet and a similar number of agents (accountants preparing returns for others). In 2004, the number of taxpayers filing electronically finally rose to more than 1 million, in line with the department's own revised targets but still at a level considerably below either the levels achieved by other tax administrations in this study or the targets in their Public Service Agreement with the Treasury. In 2003–4, nearly 12 per cent of income tax self-assessment forms were filed online, with a slightly lower ratio of employer P14 forms (Inland Revenue 2004)

Both UK revenue departments have experimented with incentivizing either citizens or businesses to use their online services, with variable degrees of success. From the start, citizens were given a later deadline when filing online (31 January rather than 30 September), if they wanted the department to calculate their tax for them—a task that Inland Revenue builds up as a great plus point, but which in fact takes an operator only an extra ten seconds or so compared with just entering the data from a tax form onto the database. Taxpayers who sent in their return by 30 December and owed less than £2,000 could have any overdue tax collected through the PAYE system in monthly chunks rather than having to pay a lump sum. Rebates were also paid far quicker for online returns. For businesses, the Inland Revenue offered a combination of selective incentives and compulsion to businesses for filing online, from 2004–5. The incentive payments amounted to £825 (tax free) over the first five years of electronic filing. This 'carrot' was backed up with the 'stick' that all businesses must file their annual staff payment returns online by a certain date—2010 for businesses with fewer than 50 staff. Those who do not will face a penalty of up to £3,000 a year, in addition to existing late-filing penalties. For medium-size firms employing between 50 and 249 staff, the ruling applies from May 2006, and there is no financial incentive on offer, while large firms with more than 250 staff must comply by 2005. For such firms, this option is relatively new. Previously, EDI was the only viable option because the Internet option offered by Inland Revenue could not cope with very large numbers of records. It was little wonder then that the new head of the two combined departments, David Varney, confirmed immediately that the extent of mandatory online filing was likely to be an issue for the department (*Accountancy Age* 21 October 2004), raising the possibility that compulsion might be introduced for individuals as well as businesses.

Turning to the Customs and Excise department (a separate entity for most of our period), it first created a basic website in 1998, but over the next three to four years this was left little changed or developed and became inaccurate. A new version of the site was eventually launched in 2002, lagging far behind the other revenue agencies covered here in terms of information or services available online. Customs partly rested on its laurels because it had been very successful in the early 1990s in introducing an EDI scheme called CHIEF, for businesses to file import and export notifications and permissions. With near-universal take-up, this system meant that Customs could claim strong electronic usage levels, even though its efforts to introduce Internet based technologies stumbled badly. Customs' scheme to encourage traders to use a pilot system for filing a simple, seven question VAT form online was a clear failure. By 2002, only 0.02 per cent of traders were filing electronically using the system (Dunleavy and Margetts 2002). Customs followed the UK government's centralized advice on securing tax returns to the letter, insisting on the use of digital certificates which had to be purchased at the price of £50. This barrier provided a clear disincentive to smaller traders, which could not be overcome by the introduction of a £50 incentive for filing online. By 2005, the percentage of those filing VAT online was still less than 5 per cent.

In Japan progress towards online taxation was even slower, with paper methods omnipresent until well into the twenty-first century. Up to 2003, Japan's citizen portal was organized by agency, rather than user intention, and provided only information rather than services (Accenture 2003: 67). But in January 2004, the government launched its 'multi-payment' network, developed through cooperation between the public and private sectors and offering a secure environment for citizens and businesses to pay fees or taxes to government. The NTA was the first service to use this system, so citizens could now pay their taxes online. In June 2004, taxpayers were offered the facility to file taxes over the Internet via the e-Tax service, building on an earlier pilot in four prefectures in the Tokai region in February. But users complained that the system was inconvenient. While tax returns could be filed online, related receipts had to be sent separately and the service covered only national taxes, so that regional levies had to be submitted to tax offices separately via regional tax forms, which could not be filed online. Effectively, therefore, the service required tax returns to be filed both electronically and on paper. Total electronic filing amounted to around 35,000 returns, less than 1 per cent of the 23 million individual taxpayers. Press commentators considered even the NTA's modest target of 5 per cent of all tax returns submitted online by fiscal year 2006 to be unachievable 'under current conditions' (*Nikkei Weekly* 21 September 2004). The same report concluded that 'merely building the e-government infrastructure—without offering the public online services that are convenient and easy to use—could wind up being a huge waste of time and money'.

6.4 The State of Play in Tax Administration IT

What are the implications of these different trajectories for the current state of tax administration in our seven case study countries? Comparing the numbers of registered taxpayers per tax agency employee (shown in Table 6.2, using data from OECD 2004, 2005) has the USA at the top, New Zealand (which has a very inclusive tax net) comes second while Japan drops away to the middle of the seven countries. Canada and Australia do well and the two EU countries, the UK and the Netherlands, come bottom on this basis. In terms of administrative costs, the USA seems far and away the most efficient country. IRS is favoured by not collecting VAT or some other taxes and by the USA having a high GDP level compared to, say, New Zealand. But the US system also deals with huge numbers of relatively

Table 6.2 Indicators of tax agency staff efficiency in 2004 and administrative costs ratios for 2000–2

| Country | Registered tax-payers per TAE | Citizens per TAE | Administrative costs of collecting 1,000 units net of local currency | | |
			2002	2001	2000
USA	1,380	2,260	5.2	4.6	4.3
New Zealand	1,200	850	11.7	12.1	14.4
Canada	669	810	12.0	10.8	10.7
Australia	639	1,020	11.9	12.7	11.1
Japan	420	2,260	16.2	15.4	14.2
UK	358	730	11.5	11.1	11.0
Netherlands	354	630	17.6	17.4	17.0

Source: OECD (2004: Table 18).

Note: TAE Tax agency employees measured as full time equivalents. The registered taxpayers number is the sum of individual taxpayers *plus* whichever is the larger of the two registered business numbers for each country.

costly individual taxpayers, over four times more than the UK, its nearest comparable state in our set of countries. Yet US administrative costs are about half those of the middle group of Anglo-Saxon countries (the UK, Canada, Australia, and New Zealand). Equally clearly from Table 6.2, Japan and the Netherlands run relatively expensive tax collection operations, with administration costs one-and-a-half times this middle group.

Looking at the IT share of administrative costs, Table 6.3 shows that it is higher in the Netherlands, running around twice the share it is in the lowest countries, the UK and Canada. The other three countries for which

Table 6.3 IT cost ratios and levels reported for the nearest years to 2004 by national tax agencies

| Country | IT costs as proportion of administration costs, latest year (%) | Per cent of IT costs on operating systems, latest year (%) | Total costs of IT in local currency | |
			Latest year	Prior year
Netherlands	24	80	629	517
USA	20	80	1,270	1,910
New Zealand	20	na	86	86
Australia	18	78	405	395
UK	13	72	(180)	(120)
Canada	12	64	420	433

Source: OECD (2005: Table 31).

Note: 'na' means data unavailable. None of the information needed is available for Japan, which is accordingly excluded from this table. The UK total IT cost numbers refer only to Customs and Excise and exclude Inland Revenue.

data is available (excluding Japan) are in the 18–20 per cent range. Most countries spend around four-fifths of their IT budget on simply operating their systems, but the ratio is lower in the UK which has been investing heavily in new systems and is below two-thirds in Canada. The last two columns of Table 6.3 show that in the most recent two year data filed with OECD, there was a big fall in US spending on tax IT, while there have been increases in the Netherlands and perhaps the UK (where the data are incomplete). In other countries IT costs seem to be static.

Turning to the web presence of tax agencies across our seven countries, Table 6.4 shows that the ATO with its large web-based expert system of tax law achieved substantially more page requests to its sites than its nearest rivals in our countries, New Zealand and Canada. There is then a large gap with the Netherlands, the USA, and a lagging UK achieving less than half the Canadian level of page requests. Finally, Japan lags far behind the other countries in web usage for tax purposes. Canada and Australia are clearly ahead in terms of handling large absolute volumes of web traffic, as is the much larger IRS operation serving a population many times larger. Again Japan has much the lowest web traffic numbers for tax services. In terms of the size of the tax administration's website, Australia claims more web pages than all the other countries put together, reflecting its expert system strategy. Both New Zealand and the USA have clearly gone for websites with relatively few pages, while the UK has a fairly large but apparently not much used set of sites.

Table 6.4 The level of use of tax agency websites and the size of these sites in 2004

Country	Page requests per registered taxpayer (individual and business)	Page requests for last year (in millions)	Size of website (thousands of pages)
Australia	12.4	153	357
New Zealand	9.4	51	3
Canada	8.1	209	51
Netherlands	3.4	31	30
USA	3.3	463	21
UK	2.1	65	85
Japan	0.6	15	36

Source: Calculated from OECD (2005: Table 12); OECD (2004: Table 21).

Note: UK numbers are for Inland Revenue and Customs and Excise combined. The Australia number given by OECD covered only eleven months, so we have pro-rata-ed this rate to give a twelve-month number, shown here. For registered taxpayers number, see the note to Table 6.2.

Conclusions

The comparative picture emerging from the range of evidence presented above suggests that four countries (the USA, Australia, Canada, and perhaps New Zealand) have reaped relatively large benefits from their IT operations in one dimension or another—the USA holding down its costs and handling large volumes of interactions with taxpayers, but lagging on web access; and the other three countries achieving creditable cost data and substantially building usage of their e-filing services. The Netherlands has a pretty good web operation but seems relatively expensive. The UK is fairly nondescript on most dimensions except holding down the administrative costs of tax collection, but then only to the general 'Anglo-Saxon' level. Japan clearly has an old-fashioned tax presence, handling interactions with relatively few taxpayers at high cost and with a badly lagging web presence.

Tax agencies are somewhat *sui generis* machine bureaucracies, carrying out a historically rather discreet function. But their struggles to modernize their sprawling IT systems and to change the ways that they interact with citizens and businesses have central significance for modern public administration and the development of e-government. The influence of NPM approaches has been less extensive in tax-raising, and the reliance on maintaining strong tax authorities with considerable in-house capacities has generally been stronger here than in other sectors. Nonetheless, tax IT has seen very large changes towards contracting in some countries, especially in the UK and to a lesser degree in Australia and New Zealand.

7

Social Security: Managing Mass Payments and Responding to Welfare State Change

In all human societies some system for distributing resources to the elderly, the sick, and dependent children is an inescapable anthropological necessity. In advanced industrial countries the key institutional means of accomplishing support is the welfare state, and between half and three-fifths of the population at any one time will depend wholly or in part on receiving transfer payments from social security agencies. The recipients of payments need to get their welfare payments reliably and on time, creating a numerically huge political constituency with a direct interest in state agencies operating within very finite limits of accuracy and reliability. Their understandable vigilance is matched by that of taxpayers, business interests, and conservative politicians, because welfare state payments account for an enormous slice of overall public spending, between 15 per cent (the USA) and 24 per cent (the Netherlands) of GDP for our seven case study countries. A final dimension of political salience is that welfare state spending is usually nationalized, creating very large-scale social security systems in all our case study countries—systems where small defects or mishaps in the administration of payments can translate into phenomenally high costs in rapid time.

Running social security IT is consequently every bit as politically visible and administratively demanding as collecting national taxation. And some of the problems confronting agencies and their IT industry suppliers are strikingly similar to those considered in Chapter 6, notably the challenge of modernizing complex systems of legacy IT. At the same time the social security arena has some distinctive traits and challenges of its own, notably in the tendency to underfund the core systems of welfare state agencies far more than is true of tax agencies, and the complexity of the different benefits and associated IT challenges which must be managed by the same national agencies. We first briefly sketch the traditional character of transfer agencies and their IT systems before mentioning the changing administrative and managerial context for welfare systems in some countries. Next, we look at the changing contractual and e-government pictures for social security IT across our seven countries.

7.1 Transfer Agencies

The central rationale for social security administrations is chiefly to make transfer payments to eligible citizens, either in relation to those individuals' historic records of contributing to social security funds for old age or unemployment insurance, or unconditionally, in virtue simply of their family or household situation and level of resources, set against a minimum level guaranteed by the state. Neither of these tasks is simple. For contributory benefits agencies must maintain records of payments-in, typically over very long time periods (such as people's complete working lives for old age pensions), and then satisfactorily establish the claimant's identity and match them to their entitlement. For as-of-right benefits, agencies must be able to assess the claimant's situation in a great deal of detail so as to exactly determine their entitlement under law. In both cases there is an obvious and large-scale risk of fraud, in which people misrepresent their identities or their situation so as to draw benefits to which they are not entitled.

Traditionally many welfare state systems also paid some contributory and as-of-right benefits over very long periods, or even indefinitely until people died, with the critical time for checking identities and eligibilities being when claimants are first accepted into benefits. This focus on initial checks still remains dominant for benefits for elderly people and the chronically sick. But it has never prevailed in time-limited benefits (such as unemployment insurance benefits in most countries)—where a key source of potential fraud is determining when people have returned to work. And there have also been major changes in some countries (notably the UK) towards much more 'active' welfare approaches for working-age people, even those who are ill or disabled or looking after children. These arrangements now link entitlement to benefits with actively seeking work, including applying for jobs and training—often with ambitious aims of linking together social security payments, employment interviews and training, and support for families with children or housing difficulties.

It might seem that the information problems of administering social security benefits could be best tackled by breaking-up their administration, so that direct controls on individuals could be managed by reasonably scaled organizations in a position to gather a lot of information about their 'clientele'. But in fact three contradictory pressures on social security systems have produced highly nationalized systems in six of our case study countries (and a partly centralized system in the USA, where unemployment insurance and old age pensions are organized at national level). These factors are the economic rationale for welfare payments to working age people; fiscal pressures for nationalization; and pressures to minimize the costs of welfare payments through economies of scale. The first is relatively briefly handled. In any economy some of the key sources of structural unemployment are the ties that limit people to looking for work in their own communities or regions. Providing nationally scaled systems of social security is a key element in fostering labour mobility, allowing people to up sticks and look for work in new areas and different regions of the country.

Second, there are strong fiscal pressures to concentrate welfare services at the most tax-rich tier of government, which means the national level, as we noted in Chapter 6. Redistributive expenditures can also be most efficiently carried out at this tier, avoiding the competitive 'race to the bottom' pressures that might otherwise operate if sub-national governments attempted to effect redistribution.

Third, because of the huge financial scale of welfare state benefits, there have been strong political and taxpayer pressures to keep the costs of administering these systems down to the absolute minimum level, by aggregating them into large, national-scale systems and using the maximum amount of automation of payments and records-keeping. The contemporary consequence of these cumulative pressures is the modern transfer agency—a strongly organized, large-scale, and mechanized/automated machine bureaucracy. The most distinctive feature of transfer agencies is that only around 5 per cent or less of the total budget is spent on their administrative processes and running costs, while the vast bulk of their expenditure goes out to claimants and benefits recipients. Such demanding ratios for organization costs can only be achieved by focusing on reasonably simplified systems for administering benefits and making full use of information systems and large-scale, automated administrative operations to cut costs per payment made to a minimum.

From the period of the New Deal in 1930s America, when Roosevelt's new social security bureaucracy made early use of punched-card systems to show that the new system could be established at reasonable cost, social security agencies have been pioneers of government automation. Among our case study countries the first computers were introduced into social security administration as early as the mid-1950s (Australia and the USA), the early 1960s (the Netherlands), and the late 1960s (Canada, the UK, and Japan). There were extensive programmes for automating paperwork systems, especially focusing on computerized indexes of contributions and large-scale, centralized payment systems in the 1970s. But the consequences of these early efforts can be traced out in the contemporary period in a set of very large-scale, national-level legacy IT systems running on old code in mainframe computers. Additionally, because they grew up piecemeal over three decades rather than being designed as a coherent whole, and with new benefits coming on stream in many countries, numerous different components of the overall social security IT system are commonly networked together in complex ways. The very large-scale of transfer agencies' IT systems means that (as with tax bureaucracies) they are almost impossible to modernize as a whole.

Additional complications have been introduced by the extensive reorganization of social welfare agencies in many of our case study countries over the last two decades. The UK, the Netherlands, and New Zealand have seen a convergence of welfare and employment policy, with an emphasis on 'enabling' strategies that seek to boost employment and employability, making use of eligibility and means testing. Such reforms have been labelled as a shift from 'sharing to earning' (the Netherlands at the end of the 1990s); 'welfare-to-work' (the UK) and a re-labelling of the welfare state as a 'trampoline' rather than a 'safety net', where welfare recipients 'bounce back' to employment (the US in the mid-1990s). These policy reforms (in rhetoric at least) have been accompanied by administrative reform, so in our period there have been extensive reorganizations and renamings of government agencies responsible for employment policy and social welfare. At the service delivery level, some countries have tried to move towards a 'one stop shop' organizational model, usually facilitated through dramatic information systems change.

In e-government terms, social security is also a difficult field for innovation. Agency staffs often see themselves as dealing extensively or predominantly with client groups that are relatively poor and hence tend to have low levels of Internet penetration. Poorer elderly, chronically sick, or disabled people are particularly unlikely to have Web access. And people with weak education or literacy levels may have a limited demand for taking up e-government services, and a stronger than average preference for wanting to retain face-to-face contacts with local offices. There are also virtually no large-scale private sector operations dealing with these client groups, so that private sector role models can be hard for welfare agencies to find. On the other hand, it is important not to overstate these problems. Like tax agencies, social security agencies also interact with very large numbers of people in work. And for contributory benefits and universal state old age pensions the spectrum of the population interacting with agencies is very wide. Both these factors suggest a considerable potential for e-government processes in the social security field, and across our period the spreading levels of first Internet and later broadband access among households reinforced the potential for advances. Yet social security agencies are not renowned for the innovative nature of their e-government provision. There are divergences across the countries in their strategies and in several countries social security agencies have struggled to reap the promised benefits from technological development.

7.2 IT Contracting and e-Government in Social Security

In the USA, the agency with responsibility for social security at federal level is the Social Security Administration (SSA). Originally part of the Department of Health and Human Services, SSA has been an independent agency since a 1994 decision of the Clinton presidency. It managed three main programmes: Old Age and Survivors Insurance, Disability Insurance, and Supplemental Security Income (SSI). By the early twenty-first century, the agency had a staff of over 65,000 employees, handling over US$400 billion annually and dealing with around 50 million claimants. SSA's central office is in Baltimore, Maryland, while the field organization is geared towards providing services at the local level, including 10 regional offices, 6 processing centres, and 1,300 field offices.

The SSA was an early innovator in IT and at the beginning of the 1970s was regarded as the most experienced user of IT in the federal government (Derthick 1990; GAO 1991; Margetts 1999). But by the end of the decade SSA's reputation had taken a severe battering, particularly after a major failure in the implementation of SSI when it was first introduced. Setting up SSI was an enormous task, involving the transfer of 3 million beneficiaries from 1,300 state and local offices to federal rolls, the hiring and training of 15,000 new employees, and the development of a complex computer system in an impossibly short timescale to meet the legislative timetable. Even ten years later, some observers considered that 'morale at the agency never fully recovered' (OTA 1986: 105). The agency now had a reputation for obsolete hardware and a computer system consisting of a 'hodge-podge of software programs developed over a twenty year period' ... which a 'thousand possible small foul-ups' could cause to collapse (OTA 1986: 121).

A plan to redress this state of affairs (called the Systems Modernization Project) took shape throughout the 1980s. It was much criticized by Congress for its incremental, piecemeal approach and lack of vision and for spiralling expenditure, totalling $4 billion on operating and modernizing systems between 1982 and 1990 (GAO 1991*a*). But by the 1990s, the agency was beginning to reap appreciable benefits. By 1994, it took ten days to receive a social security card, compared with six weeks in 1982, and emergency payments were received in five days, instead of fifteen days in 1982 (SSA 1994: 1–4). The Systems Modernization Project never achieved the initially promised 'transformational' benefits (Margetts 1999: 84–5). But by the mid-1990s, there were some signs that the SSA's systems were significantly more efficient than the UK, with a lower percentage of benefit expenditure spent on administration (1.5–5 per cent) and a much lower percentage of administration costs spent on IT (4.6–18 per cent) (Margetts 1999: 72).

In the early days of the 1970s computerization changes, SSA had a policy of using in-house personnel to carry out IT work where possible. It also tried to avoid the central contracting initiatives of the 1980s mandated by the Office of Management and Budget, including the Competition in Contracting Act of 1984. SSA were not completely successful, and half of the agency's IT budget has long gone to outside contractors. But the agency continued a policy of developing in-house expertise where possible, in contrast to almost every other federal agency. The troubled history of some large IT contracts that the agency did enter into may have encouraged them in this path. A 'special relationship' with IBM in the 1960s was plagued with accusations of lock-in. Compatibility issues lead to greater and greater reliance on the company and in 1978 the GSA put a hold on all SSA computer acquisitions subject to review. In 1981, the SSA's largest contract so far (US$115 million) was awarded to Paradyne Corporation to provide the agency with 1,850 programmable microcomputer systems. Paradyne was eventually accused by the Security Exchange Commission of rigging the tests using dummy equipment made by competitors and having sold SSA an untested prototype. SSA's response to these problems was to assume that it would always face legal battles. So it prepared for them at the outset, opening a file for the legal protest with the GSA Board of Contract Appeals at day one of a tender, and added ninety days to all project timetables for the protest.

By 2000, SSA had three major IT system contracts, all with different contractors. The agency signed a US$500 million contract with Unisys in October 1996 for the installation of workstations and local area networks, as a part of a huge IT upgrade across the organization that rolled out 70,000 PCs in 1996. During 1997 and 1998, there was concern that the contract was expensive and already providing out-of-date equipment. But SSA stuck with Unisys for follow-on work and a second phase began in 2000, with IBM as the subcontractor. Maximus won a US$350 million contract in May 2001 to provide case management, assessment, and treatment referral services to individuals receiving federal disability benefits who have severe substance abuse problems. Lockheed Martin signed a seven-year US$115 million contract with SSA in September 1998 to provide IT software support services. The agency also made progress in paying benefits electronically rather than in cash, reaching three-quarters of its general payments by mid-2001, with SSI somewhat lower at 50 per cent. SSA also joined a project in conjunction with the Treasury department to implement an Electronic Transfer Account for claimants without access to a bank account and unable to register for one.

In terms of e-government changes, SSA was relatively early among federal agencies to reap some of the benefits of the Internet. As early as 1997 SSA allowed individuals to request and receive 'Pensions and Earnings Benefit Statements' online. However, questions were raised about the privacy of the service and SSA had to replace it with a mail back facility (Dunleavy and Margetts 1999: 70). In April 1999 it was nominated by the leading US trade publication *Government Computer News* as a 'best-practice' site for federal agencies, by which time the agency's website had a range of information in both English and Spanish and a 'Top 10 services' list on the home page. During 2001, the SSA developed facilities for helping individuals

- to determine their eligibility for benefits;
- to make an Internet Social Security Benefit Application;
- to check their Social Security Account online and to change their address via the Internet.

By this time, one of the SSA's most popular Internet services was the online benefits application, where people could apply for retirement, spouse's and disability benefits via the Internet and a facility for estimating future benefit entitlements.

In the first few years of the twenty-first century, SSA received a number of positive judgements on its e-government performance. In an annual ranking carried out by Brown University of both state and federal government websites in 2003, the researchers placed the SSA the third highest of all federal sites (which in any case, do better than the US states on the e-government index). On an index running from 0 to 100 rated on contact information, publications, databases, portals, and number of online services, the SSA scored 69, below only the Federal Communications Commission (on 73) and the central government portal firstgov.gov (with 84). SSA ranked ahead of the IRS, all the other main delivery agencies and all of the other 1,600 state and federal sites surveyed (*PBI Media* 24 September 2003; *Chicago Daily Herald* 22 December 2003). In the 2006 fiscal budget, where federal agencies' e-government ratings were ranked on a three-tiered colour-coded system (with red meaning failure, yellow meaning improvement, and green signifying adequate implementation), the SSA was the only agency to improve its e-government rating from yellow to green (*National Journal Group* 7 February 2005). In June 2005, the SSA business services online website received a top satisfaction score in the University of Michigan's American Customer Satisfaction Index (ACSI) for e-government, a national economic indicator that measures customer satisfaction in both private and public sectors. Scoring 82 per cent, it outperformed federal government websites as a whole (on 73 per cent), outscored many private sector companies measured by the ACSI and exceeded the ACSI's average e-retail score of 78 per cent. The SSA retirement planner website also achieved a satisfaction score of 79 per cent (*Business Wire* 21 June 2005). In 2001, SSA received nearly 46 million form W-2 requests electronically. But by 2005, after system enhancements and improved marketing, user demand had grown to nearly157 million requests annually. There thus seems reasonable evidence that the incremental approach for which SSA were so criticized during the 1980s was the right one, in tune with the 'build and learn' approach that works best with the Internet. Indeed SSA had always placed a proud emphasis on their incremental approach, claiming that their 1980s Information Systems Plan provided for 'evolutionary rather than revolutionary changes' (SSA 1982). An unfashionable view at the time, it has achieved common currency in the e-government arena in the 2000s.

In the UK, social security administration was affected by frequent reorganizations in the last two decades of the twentieth century, after a long stable period in the 1970s and early 1980s under the Department of Health and Social Security (DHSS), their operations were later split off into the Department of Social Security (DSS). The UK government's 'Next Steps' agencification programme in the 1980s created three agencies within the DSS departmental group: a massive Benefits Agency with 68,000 staff, whose rationale was paying out benefits; the Contributions Agency, to collect national insurance payments, later merged into the Inland Revenue; and the Child Support Agency, running a separate (and always disastrous) system for collecting family support payments from divorced fathers. In 2001, a merger with some parts of the Department of Employment and Education brought the (more acceptably named, politically) Department of Work and Pensions with two main agencies, Jobcentre Plus and the Pensions Service. The department has an overall budget of around £100 billion, 1,500 frontline offices, and 125,000 staff, with an IT budget for 2004–5 of £678 million accounting for almost a quarter of central government IT expenditure (*Kabledirect* 13 January 2004).

The DHSS was an early pioneer in IT, with a computer system handling straightforward data processing tasks from the end of the 1950s. By the end of the 1970s, however, the computer systems of the DSS were widely recognized as outmoded and in need of attention. The department embarked on what was to become a fairly troubled relationship with the computer industry during the Operational Strategy, a major computerization project aimed at transforming departmental administrative operations which was probably the first UK government IT project to receive a bad press. Although it automated some operations and brought PCs into the department, it delivered few of the promised benefits in terms of staff reductions or service quality improvements and initial cost estimates of £700 million rose eventually to an estimated £2.6 billion (see Margetts 1999). Departmental IT by the late 1990s still resolutely lacked a 'whole person' or 'one-stop shop' approach, with little connectivity between systems based on single benefits, and many paper processes still in operation. The planned solution was the ACCORD project, entailing expenditure of £3,500 million over ten years to modernize and connect up the department's main computer systems.

The DSS had originally planned that their own staff would undertake most of the development work on the Operational Strategy during the 1980s, but in reality the last twenty-five years have seen an ever-increasing reliance of the agency on external companies. In 1989 the entire Livingstone Computer Centre was contracting out to EDS, after which the company took over two more of the four area centres. The department was always notable for extensive ad hoc use of management consultants (independent contractors) spending over 8 per cent of its IT budget on consultancy in the early 1990s, a higher proportion than any other department (Margetts 1999: 61). In 1994, a significant chunk of the department's Information Technology Services Agency was designated as a candidate for Market Testing in contracts worth £577 million and a transfer of 1,600 staff under TUPE rules (NAO 1996b: 1). EDS emerged with the bulk of the spoils, taking over all the department's data centres while SEMA and ICL won the contract for the provision of data network communications. In 1998, the DSS signed 'ACCORD' framework agreements with three prime contractors: EDS, Fujitsu (formerly ICL), and BT/Sema. But in November EDS consolidated its position as prime contractor, running computer systems for the whole of the Department of Work and Pensions as lead contractor in the 'Affinity' consortium (IBM, CWC, and PWC) worth £7 billion in total over 8 years, involving the transfer of around 2,000 staff. EDS also signed a partnership contract with the Employment Service worth at least £300 million over 10 years. A DSS review in 1999 cemented EDS's dominance in the growing fusion between employment and welfare, effectively cancelling relations with ICL and Sema.

The 1990s were plagued with problems for UK social security agencies. In 1995, the government's first contract awarded under the PFI, for the £144 million replacement National Insurance Recording System (NIRS2), was awarded to Andersen Consulting, after the government accepted a bid from the company almost half that of other tenders and a quarter of the public sector comparator case. The deal was initially seen by an audit office report as offering good value for money (NAO 1997) only for the contractor to stop operating the old index system as planned, but then not bring the new system into place for almost a year. During this long gap payments and pensions were being assigned by the department to citizens without full information on their contributions, at an eventual cost of around £85 million in compensation to citizens and £68 million on remedial work to the system (NAO 2001; *Computing* 29 January 2004). Another expensive fiasco was a joint project (Pathway) between the Benefits Agency and the Post Office to computerize the payment of benefits through post offices, a billion pound contract let to ICL in 1996. The project eventually collapsed completely in 1999 when it proved too complicated to integrate Pathway systems into Benefits Agency computers, and the project was overtaken by a government decision to pay benefits directly into claimants' bank accounts, at a cost of £140 million to the Benefits Agency and £180 million to ICL. ICL were later accused of 'deliberate misleading' their Japanese parent, Fujitsu, 'with respect to the risk involved' and of exaggerating the likely profitability of the contract by claiming that the return on the deal would be more than 20 per cent (*Times* 23 April 2003).

Concern over IT in social welfare continued in the public eye into the twenty-first century. In 2003, the Child Support Agency's new system was deemed 'a £456 million fiasco' (*Sunday Telegraph* 30 November 2003). The system was intended to reflect new 'simplified' rules for dealing with child-support payments, but by the time it was supposed to have been live none of the agency's 1 million cases had been shifted from the old system to the new. Even by 2005, the agency's annual report revealed that computer problems were leading to mistakes in one out of four cases, an administrative cost per case of around £200 and with 12,000 new cases being processed by hand. A key public sector union claimed that 'staff were leaving in large numbers because of the stress of dealing with the computer chaos' (*Independent* 21 July 2005). In February 2005, 'one of the most damning reports ever seen on government IT' was produced by the House of Commons Work and Pensions Committee,' outlining the 'catastrophic' implementation of the new system at the CSA, with a backlog of 30,000 families waiting payment building up each month. The new system was 'nowhere near being fully functional' (with EDS and the CSA disagreeing as to when it would be) and 'the number of dissatisfied, disenchanted and angry customers' continued to escalate. Meanwhile, DWP was withholding millions of pounds of payments to EDS, which was contesting the grounds for withholding payment. The report concluded that 'instead of focusing efforts on building a partnership with the IT supplier to achieve the business change required to implement the new system effectively, DWP officials were simply trying to use old Private Finance Initiative rules to offload risk to the supplier and avoid blame if anything went wrong' (*Computer Weekly* 1 February 2005). DWP had not considered the consequences of a worst-case scenario, where EDS decided to write off the contract and walk away from the project.

In spite of the numerous high-profile problems associated with IT in social welfare in the 1990s and 2000s and the involvement of EDS in many of them, both large contracts and EDS remained popular with UK social security agencies. In 2002, the Post Office signed a £1 billion contract with the company to allow benefits to be paid electronically through bank accounts, claiming that it had 'learnt the lessons' from the Pathway debacle (*Computer Weekly* 4 April 2002). The deal formed part of the UK government's universal banking service, with around 3 million customers expected to use the basic bank accounts. By this time, 80 per cent of the department's IT projects were being carried out under the Affinity Accord programme, headed up by EDS, signed in 2000 for ten years. The Department's strategy was stated as having shifted 'from very large-scale complex projects'... to a 'much more piecemeal approach arranging smaller contracts with more suppliers, reducing the scope, duration and complexity of individual projects'. But some questioned the viability of such a strategy when the department had just employed an IT director from the financial services community with specific expertise in managing very large-scale IT contracts for JobCentre Plus (*Kable Direct* 13 January 2004). Indeed, by 2005 it seemed clear that the 'bites' were going to be large. In November 2004, the DWP signed a £27 million contract with Fujitsu Services to develop a resource management system, as well as its existing £70 million contract with Capita to manage IT for social security and disability claim forms. In March 2005, DWP signed a £500 million seven-year contract to set up new IT systems for medical assessments and advice covering benefits claimants, with Atos Origin.

Meanwhile, social security administration in the UK remained stubbornly paper-based up to the end of the twentieth century. The key agencies of the department built websites in the late 1990s, but these were conservatively designed and for a long time provided strictly limited functionality (Dunleavy and Margettts 1999) with intranets virtually nonexistent. The Benefits Agency devoted a tiny percentage of its huge budget to web-based initiatives, significantly less than in the other countries. In 2002, there was political and press concern that a new Pension Credit scheme to provide a guaranteed income for pensioners, due to be launched in October 2003, would run on a system described by the Secretary of State for DWP as 'very decrepit'. MPs claimed that the introduction of the credit, affecting around 5 million pensioners, could be delayed because of the software not being able to deal with the complexity (*Computing* 18 April 2002). In 2004, the scheme was indeed labelled as a failure by the National Pensioners Convention who described it as 'undignified' and 'very, very confusing', with both the sophisticated telephone contact centres and website suffering from low take up levels (*Kabledirect* 11 November 2004; *Government Computing* 16 October 2003). In 2003, the Work and Pensions Select Committee produced a highly critical report on the department's IT and embarked on an inquiry into the department's systems which reported to widespread press commendation in the autumn of 2004. An NAO study at the beginning of 2005 suggested that DWP had lost £9 billion over the last three years through benefit fraud and error. In response, the department outlined an IT 'transformation programme' as part of its five-year strategy, with a number of planned e-services of the kind that social security agencies in other countries have been providing for years.

In Japan, the social security system is managed by the Ministry of Health, Labour, and Welfare and the Social Insurance Agency (SIA), with the SIA formed as an external organization in 2001. In 2003, there were around 17,000 staff in the agency, including local offices. In Japan, as for tax administration, there is a long history of computers for social security administration, with a pensions system developed in the 1960s. Between 1967 and 2003, the SIA spent 1.17 trillion yen on systems development, and the social insurance system is the largest and most expensive 'by far' of the computer systems across Japanese ministries (*Yomiuri Shimbun* 26 January 2005). As for all central government, computing has always been outsourced: in fact, officials pointed out that it was difficult for the SIA to do more outsourcing in line with current central government policy from the Cabinet Office, as they have always done as much as they can. Indeed, officials in the SIA 'have no knowledge of how the system works' (*Yoriumri Shimbun* 20 November 2004) and a senior official at the agency admitted publicly: 'Those in charge of the system are secretarial workers, so they are not trained to understand the workings of the system'. While most other Japanese ministries and agencies put codicils in IT contracts that require contractors to give them the specifications for the structure and design of systems, SIA do not do so and they remain with contract providers.

Of the numerous large-scale systems run by the agency, the largest is the main social insurance online system, the latest version of which was introduced in 1980, controlling data on both the employees' pension plan and the basic pension scheme. The system was originally developed by Hitachi (as sole contractor from 1968), but NTTD was invited to join in maintaining the system in 1980 and became the prime contractor in developing and maintaining the system. By 2003, some ministry staff were involved in managing the system, but contract staff predominantly worked within the agency. The Social Insurance Operations Centre was housed in a four-story building owned by NTTD in Mitaka in western Tokyo, operating computers procured by NTTD for the SIA. NTTD and Hitachi held the right of ownership and the copyright to the system. All social insurance records were dealt with in one system. They were planning a new Web-based system, but still by 2003, citizens had no option but to go into social security local offices to have any dealings with SIA. Officials considered that the new system would not be cheaper, but could mean less work for local office staff and potential savings for government.

During 2004–5 the agency received sustained criticism from the Diet and a prestigious Tokyo newspaper for its 'lax control over computer system development and cost effectiveness' illustrated by its 'close ties with its information technology contractors and dubious payments to the contractors' (*Yomiuri Shimbun* 26 January 2005). The 'scandal-plagued' agency was accused of having violated the Law of Accounts for its inadequate contract and accounts management (*Yomiuri Shimbun* 29 November 2004) and its relationship with NTTD was particularly criticized: 'retired agency officials have landed jobs at the telecommunications firm under the *amakudari* (descent from heaven) practice, and serving employees have received more than 100 million yen for editing books (social insurance and computer manuals) for an NTT group company' (*Yomiuri Shimbun* 10 January 2005). Of the 92 billion yen received in payments by the two companies in 2004, 10.6 billion were paid for services claimed to have been done by the contractors but not stated in the contracts (*Yomiuri Shimbun* 10 January 2005). Part of these arrangements (8.6 billion yen) appears to have been a PFI-type deal, whereby NTT paid the entire cost of establishing a system while SIA paid back the cost through monthly fees. But the cost effectiveness of the agreement could not be determined due to the absence of design specifications. While other Japanese ministries (such as Construction and Transport) and agencies (such as the Patent Office) hire systems engineers to review cost estimates submitted by contractors, including time and unit cost for establishing systems, SIA does not and continues to make payments without reviewing invoices. The newspaper claimed that this procedure caused the ballooning of costs and by 2003, the agency owed NTTD about 200 billion yen. Meanwhile, a chief information officer in charge of monitoring the government's IT procurements claimed that NTTD's statement that manpower equivalent to 6,360 engineers was needed on an annual basis to maintain services was unconvincing. In March 2005, in a survey of Japanese government IT systems which identified 95 billion yen overspending, the SIA came out as the worst culprit, with estimates that the running costs for its online insurance system could be cut by 52 billion yen (*Yomiuri Shimbun* 15 June 2005). The survey found that the costs for the computer centre, facilities, terminals and networks, which usually decline over a few years, had not changed appreciably from 1999 to 2003, highlighting the ministry's 'lack of cost consciousness'.

Meanwhile, the SIA continued to offer little in the way of electronic services. Social welfare was not mentioned in the report on Japan's surprise leap to joint third in the Accenture (2005) rankings of e-government, although by this time e-filing of taxes was available across Japan and the Ministry of Finance had e-enabled permit fees, fines, and taxes. In general, e-government in Japan has been geared at citizens paying government rather than vice versa.

In New Zealand, the Ministry of Social Development was established in October 2001 through the merger of the Department of Social Policy and the Department of Work and Income (itself formed from earlier departments of income support and the Employment Service, merged in 1998), to deliver income support and employment services to around 1 million citizens. Along similar lines to the UK, 170 integrated service delivery offices were established under the auspices of the agency known as Work and Income (WINZ), offering a single point of contact for work-search support, income support, and in-work support. In 2003, a reorganization seemed to bring social welfare agencies back to a situation similar to that before the 1980s NPM reforms, when relevant agencies, such as the Department of Child, Youth and Family Services, were 'clustered' around the Ministry.

As in the UK, EDS was the dominant contractor in New Zealand's social welfare IT systems throughout our research period. The Department of Social Welfare signed a contract in April 1997 with EDS to manage the computer systems responsible for processing N$8 billion of social security benefits annually (CSC and Unisys were the failed bidders). EDS also took over a former Department of Social Welfare computer centre in July 1997 through a contract to develop the Social Welfare Information for Tomorrow Today (SWIFTT) system. Also as in the UK, EDS seems to have consolidated their position during the merging of social security and employment domains, although Unisys continued to provide some mainframe assistance to WINZ (subject to delayed Web-based service provision plans).

WINZ has a troubled history with IT, in part due to its organizational history of 'spin-offs' and mergers. The creation of the Work and Income Department in 1998 presented the new agency with the 'unenviable' task of merging 'two almost incompatible computer systems' (*New Zealand Herald* 1 September 1999)—Swift (NZ$50 million), which made benefit payments and Solo ($31 million) which handled case management for the unemployed. A project to develop 'Focis', a system to integrate the information systems capabilities of Income Support and the Employment Service at a cost of NZ$38 million ran into problems in 1999. In 2000, the Department was landed with an 'unexpected NZ$30 million bill for two new Unisys mainframe computers needed to ensure that rising numbers of beneficiaries get paid' (*Infotech Weekly* 2 October 2000), when the existing mainframe ran out of capacity before a planned change to a different (and cheaper) hardware platform kicked in. By this time the cost of Focis had risen to NZ$77 million and the Department's capacity to manage its IT was in question: 'WINZ has pretty much outsourced all of their advice so they are to a large extent captured by EDS and Unisys' (*Infotech Weekly* 16 August 1999). At one point job boards were removed and visitors to WINZ offices were expected to queue to use a computer to find out about vacancies, a widely unpopular development which caused some politicians to argue that the management of the agency 'did not understand what computers were good for and what they were not good for' (*New Zealand Herald* 10 August 1999).

More recently, WINZ has found e-government a challenge. The agency ran into major processing problems in the handling of student loans in 2000; an independent review revealed largely paper-based processes and an inadequate website. Also in 2000, WINZ's website was described by a committee of chief executives looking at IT issues as 'woefully limited', in spite of the department's huge investment in IT (*New Zealand Herald* 16 June 2000). A round up of the 'IT year' in the *NZ Herald* at the start of 2004 showed how the Ministry of Social Development's reputation for e-government continued in the doldrums, announcing that 'the project to watch' was the Ministry of Social Development's replacement of its Swift and Trace systems: 'before it's even started, the job threatens to cost $177 million, making it one of the biggest computer projects undertaken in New Zealand. Already the planning phase is shrouded in secrecy. Somehow you just know it's going to get worse' (*New Zealand Herald* 9 January 2004).

In Australia, the agency Centrelink is responsible for social security benefit provision, providing services to more than 6 million Australians, formed from an amalgamation of services from several departments in 1996. In 1999–2000, the agency dealt with approximately AU$44 billion of payments, around 11 million transactions a day and supported a network of around 22,000 public sector users (ANAO 2001).

Centrelink is the fourth biggest IT operation in Australia, with a huge operational budget, an IT department of around 1,750 staff of which at least 400 are contractors and annual expenditure of about AU$320 million annually maintaining and upgrading systems. Some of these systems have received public attention for their aged and unwieldy nature. Even by 2004, Centrelink's central data store was an aging database (a Computer Corporation of America Model 204) running on an IBM mainframe installed in the mid-1980s (*The Australian* 16 March 2004). In part due to its multi-organizational past, the agency operates numerous database platforms in addition to a wide range of hardware and operating systems leading to a 'plethora of inflexible back-end systems' and was still in 2004 'one of the largest—and last—users of the ageing, barely alive, Novell NetWare network operating system' (*The Australian* 16 March 2004).

In 2005, Centrelink's chief information officer Jane Treadwell left after seven years to become the CIO for the state government of Victoria. Hers had been a controversial tenure, as 'one of the first of a new breed of information manager drawn not from front-line technology ranks, but from a management consultancy', the global management services specialist McKinsey. Under her command, Centrelink developed a reputation for being 'fiercely independent in its technology operations and particularly in asserting its rights to retain products and technical standards that have fallen from vogue elsewhere' (*Canberra Times* 29 March 2005). The agency for example was one of the few large organizations using Lotus SmartSuite on all desktops and it had very few Microsoft products.

Partly due to Ms Treadwell's lobbying and that of the departmental chief executive, Centrelink was able to steadfastedly reject inclusion in the failed clustering initiative of the 1990s to a greater extent than any other agency, even the ATO. The agency argued that its IT operation was 'too important to the well-being of too many welfare recipients to risk moving it to a private sector service provider' (*Canberra Times* 29 March 2005). Originally Centrelink was involved in 'Cluster 1', covering social welfare and family through the Departments of Family and Community Services, Employment and Education, worth around AU$1 billion in total. But extensive lobbying delayed it until 2001, when the Humphrey report led to case-by-case contracting and Centrelink announced a strategy of 'selective sourcing'. In August 2003, the agency published plans to offer more than AU$400 million in business through five tenders, for desktop services, its nationwide data network, and a panel contract for systems integrators, which could itself generate business worth hundreds of millions, but using initial contracts to assess partners. The agency justified the strategy by pointing out that 'because system integrator relationships were strategically critical to Centrelink', the agency wanted to use initial contracts to assess partners: 'we need people that understand the way we do things—that understand the Centrelink culture . . . if you find a partner you can't deal with, you want to be able to resign' (*The Australian* 26 August 2003).

Centrelink was early to quickly develop a website, an intranet, and online services. Even in 1999, its site was well used and had innovative facilities; officials would ring back citizens who sent an email, for example (Dunleavy and Margetts 1999). In 2002, Centrelink was put forward as a 'working model for the 'whole-of-government approach' by the consulting firm Primavera, as one of those government agencies 'leading the pack' in terms of delivering on the whole of government promise of better service delivery through improved collaboration and reduced duplication of infrastructure and resources. The consultancy claimed that the agency demonstrated horizontal integration of different federal agencies and was entirely 'citizen-centric' in that users could access services and information without having to 'enter the bureaucratic maze or necessarily understanding how the government agencies and departments are arranged'. The agency was particularly congratulated for its single interface for the end user, in spite of involving twenty agencies.

But by 2004, the agency's e-government past seemed to be catching up with it when it was described as 'choking in an expensive jungle of technology systems' (*The Australian* 16 March 2004) as it embarked on a five-year, AU$312 million programme to upgrade and refresh its IT, involving outsourcing of its desktop operations. The agency was criticized for spending millions of dollars with Sun Microsystems on web services, while 'IT chiefs thresh about in a jungle of technology platforms—some dating from 20 years ago', the continuing legacy of the agency's organizational history. Although the 'IT Refresh' programme was intended to systematize the agency's infrastructure, the CIO insisted that the aging 'Model 204' central database was not to be touched during the upgrade programme, causing one vendor to complain: 'In some ways IT Refresh should have been called IT More of the Same . . . They seem to have one of everything' (*The Australian* 16 March 2004).

In Canada, social welfare and security has been administered by HRD Canada since 1997, responsible for employment insurance, income security, employment programmes, corporate services, homelessness, and labour services. HRDC provides social services to 30 million Canadian citizens through 320 offices across the country. During the 2000s, the Department was divided up into Social Development Canada, dealing with social welfare, while employment and training and education issues were dealt with the Human Resources and Skills Development Canada; the agencies were then merged again as Human Resources and Social Development Canada in 2005.

Like many social security agencies, HRDC was an early user of large-scale mainframe computer systems and by 2003 still relied on a 'patchwork' of systems dating from the early 1970s. The systems were written to operate on the hardware used by the department at the time, first Burroughs and then Unisys (never IBM), using the now outdated COBOL language. By 2003, many of the department's systems still used Cobol programs dating from that time, including the main program paying out unemployment insurance: so when it goes wrong or faces a new challenge, such as the millennium problem of 2000, 'Cobol programmers have to be brought out of retirement', as one interviewee put it. Unlike their UK counterparts, however, the Department was keen to pursue e-government while leveraging older mainframe systems to extend their usefulness in the new environment. 'We procured commercially available "middleware" software to extend the reach and convenience of using legacy systems without requiring major re-engineering', moving towards a situation where a single business event would drive updates to multiple separate systems that formerly did not 'talk' to each other, as the assistant deputy minister of the agency put it in 2002 (Milne 2002: 18). Web-based technologies have also progressed gradually since the time when 'someone in HDRC put up a website' and the department's current e-government strategy has evolved from there, to a kind of 'patchwork quilt' of websites. The intranet has evolved in the same way. By the early 2000s, the department was trying to 'clean up' and 'standardize'. HRDC as a whole managed Internet issues corporately, but websites had been developed by program areas in a decentralized way.

In common with other Canadian departments, HRDC has not been an enthusiastic outsourcer, limiting contracting out to specific projects. In 1997, the department's manager of network support services was quoted in the trade press extolling the benefits of 'out-tasking', a 'happy medium' involving outsourcing selected portions of the IT infrastructure, 'leaving managers to focus on strategic issues of business' (*ComputerWorld Canada* 12 September 1997). This attitude may in part have been shaped by the department's first experience of outsourcing, the problematic Income Security Program Redesign, a contract with EDS Canada to automate distribution of Canada Pension Plan cheques, disability benefits, and child tax benefits. At the end of 1997 and after spending C$365 million (on a project with an original budget reported as C$103 million, *Canadian Business and Current Affairs* February 1996) HRDC announced it would not renew its contract with EDS, that the project was not going to meet its 1998 deadline and that the department would handle the new system itself (*Financial Post* 15 November 1997). The next announcement of a major contract was not until November 2001 when the Department awarded a contract to replace its network to CSC in a five to seven-year contract of around C$96 million, which the company's president in Canada described as an 'important contract win for CSC in the Canadian federal government information technology market' (*Canada News Wire* 15 November 2001).

In contrast to several of the other social welfare agencies discussed here (particularly the UK) HRDC had an early success in connecting the adoption of IT with staff reductions. Faced with an expenditure reduction target of C$200 million (the equivalent of around 5,000 full-time staff) in the mid-1990s, the department made plans to transform its Service Delivery Network of 800 front line and regional offices, and numerous call centres and mail service centres (handling 60–80 million telephone calls and 100 million items of correspondence annually) into an Electronic Service Delivery Network (ESDN). This involved significant new investment in IT and the automation and consolidation of numerous operations, including the reduction of the number of local offices to 320 by 1998. Building on a 1992 pilot project, the department also introduced a new generation of electronic self-service kiosks, through which citizens could file Employment Insurance (EI) applications, find labour market information, and search for job opportunities. The number of kiosks expanded dramatically, from under 2,000 in 1995 to over 5,000 by 1998, and HRDC relied extensively on this kiosk technology and investment in telecommunications in order to meet staff reduction target (Longford 2002: 7), halving workforces in some area offices. Overall, HRDC external expenditures on IT goods and services increased by 120 per cent, from C$101 million in 1994–5 to C$221 million in 1999–2000, while at the same time its personnel expenditures declined from C$1.4 billion to C$1.2 billion, a drop of almost 15 per cent, and its total employment declined by 21 per cent (Longford 2002: 8). The department's employment reduction goal of eliminating 5,000 FTEs was achieved within three years, leading to annual departmental savings of C$195 million in personnel costs and enthusiasm for IT investment as a way of lowering labour costs.

Perhaps for this reason, HRDC built on its early success with kiosks to be innovative in developing services on the Internet, launching a benefits website *www.canadabenefits.gov.gc.ca* in 2001, listing information and services, such as pensions, employment insurance, and housing, from federal, provincial, and territorial government departments, Crown corporations, and agencies. The site was identified as innovative, offering a 'whole of government' approach to benefit provision in Accenture's 2003 e-government study, acting as a 'one-stop shop where Canadians can easily find the information they are looking for, even if they do not know the exact name of the program or even which department of government provides it'. HRCD developed a strategy of converting kiosks into Internet terminals where citizens could access the website, from which information dropped straight into legacy systems, as data from the kiosks had done. By 2003, the site was receiving an average of 30,000 visitors monthly and citizens from several states (3 million a year) could apply for employment insurance online. Another successful part of social welfare provision was the Job Bank (*www.jbbank.gc.ca* which soon became the most popular part of the Canadian government site, even in 2001 receiving 48 per cent of the site traffic with 1,000,000 visits a day and more than 28 million user sessions a year (Accenture 2002). As with many of HRDC services, the Job Bank service had previously been delivered through kiosks located in mainly government offices. All the gold, silver, and bronze medals for innovative service delivery to citizens and businesses for the trade conference GTEC 2004 were awarded to Social Development Canada or HRDSC e-government initiatives, as were gold and silver for 2005. In 2005, SDC consolidated 170 websites into a single site. Alone among our case study departments and no doubt in part reflecting the high Internet penetration in Canada, the department has been part of a project which developed a successful portal for 'seniors', Seniors Canada On-line. It was introduced in 2001 to provide a 'single-window to on-line information regarding benefits and information for seniors, their families, caregivers and supporting organizations'.

Not all the department's initiatives have received acclaim. HRDC reported gains in service quality for its IT investment that facilitated the impressive staff reductions outlined above (HRCD 1999; Longford 2002). But at the same time the automation was linked to the implementation of the Employment Insurance Act and a 37 point drop in the percentage of officially unemployed Canadians eligible for EI benefits: 'for many citizens, in effect, improved service at HRDC amounted simply to having their EI benefit claims rejected *faster'* (Longford 2002: 13). The department was much criticized by (among others) the Privacy Commissioner of Canada on privacy grounds for its policy, from 1995, of routine data matching of insurance claim records and Traveler Declaration Cards supplied by Revenue Canada in order to identify fraudulent claims. The Commissioner also, in 2000, reported on HRDC's development of its Longitudinal Labour Force File, a detailed research database containing information from across government on over 30 million individuals and at a level of detail described by the Commissioner as 'a de facto citizen profile'. The department dismantled the database in response to the ensuing public outcry (Longford 2002).

Overall, however, e-government has brought benefits to social welfare agencies in Canada. HRDC was an early user of the Secure Channel, automating the communication of the 'employment record' between government and business, which previously had to be impact printed in triplicate and was the 'most troublesome form ever created by government', as one interviewee put it. Future developments rested on the success of the (at times, troubled) Secure Channel development, in particular with respect to security and the potential for reducing the error rate in EI, and the 'Service Canada' initiative developed by CCRA (see Chapter 6), but also involving welfare agencies. Service Canada is intended to be a one-stop shop for a range of government services, which is to provide a 'My Account' facility to give Canadians a single view of their accounts, programs, and benefits with government. It could involve CCRA in the paying out of benefits.

In the Netherlands, the Ministry of Social Affairs and Employment is responsible for both social welfare and the majority of labour market policies. This integration between employment and welfare functions also exists at local level, where provincial and local government organizations work with social partners from the private and non-profit sectors. Key stakeholders are so-called UVIs, state bodies responsible for the administration of welfare payments and employee insurance.

As in our other countries, social welfare in the Netherlands has a long history of using IT. Social welfare in the Netherlands was long dominated by two computer services providers, both 'home grown'. By the early twenty-first century, Pink Roccade, the former Dutch government national computer centre that was partially privatized in 1999, was holding the largest social welfare contract, an agreement worth approximately NLf400 million. The company's position was further strengthened by its successful NLf400 million purchase of ASZ (Automatisierung Sociale Zekerheid), the IT division of one of the largest social security and employment insurance providers (UVIs) in the Netherlands, GAK Group. This takeover gave Pink Roccade control over all IT provision for GAK's payments and services. This deal with ASZ sparked criticism from the Secretary of State Hoogervorst from the Ministry of Social Affairs and Employment, who suggested that it would result in GAK being far too dependent on Pink Roccade, amid more general complaints about Pink Roccade's monopolistic access to public sector contracts. The other major player in social welfare was the Dutch company Ordina, which in 2000 took over the specialist social welfare systems integrator Relan ICT (with a workforce of around 575,375 in permanent employment), the IT daughter company of the Relan Group. Relan ICT was one of the largest providers of IT services to the Dutch social security market and owned two large UVI organizations, GUO and CADANS, responsible for social security and EI payment. This deal, which gave Ordina access to GUO and CALANS in the same way as Pink Roccade's role as prime contractor gave the company access to the GAK group, was aimed at establishing Ordina's position in social services IT provision. The new organization branded itself specifically for social welfare provision, Ordina Sociale Zekerheid BV.

The terrain was then set for a battle between Ordina and Pink Roccade for capture of the IT services market in social welfare, particularly after all UVIs were combined under one umbrella organization (UWV) in 2002. From that time, both Ordina and Pink Roccade were also being eyed by other more internationally based computer services providers for potential takeover, their role in social welfare a key selling point. In September 2004, Pink Roccade signed a letter of intent to acquire a data centre from Ordina with the specific hope of 'winning over Ordina's biggest client, UWV, when it retenders for outsourcing business in 2006' (*ComputerWire* 22 September 2004), taking over 40 of the 60 employees in the UWV operation with the remaining 20 to be retained by Ordina. At the time, Ordina admitted to not having the scale in outsourced data processing services to continue to service UWV, but planned to continue to provide systems integration and application development. However, by early 2005 Getronics and Ordina were involved in a bidding war to take over Pink Roccade (*Datamonitor* 25 January 2005) eventually won by Getronics (*VNU Net* 14 March 2005).

The most important central initiative was OL2000 (Public Counter 2000), developed by the Ministry of the Interior in the first half of the 1990s as a move towards integrated service counters (Government Service Centres) or one-stop shop from government and non-profit organizations to citizens and businesses. In 1996, OL2000 was extended, reorganizing public service delivery towards the demand patterns of citizens, with IT performing a more important role than the previous initiative, which was organized around physical counters. Because of local government autonomy in the Netherlands, it would be unquestionable for the central ministry to mandate the concept, but the Ministry provided funding and some project management capacity. Local community projects, usually a collaboration between private sector, non-profit, and government organizations, put in proposals to bid for this funding. From 1999, OL2000 tried to develop national cover by stimulating all local governments to do the same, with particular focus on four counters: 'business', 'building and housing', health care, and 'work and income' (with funding from appropriate ministries). The aim was to develop virtual counters, using knowledge systems, electronic kiosks and the Internet, which would act as generic counters for future initiatives.

Meanwhile, it is difficult to summarize the extent to which social welfare in the Netherlands is e-enabled, given the lack of standardization or centralization in this (as in any) area of Dutch social administration. But by the early twenty-first century, there were some indicators that it was progressing well. The European Commission's assessment of e-government services for citizens in the Netherlands gave the Centre for Work and Income and the Social Insurance Bank maximum scores for 'sophistication' in its 2005 report on e-government in the Netherlands (see *europa.eu.int/idabc/en/document/1237/422*). User satisfaction with the OL2000 services available was high (UNPAN 2004), including a job-seekers bank on which people registering with a Centre for Work and Income would automatically be included (anonymously or named), and users were notified of appropriate job opportunities. There are other moves towards 'zero-touch delivery'; for example, the child benefit process is started automatically the moment the authorities (via the municipality) are notified of a child's birth. Municipalities electronically notify the Social Insurance Bank, which contacts the parents automatically.

Conclusions

A number of generalizations emerge from these assessments of IT in social security administration in our seven countries. These agencies have been under particular pressure to attain staff cuts from computerization and to outsource their information systems. They struggle reputationally, most often heard of when they go wrong. They are open to reorganization from the centre, particularly the relationship with employment agencies and prone to organizational fragmentation in countries with radical NPM reforms, particularly the UK and New Zealand—although re-aggregation can occur when problems reach public attention.

In all our countries, social security agencies were early users of technology but lagged behind other agencies during the last twenty years of the twentieth century. With client groups with low levels of Internet penetration (particularly pensioners), several agencies have been slow to innovate in delivering services electronically, perceiving fewer gains than the tax agencies discussed in Chapter 6. Incentivization is difficult too, with compulsion considered inequitable to the point of non-viability. More recently, there are signs that some organizations have been more successful with their e-government efforts, particularly during periods where organizational configurations have been relatively stable, in the USA, Australia (to 2005) and Canada (to 2004). Because their operations are central to most of government's interactions with several key client groups, social security agencies have much to gain from e-government's potential to 'join-up' across government agencies and to facilitate a 'whole of government' approach. All have used the rhetoric of 'joining up', a 'whole person concept', and 'one-stop shops' and some have realized this potential (the Netherlands, Canada, and Australia).

At the same time as these similarities, the comparative picture suggests that three countries emerge as winners in the terms of using IT to run relatively modern and robust social security systems. In Australia, Centrelink has developed a good reputation for IT strategy and development and even innovation. It managed to escape the failed clustering initiative, due in part to its own sustained lobbying, which could be argued to have been a contributory factor in Centrelink's emerging reputation for its 'whole of government approach'. Likewise, Canada's HRDC was an early and successful user of IT, and its sustained build up of internal expertise and policy of using only limited forms of outsourcing seems to have reaped some of the benefits of e-government. In the USA, the SSA seems to have rescued its reputation from the damage of the high-profile disasters in 1970s and its cautious, evolutionary, and incremental approach (sustained in defiance of central federal agencies) seems to have paid off, with the agency developing a good reputation for e-government in the twenty-first century. In the Netherlands, a more mixed case, reorganization has brought centralized initiatives, which have shown some measure of success. The fierce competition for business in the social welfare sector, with Getronics the eventual winner, looks like the provider market has also consolidated in a way unusual for the Netherlands. But in all four of these countries, the social security agencies have determinedly maintained internal expertise, directly contravening central outsourcing policies in the case of Australia. This strategy may well have played a role in minimizing contract relationship problems, reinforcing our argument that the contract regime is what matters.

In three other countries (Japan, the UK, and New Zealand), social welfare agencies have suffered from all the problems that we might have predicted from the defining features of social security administration noted in the introduction. In New Zealand, frequent reorganizations, first towards fragmentation and then back towards consolidation, have had strong effects on the Ministry's IT systems, which have been plagued with project management problems, cost over-runs, poor reputation, and lack of internal expertise, leading to minimal e-government achievement. In Japan, social security administration remained almost completely paper-based throughout our study period. The agency's expensive mega-contract with two key providers, with allegations of corruption and dangerously low levels of internal expertise seems to have contributed to this result. In the UK, IT in social welfare is littered with problematic large-scale projects and contracts, while remaining inefficient and paper-based even by 2004. Contract providers (particularly EDS) seem to have escaped unscathed from their strong association with this troubled period.

The sheer scale of welfare state administration means that governments have a great deal to gain from computerization in this area, in terms of increased productivity, efficiency, and service quality. For a significant subsection of the population in each of our countries, this is the branch of government they care most about in terms of its ability to keep operating swiftly and accurately. However, social security agencies battle against their lack of status compared with other departments and agencies, their political visibility (which puts them first on the list for central reorganization and outsourcing initiatives) and the size and complexity of their task. Three of our countries seem to be overcoming these challenges and reaping some at least of the potential benefits, while others continue to struggle. For all of them, huge and complex information systems and a range of contract relationships are completely and irreversibly central to welfare administration and policy development.

8

Immigration: Technology Changes and Administrative Renewal

Like taxation, the ability to control entry to and exit from a territory is one of the critical defining features of a state. Established early on in the evolution of the modern state, the immigration control function has until recently been a set of organizational procedures focused on the issuing and physical checking of paper passports and other documents. The advent of the Internet and new electronic means of documentation and identification have both had remarkable impacts on the field, however. Some advanced industrial countries (especially the USA and the UK) have now moved to implement strikingly high-tech schemes of regulating immigration that are still being rolled out. They dramatically increase the role of ICTs in control processes. We first briefly sketch the changing administrative and managerial context for immigration control and some of the problems it poses for the demands placed on IT in this policy area. Next, we look at the changing contractual and e-government pictures for immigration control across our seven countries.

8.1 The Changing Context for Immigration Control

Traditionally, immigration bureaucracies have been another variant of Mintzberg's machine bureaucracy, characteristically taking the form of an old-fashioned, heavily staffed and hence quite large regulatory bureaucracy. The critical tool for their operation is authority—the legal and regulatory competence to refuse entry or exit to non-eligible persons—as determined by the legislature and executive. As Hood (1983: 54) describes it, authority is the 'ability to command and prohibit, commend and permit, through recognized procedures and identifying symbols'. In this sense immigration bureaucracies are at their root coercive, deploying a great deal of discretionary power against persons whose documentation does not meet requirements or whose purposes or behaviour arouse suspicion. At the same time, immigration bureaucracies in advanced industrial countries operate in a heavily legalized environment, where decisions have to be made accurately and often swiftly in order to forestall legal challenges and potentially expensive litigation.

The other defining feature of the immigration environment is that the problem or exception cases requiring time-consuming handling and investigation are typically a relatively small fraction of the overall flows of people in and out of the country, flows that are often critical for its economic well-being or overall position in the world. The flux of air travellers especially, but also sea passengers and cross-border flows between different countries on the same continent, has grown rapidly in the modern period to encompass hundreds of millions of cross-border journeys every year. This is the 'oceanic' context within which immigration bureaucracies must constantly search for anomalous or ineligible individual movements to inspect and intercept. This necessity introduces significant constraints in how these agencies behave, since they cannot afford to disrupt large flows of legitimate travellers too much, for instance, by creating large queues at airports or borders. Immigration checks therefore have to be quite slickly and scalably organized. They have to be operated quickly and the agencies involved have to develop a strong 'customer service' orientation for handling the millions of legitimate travellers they briefly interact with—an orientation that is otherwise not very evident in the remaining aspects of their work. Once ineligible or 'problem-case' people are identified, however, immigration bureaucracies often treat them in a strongly authority-based, even coercive way. And in aspects of their operations that do not involve their own citizens or overseas short-term travellers, these agencies may not show much of a 'customer care' stance. For instance, immigration forms and documents are usually long and complex and agencies require them to be filled in completely and exactly, with gaps or non-compliance in providing full information leading to rejection.

To get some idea of the loads on different immigration agencies, Figure 8.1a shows the average annual flows of foreign population and foreign workers into our seven case study countries. Monitoring and processing just these movements alone creates substantial workloads for the immigration bureaucracies in each of our case study countries, but, of course, disentangling these cases from short-term travellers and domestic citizens adds additional complications. In the years 1992–2001, some 21 million foreign people joined the United States' population. And the OECD in 2004 estimated that the stock of international migrants in the USA was nearly 35 million (almost three times larger than the country with the second largest stock of immigrants, the Russian federation). Canada, Australia, and the UK also had substantial numbers of international migrants in their population while both the Netherlands and New Zealand had substantial inflows in this period. Japan is widely seen as a relatively closed country, but Figure 8.1a shows that around 270,000 foreigners became resident in Japan and around 110,000 foreign workers entered the country each year in our period. The figure also highlights a second key feature of immigration control operations. In addition to regulating very large numbers of movements, these bureaucracies must also be able to handle marked fluctuations in the numbers of people seeking to immigrate. For instance, the number of foreign people accepted for entry in the USA varied between 2.1 and 4 million people a year in our period, and even in Japan they fluctuated between 210,000 and 351,000 people admitted in a year. This large range means that both agency administrations and their IT systems have to be easily scalable, coping with very different and often sharply changing volumes of work. Admissions of foreign workers also show strong variations year on year, reflecting employers' changing needs at different stages of the economic cycle. Again it is politically sensitive for immigration controls to become so protracted or onerous that businesses find themselves unable to quickly attract the right overseas staff or for controls to interfere with longer run customers for a nation's businesses or universities.

Figure 8.1b shows that admittances of asylum seekers were also substantial in most countries. The USA admitted between 42,000 and 154,000 asylum seekers a year in the period covered and the UK between 28,000 and 111,000 people a year. At the other end of the spectrum it is clear that Japan has admitted almost nobody as an asylum seeker, with the numbers involved varying from just 50 to 350 people a year. In relation to their populations, the Netherlands and Canada had the most generous policies on admitting asylum seekers. Again the variations in this load created substantial problems for some immigration bureaucracies, notably in the UK where the load of annual admittances doubled in the space of three years from 1997 to 2000, and the numbers of rejected asylum seekers also mushroomed.

(a) Annual inflows of foreign population and foreign workers

Country	Foreign population (000s)		Foreign workers (000s)	
	Mean annual inflows	Range from minimum to maximum flows	Mean annual inflows	Range from minimum to maximum flows
USA	2,307	1,859	442	576
Canada	282	72	77	28
Japan	269	141	105	63
UK	263	204	48	48
Australia	241	259	52	54
Netherlands	81	28	na	na
New Zealand	42	37	45	38

(b) Flows of asylum seekers

Country	Mean annual inflows	Range from minimum to maximum flows
USA	93	112
UK	66	83
Netherlands	36	34
Canada	28	21
Australia	9	8
New Zealand	1.2	2
Japan	0.2	0.3

Figure 8.1. The flows of people into our seven case study countries, 1992–2001

Source: OECD (2004).

Notes: In a few cases data is not available for the early part of the period and mean averages and ranges are computed from 5 to 9 years' data instead.

There are finally general trends for the loads on immigration authorities to grow in a secular way over time, with rising levels of air travel especially and a growth of asylum seekers worldwide in the late 1990s as a result of conflicts and displacements of people. Countries with large proportions of international migrants in their populations also tend to generate increased immigration over time, especially via flows of temporary workers or relatives looking for support from their families.

Immigration authorities (like their counterparts in customs functions) have generally tried to cope with these multiple demands by reducing the extent of physical and volumetric controls (such as 'inspect everyone' or 'inspect closely every tenth passport'). Instead, they have shifted over since the early 1990s towards relying more and more on risk-based intelligence and assessments so as to better target inspections and interventions on problem cases. They have also moved away from initially very paper-based and cumbersome methods of looking out for problem cases (such as voluminous paper 'watch lists') towards relying instead on electronic information systems with greater capacities, faster response times, and more automated forms of checking. Towards the end of our period these changes extended to the general use of machine-readable passports.

A critical factor greatly intensifying these changes was the 'war on terror' and renewed emphasis on 'homeland security' launched in the USA after the 9/11 massacres in New York and Washington. All nineteen terrorists involved escaped detection as suspicious by immigration authorities on their initial entry. Indeed, one of the bombers was even issued with a visa extension by US authorities some months after his death in the suicide attack. From 9/11 onwards, and following subsequent bombings in various countries across the world, including Bali, Madrid, and London, there was a strong focus on enhancing security in international travel. Systems of border control were placed centre stage, with much debate over the most effective kind of identity documents. New schemes for tracking foreign nationals, identifying travellers and enforcing border control abounded in all our case study countries. Longer-run developments towards forcing airlines to notify all passenger names and ID numbers in advance of people boarding flights were greatly accelerated and intensified. In America, the immigration control function was incorporated in the vast new Department of Homeland Security, set up in response to the debacle. And the USA pioneered a big push to introduce biometric identification, linking individuals to their documentation not just via a photograph, signature, and hard-to-forge document, but for the first time also via their fingerprints, or iris scan, or face shape or other unique biological identifier. Our period ends with these changes still undergoing implementation, but with some countries (notably the UK) apparently anticipating a revolution in the state's control and surveillance capabilities.

8.2 IT Contracting and e-Government in the Immigration Sector

Shortly after the World Trade Center came crashing down, a contingent of tech industry heavyweights...flew to Washington to meet with administration officials. And during the following twelve months, a hundred or so tech leaders held a flurry of follow up meetings with the Defense Dept. The subject at hand: how best to marshal the strongest ideas from Silicon Valley in the new war against terrorism ... tech heads salivated over the prospects of an unexpected and promising new multibillion-dollar market. (*Business Week* 16 September 2002)

Massive expenditure rises on homeland security (particularly in the USA where total expenditure was estimated at between $98 billion and $138 billion for 2003) brought increases in government IT expenditure as a whole, and border control in particular. Big players like IBM and Hewlett-Packard recorded major growth in federal government markets. The USA also imposed a demanding deadline for introducing electronic passports on all those overseas countries with which it ran visa-waiver schemes, prompting a rush to comply by their governments. This in turn brought a host of new players into the government IT market, including microelectronics companies producing smart card chips capable of storing biometric data, and biometric consultancies and firms that specialized in screening large number of people and verifying identities. By 2004, the global market for biometric products was around US$1 billion but was expected to grow to more than US$4.5 billion (*Guardian* 18 June 2004).

But despite appearances, none of these contracting or ICTs changes came out of the blue. The 9/11 effect primarily accelerated developments that might have happened on a slower timescale anyway. And they rested on a developing background of government–IT industry relations that had been changing immigration rapidly from its previous low-tech configuration that endured long into the Internet era. We look at this transition in each of our case study countries in turn.

In the United States, the agency with responsibility for immigration control at federal level was traditionally the US Immigration and Naturalization Service (INS), part of the Department of Justice. The INS incorporated US border control, with over 8,300 agents by 1999. Tracking all those who enter and exit the USA is a massive task. There were some 440 million entries in 2002, with 61 million citizens and 279 million non-citizens involved in the movements (Koslowski 2004: 16). The relative sizes of these numbers speaks volumes regarding the relative insularity still of Americans, only one in six of whom has a passport, compared with the UK's figure of 83 per cent. They also of course reflect the centrality of the USA in the business, government, and academic worlds and the flow of business travellers, immigrant workers, and tourists to the key metropolitan centres of world commerce. The US border control system has to cover nearly 7,000 miles of borders along Mexico and Canada, including more than 300 land, air, and sea ports. Spending on border control rose rapidly even before 9/11, from US$261 million in 1990 to around US$1 billion for

2000. Tracking immigrants within national boundaries is also a challenge. In 2000, the INS estimated that there were around 5 million illegal immigrants inside American borders, 700,000 in Texas alone (*Ottawa Citizen* 13 February 2000).

INS had long operated a range of computerized immigration control systems, some of which had a reasonable record on joining up across agencies. An early example was IBIS, a shared IT system to assist law enforcement officials at US borders developed by the INS, US Customs, and the State and Agriculture Departments. It pooled information with systems within each of the departments, for example, passport information on incoming airline passengers gathered abroad via the Advance Passenger Information Service (APIS). In 1995, the INS created INSPASS, an automatic teller machine for frequent international travellers. Users had to insert an ID card, put their hands in a slot and if recognized by the system they would be cleared in thirty seconds. Each inspection machine cost $35,000, but replaced over four inspectors. As early as 1995, 500,000 American travellers were cleared in this way on entering the USA from abroad (*Washington Post* 9 October 1995). By the early 2000s, APIS was used to offer 'blue lane' expedited services to those US-bound passengers who gave passport information to laptop-equipped airplane personnel for transmission via the Internet to INS inspectors at the port of arrival (Koslowski 2002: 20). Later, the programme was extended beyond US borders to include travel to the Netherlands, allowing passengers to use their credentials both at airports in New York and Amsterdam. These systems meant that American border controls were far more automated compared to those in other countries, especially the UK during the same period (see below).

However, some aspects of the immigration system were heavily criticized. The Non-Immigrant Information System (NIIS) updated entry and exit record databases to identify visa overstayers. Congress mandated this change in 1996 legislation (Koslowski 2002: 15) but later pushed back the deadline for implementation of the law after strong lobbying by US business groups from states bordering Canada. They argued that even the most sophisticated smart card technology would back up traffic at the border for hours. In 2000, full deployment of NIIS was put on indefinite hold. The existing visa-tracking system for plane passengers consisted of a paper form stamped at the port of entry that was supposed to be returned to the airline on departure and entered manually into a database. But due to lost forms, incomplete data, and people entering or exiting by land borders, the system was basically ineffective. It was much criticized after 9/11, when there was no effective way of knowing if those involved in the attack had overstayed their visas.

Another much-criticized system developed by the INS was the single-fingerprint biometric identification system (IDENT), a database containing records of undocumented aliens, including a photo and digitized fingerprint. The system cost around US$85 million. IDENT was intended to enable border control authorities to check any previous encounters with the INS or criminal records of those crossing borders. However, in spite of years of effort and congressional concern, the system was never integrated with the FBI's Integrated Automated Fingerprint Identification System, even though the INS and the FBI were both agencies of the Department of Justice, and so might have been expected to coordinate their systems. INDENT collected two index fingerprints from travellers, while the FBI has long used 10-fingerprint systems, as recommended by the National Institute of Standards and Technology. In addition, federal, state, and local law enforcement agencies still do not have access to IDENT, and the FBI and DHS fingerprint systems are still not fully interoperable.

During the late 1990s, the INS accelerated its purchase of IT (Koslowski 2004: 16), awarding three contracts totalling US$750 million over a five-year period in 1998 alone. Indeed, border control has long been big business in the USA, with increasingly high-tech gadgetry being employed. Between 1994 and 1999, the US Border Patrol increased its equipment spending from US$2 million to US$90 million. There are now more than 10,000 motion sensors buried beneath crossing points and trails: when they are crossed, vibrations from footsteps trigger an alarm to nearby Border Patrol stations. Night vision scopes are used to detect heat and spot objects as small as a mouse from an elevated position. Agents also used night vision goggles (priced at over US$2,000 each).

After 9/11, the whole security field changed in the USA as those agencies dealing with any aspect of security, including immigration control, were reassembled into a giant conglomerate Department of Homeland Security (DHS). In March 2003, the INS moved to the new department under the title of US Citizenship and Immigration Services (USCIS), the priorities being to promote national security, work to eliminate immigration case backlogs, and improve customer services. By this time USCIS comprised 15,000 federal employees and contractors working in around 250 headquarters and field offices around the world. The centrality of immigration controls increased after it transpired that although the nineteen highjackers had entered legally on business, student and tourist visas, one with a student visa had never attended college and three had stayed in the USA after their visas expired (Koslowski 2002).

Expenditure on homeland security shot up and the IT industry clustered around, particularly after the Bush administration's US$38 billion request for anti-terrorism funding received congressional approval. Washington agencies were 'saddled with the huge chore of evaluating proposals', with the Technical Support Working Group receiving 12,500 proposals alone (*Business Week* 16 September 2002). A significant proportion of the effort and expenditure was again geared at systems for border control. The president's 2003 budget included $380 million to finish building by 2005 a new system to track immigrants both on entry and exit, to identify those that had overstayed visas and those that should be denied entry. The Attorney General announced that by 1 October all US ports would be able to take fingerprints of 'high-risk' visitors from countries such as Iran and run them against a database of known criminals and terrorists. The system was later re-launched as the US Visitor and Immigrant Status Indicator Technology (US-VISIT). In its first phase of implementation, US-VISIT collected digital photograph and fingerprint scan biometrics from those individuals travelling on a visa to the USA and then ran watch-list checks on the data collected (Koslowski 2004: 18). The system basically consists of legacy INS systems and various applications. It is not without critics. It was accused by the *Washington Post* (23 May 2005) of being 'poorly coordinated and ineffective', including a fingerprint system based on the original IDENT system that did not use the federal government's biometric standard. Meanwhile, major work remained in the huge task of overhauling all the computer systems that fell within the new Homeland Security Department, involving 'crafting a plan to link thousands of disparate government computer systems and finding ways to tie the feds with state and local governments and the private sector' (*Business Week* 16 September 2002).

For the huge US-VISIT system, the prime contractor appointed in May 2004 was Accenture, beating Lockheed Martin and CSC to win a ten-year deal estimated at up to US$10 billion. The company and its subcontractors (dubbing themselves the Smart Border Alliance) promised to create a 'virtual border' that would electronically screen millions of foreign travellers. The contract was described as an 'indefinite delivery-indefinite quantity contract' and Accenture and Homeland Security were criticized for Accenture's role in the tendering process itself. The company advised the leader of the US-VISIT programme to 'limit the number of bidders, and streamline the procurement approach' (*Washington Post* 23 May 2005), they moved into Homeland Security premises the year before the contract award and hired the procurement expert Stephen Kelman (who advised the Clinton administration) as a consultant. From 2001, when it separated from Andersen Consulting, Accenture was 'refashioning itself into a homeland security specialist' (*Washington Post* 23 May 2005), and the manager of the US-VISIT contact cited the company's experience in building similar border management systems in Ireland, New Zealand, and Canada (*Financial Times* 3 June 2004).

Meanwhile, EDS was long a big player in the field of homeland security, supporting many of the departments and agencies now forming part of DHS. The company was awarded six task orders under the Starlight programme in a team with Sytel, during the 2000s. These included three task orders totalling more than US$51 million for IBIS in August 2003 and for Immigration and Customs enforcement in November 2003. In April 2004, the Sytel/EDS team was awarded the Student and Exchange Visitor Information System (SEVIS), also under Starlight, an Internet-based system to monitor foreign students. When EDS won a contract for new systems for immigration and customs enforcement in November 2004, news wires suggested that the services the company was delivering to DHS 'touch most of the agency's core operations' (*Canada Newswire* 18 November 2004). Another major player was Lockheed Martin, winning a US$350 million award to integrate all security measures at the 429 largest US airports.

One policy move from the USA in the area of border control impacted upon the IT strategies in this field of all our other case study countries. From October 2004, the US government required countries whose citizens could enter the USA without a visa to have an electronic passport programme in place, with tamper-resistant and machine-readable passports carrying biometric data. Contactless chips were chosen by the International Civil Aviation Organisation (ICAO, a UN affiliated agency that sets travel documents standards for 188 member nations) as the best way to store biometric data for verifying the identity of travellers. This deadline caused a global rush to produce new combinations of passports, national ID cards, driving licences, chips and biometrics in a 'shotgun' wedding of passports and smart cards (*Card Technology* October 2004: 50): 'Passport agency officials have been criss-crossing the globe attending standard-setting meetings and vendor operability tests, all aimed at creating a system that would allow, for instance, a chip-based passport issued by Pakistan to be read by border guards in Brazil'. The American deadline was extended to 2005 as it became clear that many of the twenty-seven

Visa Waiver nations (which include all our other case study countries) would not meet the deadline. Indeed, the USA itself only awarded the contract for chip-based biometric passports complying with the ICAO standards in September 2004. The privacy lobby objected vainly. The UK-based organization Privacy International claimed that 1 billion travellers would have their biometric data captured and stored by 2015. They also argued that national governments were 'policy laundering' by using the standards set by the ICAO at the behest of the USA as a justification for introducing biometric-based passports of their own without a thorough debate at national level (Davis 2004: 50).

To some extent the US position here is highly contradictory. If EU member states do not issue passports compliant with the ICAO standard by the new deadline and the USA drops a current EU member state from the visa-waiver programme, the member state could retaliate by requiring visas of US nationals to meet the provisions of the EU's common visa policy, ending visa-free travel between the US and the EU (Koslowski 2004: 21). But as the same author points out, if several EU member states sending large numbers of visitors to the USA were to drop out of the waiver programme, the State Department would actually be unable to process these additional applications for visas, one of the key reasons that the October 2004 deadline was pushed back. Intermediate measures were put in place, with border control procedures for waiver country travellers entering the USA, including fingerprinting and photographs. Meanwhile, in 2005 the deadline was pushed back again to 2006, a date that the USA itself seems likely to be pushed to meet, given that by the beginning of 2006 it had issued only a pilot group of diplomatic e-passports, planning to start rolling them out for citizens later in the year.

Across the enormously long northern land border of the USA, in Canada, the responsible department is Citizenship and Immigration Canada (CIC). Its tasks include managing the flow of people into Canada, including visas, refugees, immigration control, and implementing the Canadian Citizenship Act. The department existed in an earlier form in the 1980s, but the Citizenship role was then moved to the Culture department and Immigration to the employment service. In 1993, the two functions were reunited and the modern department was reborn. It employs 6,020 staff, including 560 immigration officers, and detains about 9,000 people a year. The department receives around 4 million phone calls and 1.5 million applications per year for citizenship and immigration services from over 3 million clients worldwide. The Foreign Ministry has responsibility for passports and some other initiatives relating to immigration and border control. Canada's immigration issues are to some extent linked to those of the USA. Some commentators have suggested that it will be impossible to process incoming visitors and shipments without backing up traffic leading to gridlock on the Canadian side—unless more bridges are built between Canada and the USA, or large areas around either end of the bridges are cleared for secure areas (Koslowski 2004: 19).

In the mid-1990s, the new department developed the idea of continuously dealing with files for potential immigrants. But they had inherited around eighteen different legacy IT systems that did not communicate with each other, and some of which 'were built by people who were by now dead or retired'. Ineffective coordination between them led to 'inefficiency, mistakes and people with criminal records getting into Canada', as one official put it. So, the idea of an integrated system was mooted. The new system was delayed by the work necessary to rectify Y2K problems and the department's technological backwardness: it was not even Windows-based until 2001. But in that year work started on a new web-based system, called the Global Case Management System (GCMS). It was to consolidate all previous legacy systems and to link via interfaces to the police and intelligence agencies, to Highway Patrol, Customs, and the nine Canadian Provinces. It was originally considered that there were no commercial products available and that the system would be developed in-house. But after a year and a revisiting of available possibilities it was put out to tender. The US company SIEBEL won the contract, because of its experience in case management and of working for the US federal government, with Accenture, IBM, and Microsoft as subcontractors, in a contract worth $200 million over five years. The first release of the citizen aspects of the system was in 2004. The department continues to review and maintain business requirements, and the Information Management Technology branch of the department takes up about 15 per cent of the department's resources, a substantial amount.

In 2002, the Canadian government introduced a Canadian Permanent Resident Card for non-citizens, also called a 'Maple Leaf' card, which became the required proof of status document for every permanent resident returning to Canada on a commercial carrier, replacing an earlier paper form that was easily and frequently duplicated. The plastic card is magnetic but not 'smart' and has an optical stripe with all the confidential data from the cardholder's Confirmation of Permanent Resident form. It is encrypted so as to be accessible only to authorized officials and includes a laser-engraved photo and signature and 'tombstone data'. Since October 2001, the card evoked controversy (shown by the 212 press articles that have appeared on the subject), as earlier plans to introduce the card were fast-tracked as a C$17 million part of the government's C$250 million security response to the 9/11 terrorist attacks. Some critics claimed that there was no real connection between the new immigration measures and stamping out terrorism, arguing that improving the police force and going after terrorist organizations made more sense than 'harassing refugee claimants' (*Vancouver Sun* 13 October 2001). Immigration officials were accused of fast-tracking the card after intense pressure from the USA post-9/11 to clamp down on illegal immigrants, thereby damaging 'the integrity of the immigration programme' (*Canadian Press Newswire* 20 July 2003). The project also ran into severe delays. A leaked document revealed that the department planned to phase the assessment of the 1 million card applications expected from existing permanent residents over five years, after previously saying a year earlier that the replacement of the fraud-prone paper document was 'urgent' (*Toronto Star* 8 May 2002).

The following summer there were reports of long lines of people trying to get their cards and local CIC offices extending their working hours (*Winnipeg Sun* 1 December 2003). Six months later there were various reports of the card itself being forged (*Edmonton Journal* 22 July 2003), and in November, controversy centred on the quality of the photographs taken of immigrants, when it transpired that 90 per cent had to be retaken on arrival (*Toronto Sun* 27 November 2003). In December, there was chaos as residents faced being unable to return to the country after winter holidays (the deadline was 31 December) and it transpired that it was taking twelve weeks for an application for the card to be processed (*Ottawa Citizen* 9 December 2003; *Calgary Sun* 2 January 2004). Almost half of Canada's 1.5 million landed immigrants did not have the card by the deadline of 31 December 2003. By January 2004, the *Times Colonist* was writing of 'a fog of bureaucracy: misinformation, mishandlings and misunderstandings', as the scale of public confusion about the scheme became clear, in spite of an expensive information campaign.

The contract for the resident cards was awarded to the local firm Canadian Bank Note Co. Ltd, who in turn subcontracted to a subsidiary of Drexler Technology Corporation. The contract guaranteed the purchase of 3.1 million cards by 2007 at a price of US$4.50 per card. In May 2004, the company Drexler Technology Corporation received an order for C$1.8 million worth of production cards, the fifth card-production order received under a five-year subcontract awarded in 2002, making its total of orders worth C$9.4 million. The company also supplies cards to the US Department of State, Homeland Security, and the Department of Defense.

In 2003, the government started investigating the possibility of adding fingerprints to the Maple Leaf card. The Minister for Immigration and Citizenship has put forward a public interest argument for extending the Maple Leaf card as a voluntary national ID card, which might be used for travelling to the USA (*Montreal Gazette* 7 February 2003). But he faced accusations that he was again bowing to US pressure, this time to introduce biometric identifiers harmonized with those in the USA, along with claims that the national ID scheme could cost almost C$7 billion (*Canadian Press Newswire* 7 October 2003) amongst widespread scepticism.

To some extent the long development period for GCMS and the concurrent work on the Secure Channel has held up initiatives. By 2003, the departmental website explained what was needed to apply for immigration status and how to download forms, but not how to save the forms or to send back them online. In any case, once forms were submitted, all the data given had to be re-keyed into departmental systems. Eventually, it will be possible to apply for visas for Canada online. But meanwhile some online initiatives have been successful. One allowed CIC's clients to notify the department of a change of address. Another initiative launched in May 2002 was the Client Application Status (e-CAS) service. It provided information for foreign students seeking student visas, foreign nationals applying for permanent residence as a member of the family or spouse of an existing citizen, or those seeking status as an independent immigrant. It also allowed applicants to monitor the status of their applications. It uses 'shared secrets' and a client identity number to quickly access the system, which then tells you whether or not the application is received, what stage of the process it has reached, the decision made, and whether an interview has been scheduled. Even after three weeks of operation, the system had delivered application status information to more than 43,000 clients. The system has the same level of security as Canadian banks.

After the US-VISIT programme was established, it was announced that for the time being Canadian nationals would be exempt from mandatory enrolment in the programme. The Canadian government introduced a pilot of Canpass, a similar project to the US Inspass in 1993. After the 9/11 attacks, Canada and the USA entered into various cross-border agreements, which some claimed gave the police and immigration agencies wide leeway on information sharing (*Inter Press Service* 14 July 2004). There were complaints that officials north of the border were 'being kept out of the loop 90 per cent of the time' and calls for 'an audit' of the impact that the US Department of Homeland Security was having on Canadian immigration policy. The leader of a civil liberties group claimed that the Canadian government would be 'forced' to adopt a version of US-VISIT being developed by Accenture, a controversial name in Ontario where the company's inflexible social welfare system was reported to have cost the administration C$7.6 million to fix.

The only other country in our sample to have to cope with an extensive land border as well as air and sea arrivals is the Netherlands. Here the INS within the Ministry of Justice is responsible for immigration control, while the Ministry of Foreign Affairs implements the visa policy. Each year the INS processes over 38,000 cases for naturalization and 20,000 cases for asylum, as well as over 61,000 regular cases. In the Netherlands, citizens have long carried a national ID card. In 2001, the government introduced the 'New Generation Travel Documents'—an initiative to make all Dutch travel documents highly secure against possible misuse—making use of the most advanced technologies available at the time.

As in our other countries, the INS has a long history of using IT. Even by 1998, the Dutch government was making various orders for projects involving chip technology and biometrics, including one from the Justice Ministry to supply asylum seekers with identification cards and another from the Defence Ministry to supply Dutch Army personnel with chip passports (*Extel Examiner* 29 May 1998). The Defence Ministry in particular was advanced in thinking about these kinds of technologies. As in other aspects, the Netherlands was aided by the innovativeness of its private sector in technological development. At this time the country possessed one of the most advanced markets for chip technology, with 12 million chip-based bank cards in circulation by 1998, 500,000 cards in the health sector and 200,000 issued by the Justice Ministry.

From July 2001, the Netherlands became the first in the world to introduce a border control smart card programme, with an iris reader. It also joined the raft of countries which tried to speed up border checks for frequent travellers. A project using smart cards called Privum enables travellers who have undergone voluntary background checks to use special security lanes at Schiphol Airport, similar to the US frequent flyer programmes outlined previously. Participants pay 99 euros per year to participate; there were about 15,000 members by 2005. The systems integration for the project was carried out by CMGLogica, whose business development director viewed the widespread introduction of electronic passport schemes triggered by the US deadline with enthusiasm: 'In the future, there will be many passports around the world that include biometrics. There will be a very big market then' (*Card Technology* 1 April, 2005).

The Netherlands benefits from one of the most successful systems of immigration control developed at the EU level—the Common European Asylum System. This system is facilitated through EURODAC, an EU-wide database that stores and compares the fingerprints of asylum seekers and illegal entrants. It has been operational since January 2003, and it is operated by the European Commission on behalf of the member states at a total budget of €13.6 million annually. In July 2005, a second evaluation report of the system concluded that it was 'efficient and cost-effective' and had 'confirmed its role as a key asylum management tool for the EU'. In 2004, the database successfully processed 232,200 fingerprints of asylum seekers, more than 16,000 fingerprints of people crossing the borders irregularly and 39,550 fingerprints of people apprehended while illegally on the territory of a member state (*European Biometrics Portal New Section 29 June 2005*). The system comprises a central unit hosted within the European Commission and equipped with a computerized fingerprint database. It has an electronic data transmission application allowing member states to exchange information about asylum seekers and illegal entrants. The database is only for the purposes of evaluating and analysing asylum: it cannot be used by police or law enforcement authorities in criminal investigations. Impressively, the unit was available 99.9 per cent of the time during 2004, operating twenty-four hours a day, seven days a week. And no data protection problems have been raised by the national data protection authorities. In 2004, it identified that 13 per cent of visa applications were duplicates, clearly demonstrating the need for the system.

The Netherlands was the only one of our case study countries to join the Schengen agreement, under which participating EU countries (France, Germany, Belgium, Luxembourg, the Netherlands, Spain, Portugal, and Austria) agreed to lift their national border controls from March 1995, and thereby take part in the information systems operated as part of the agreement. The Schengen information system allows police within the countries involved to swap data. In 2005, trials began for the Visa Information System (VIS) net to be deployed throughout the Schengen area, to enable the exchange of visa data in relation to Schengen uniform visas and national visas among the Schengen states. Like EURODAC, the VIS is composed of a European central database of information about the personal identification of visa applicants, the status of visas, the authority that issued the visa and records of persons' liability to pay board and lodging costs, all connected to national systems. Biometric data will be added to the VIS in a later phase. In combination, these initiatives brought 'European defense contractors scurrying to reorganize to meet new homeland security requirements (*Aviation Week and Space Technology* 24 November 2003).

In August 2004, the Dutch Ministry of the Interior began a six-month test of the ICAO standard chip-based passports, with a goal of recruiting at least 15,000 volunteers to apply for a chip-based biometric passport or national ID card at the same time as they renew their current 'chip-less' documents. A €10 discount on the passport was offered as an incentive to attract volunteers. The scheme involves a digital photo and two finger-prints of each volunteer. Contracts went to the company SDU Identifica-tion, which provided both passports and ID cards. The company then produces a passport and ID card, as it would if chip-based documents were the norm. However, a report published in September 2005 found that the quality of fingerprint information used in the tests was sometimes poor and that the biometric documents were less robust than traditional passports. The quality of digital photographs was also a problem, with 1.6 per cent of photographs being unsuitable for automated biometric match-ing. This may sound very small, but any 'exceptions handling' of just a few per cent can have serious consequences in highly geared and automated immigration control systems. The programme was put on hold while the Dutch government proposed to investigate the situation in other EU countries currently developing biometric passport programmes (*eGovern-ment Observatory News* 20 September 2005).

The UK is the only other EU country, and has been affected by some of the same influences as the Netherlands. However, the UK's island situation (shared of course, by Australia, New Zealand, and Japan) creates some additional advantages compared with any of the land-border countries. In our period UK immigration control was administered by the Immigra-tion and Nationality Directorate (IND), an agency within the Home Office. Two other bodies also played a role, however, the Passport Agency (also within the Home Office) and the Foreign and Commonwealth Office (FCO). The IND also worked closely with HM Customs and Revenue Agency (formerly a separate agency, HM Customs and Excise but merged with the Inland Revenue in 2005) in the administration of controls in airports and ports. The IND's role was to consider all applications from people wanting to come to the UK for whatever reason, from a short holiday to permanent residence. It also determined applications from asylum seekers, granted refugee status to successful applicants, and removed those people whose claims failed. In 2004, UK Immigration Officers facilitated the arrival of nearly 90 million passengers in the UK, more than 12 million of whom were subject to immigration control.

In 2004–5 the IND had an overall budget of £1.7 billion and around 15,000 staff.

In sharp contrast to the USA, the process of immigration in Britain up to 1995 was almost entirely manual (Margetts 1999: 10). Each immigration officer had a paper index of suspect persons against which to check the name of every non-EU passenger arriving at the control desk. The index was in book form, containing some 10,000 entries, and each officer's book had to be updated manually every day at a cost of over £1 million per year in staff time. The number of entries had to be limited to make the index possible to handle, meaning that those included represented less than 2 per cent of available information. The Immigration Service at the time admitted that speedier control checks and an end to manual updating of the index would release over fifty years of staff time each year at the major ports, while thousands more passengers might have been scrutinized more closely. After 'several years' of trying to computerize the process (NAO 1995a: 27) a system was finally implemented towards the end of 1995, many years after a similar system had been developed in the USA.

Once the IND's new systems were put in place, however, they were plagued with problems, particular problematic contract relationships and most specifically with the company, Siemens Business Services, a company that 'hardly existed in terms of central government contracts until the mid-1990s'. In 1997, the Directorate awarded the company a £77 million project to install a new computer system to process asylum applications. The system was delivered eighteen months late in 1999, but was unable to cope with the workload. A backlog of 200,000 cases built up and 600 immigration officers had to be hired to cope with the chaos. The project was attacked (by the National Audit Office) for being 'too ambitious', and it contributed to the 'shambolic' state of the department (*Independent* 30 June 1999). Press commentators also argued that in combination with changes of rules denying welfare benefits to asylum seekers, the IT system produced 'social diaster... Tens of thousands of asylum-seekers were stranded on miserly food vouchers for years, as they waited to know if they could stay and earn a living' (*New Statesman* 9 July 2001). Eventually, the system was scrapped in 2001. In 2004, the IND's contract with Siemens Business Services expired and the company finally lost the IND contract after tendering unsuccessfully against Fujitsu and Atos Origin (formerly Schlumberger Sema), the latter being successful. Atos took over responsibility for service provision at the beginning of November 2004, when the previous contract expired, in a six-year contract worth around £200 million, supporting around 8,000 users across the IND.

Later the Passport Agency entered into a £120 million, ten-year contract with the same company, Siemens Business Systems, in the government's first PFI contract, to improve security checks on passport applications and reduce the number of staff employed at agency officies. This contract also ran into serious problems. By June 1999, there were reports that there was a bottleneck of 565,000 applications, and huge queues outside passport offices. Applications that before outsourcing had been processed at an average eleven days were now taking thirty-five to thirty-nine days and the agency had to take on 400 extra staff to cope with new work patterns (*Independent* 30 June 1999). Although the Passport Agency eventually pulled out of this crisis, it did so at a price: by raising the costs of passports very substantially and making major new investments.

In 2003, the Home Office announced plans to strengthen its border control using new technologies. Pilot tests began under which the passports of airline passengers travelling to the UK were screened on departure with new scanners to identify passengers posing a security risk by checking them against international enforcement databases. Another pilot project was to use biometric data to control immigration and asylum, through which people applying for a UK visa in Sri Lanka would be required to provide a record of their fingerprint. In 2004, the Home Office signed a five-year contract with Sagem SA to provide IRIS (an iris recognition immigration system), to be rolled out across a number of key UK airports, starting with Heathrow. Enrolment for the scheme would be voluntary, with enrolled passengers entering the UK through a special immigration control incorporating an iris recognition camera.

Throughout the years following the 9/11 massacres, discussion of computerization with respect to immigration in the UK focused on controversial government plans for a national identity card. It was intended to play a key role in immigration control, although it was never very clear exactly how it would do so. The eventual proposals included a 'smart' ID card containing two biometric identifiers (most likely to be iris recognition and fingerprints) and a national register of UK citizens. The card would be voluntary in the first instance (at least for people not travelling abroad and hence not needing passports), taking the form of a biometric passport that would be upgraded when it came up for renewal, plus a supplementary card issued at extra cost. A card on its own would be available for those people with no passport. It reflected perhaps the sorry state of the UK government's information systems that no existing system was considered viable as a basis for the national identity register, which was to be a brand new system created from scratch by interviewing in person every passport and ID card applicant and recording their biometrics. The scheme aroused controversy over the threat to civil liberties and the cost of the scheme, estimated at around £6 billion in government reports but at £11 billion by an influential report produced by the London School of Economics, that also noted that 'worst-case' costs could rise as far as £18 billion. In spite of very acute controversy in Parliament, including conflicts between the House of Lords and the lower chamber, the Bill was finally passed into law in April 2006. However, the government was forced to make two substantial concessions to stave off criticisms: that the ID card scheme could not be made compulsory without introducing a specific new law to do so (not expected before around 2013); and that Parliament would get detailed briefings on its costs every six months of the scheme's projected ten-year life (from 2009 to 2018).

In February 2005, the Home Office also presented the government's five-year strategy for asylum and immigration, called *Controlling our borders: making migration work for Britain*. Its implementation would rely heavily on new technologies. In addition to the role of the national ID card, the proposed programme included fast-track processing of all unfounded asylum seekers (using electronic tagging where necessary) and strong border controls. A new e-Borders programme was a key element, including fingerprinting all visa applicants and electronic checks on all those entering and leaving the country. The e-Borders programme was to be rolled out as project Semaphore, allowing the UK authorities to identify and address risks for e-Borders on ten 'high risk routes covering 6 million people'. In theory, the e-Borders scheme meant that the authorities would be able to refuse passage on aircraft coming to the UK of people whose status they did not accept, thereby removing the need to deport them and forestalling any claims through UK courts, since the people in question would never make it into the country. A critical factor here is that information from remote airports is processed in real time very speedily, in order to remove unaccepted passengers from planes before they take off. Project IRIS (Iris Recognition Immigration System) was to be introduced to provide fast and secure automated clearance for certain categories of regular travellers through UK immigration control. And an I-visa scheme designed to keep track electronically of all foreigners within the UK completed the UK's commitment to new, high-tech IT-based schemes.

In Australia (as in the USA and Canada), the immigration control function was historically a key part of nation-building. It now forms part of the portfolio for the Department of Immigration and Multicultural and Indigenous Affairs (DIMIA). (Originally a separate Department of Immigration and Naturalization, the department's new name reflects a merger with the Department of Aboriginal Affairs in 1990.) The organization's mission statement is: 'Australia, enriched through the entry and settlement of people; valuing its heritage, citizenship and cultural diversity; and recognising the special place of Indigenous people as its original inhabitants'. DIMIA has responsibility for the delivery of the annual Migration and Humanitarian Programs; programmes to combat and deter people smuggling activities; proactive negotiation with overseas governments, international organizations and other agencies to stem unauthorized entry to Australia; detention demands; implementation of Integrated Humanitarian Settlement Strategy arrangements to support humanitarian entrants to Australia; programmes to equip migrants and refugees to participate equitably in Australian society; and the coordination of government policies, programmes, and decision-making processes in relation to reconciliation and indigenous affairs. The department had an annual operating budget in 2005 of around AU\$700 million. The character of the immigration issue has significantly changed for Australia in recent times, with 'plane-people' outstripping 'boat-people' by seven to one at 14,000. The number of illegal immigrants in Australia who had overstayed visas after arriving legally was estimated at over 53,100 in 1999 (*The Australian* 25 November 1999).

Unlike our other case study agencies in Australia, DIMIA was unable to escape the clustering initiative for the outsourcing of IT. In fact it was included in the first cluster (known as Cluster 3) offered for tender in 1997, together with four smaller agencies. The contract, for five years and worth \$250 million (*Canberra Times* 28 July 1997) was won by the American company, CSC, with EDS and Fujitsu as failed bidders. CSC provided more than 10,000 desktops for the Department of Immigration. After initial claims that CSC was costing the department more rather than less (*The Australian* 17 August 1999), in December 2001 the Australian Auditor-General found that alone among three clusters examined in an audit office report, Cluster 3 had reduced its IT costs by more than 25 per cent (*The Australian* 7 September 2000). However, CSC also incurred penalties of AU\$2.4 million for not meeting its contract requirements to Cluster 3 in the two years after it took over service supply, and scientists across the country had protested against efforts to outsource their IT infrastructure (*The Australian* 5 September 2000). In September 2001, Optus won a AU\$65 million contract to provide a fully managed voice-and-data solution to Cluster 3. EDS is the major provider to Customs, which works with DIMIA in ports.

As in the other countries, a raft of smaller companies entered the immigration market later in our period. In 2005, the Australian system integrator Ethan Group and the Washington-based company Daon were chosen to support DIMIA in operational biometric trials, a strategy set up to investigate how biometric technology might enhance the integrity of the immigration system. Daon is a provider of identity assurance software products, particularly authentication through the linking of identity documents with unique physical characteristics using facial recognition, fingerprint, and iris scanning. In addition, some larger companies (like Siebel) started using their success in this field to penetrate new markets (*Canberra Times* 28 May 2004).

In 2003–4, the federal government allocated AU$9.7 million for biometric applications research and development across the Departments of Foreign Affairs and Trade, the Australian Customs Service, and DIMIA. In 2004, the Immigration Minister launched the Biometric Testing Facility, saying it had great potential to enhance Australia's border security effort, but there was no clear timeframe for introducing the new technologies (*Australian Associated Press* 21 July 2004). The laboratory is based in the offices of the department's IT support provider, CSC, and initially DIMIA's 28-strong biometric team used other departmental staff as guinea pigs. There were various reports that the lab heralded the development of an 'Identity Services Repository database' to store biometric identifiers from visa applicants and immigration detainees. Customs received AU$3.1 million for a trial of an automated border control system called Smart Gate, which took a photograph of an individual, encoded it in a template and cross-checked it against passport details. The Department of Foreign Affairs and Trade, meanwhile, is investigating a biometric passports project. The three projects were 'likely to be wrapped together to develop a seamless border control system' (*The Australian* 29 June 2004).

Overall, however, by 2005 Australia seemed to be lagging behind other countries in any kind of strategy for using these technologies and the visa application process was largely paper-based. Photos filed with overseas embassies were not immediately available in Australia, and there were no plans to fingerprint all visitors, unlike the USA. In July DIMIA ran into major and much publicized problems, as a report produced by a former federal policy commissioner (the Palmer Report) identified a number of systemic failures in the department which had led to several serious miscarriages of justice. This led to a public apology from the Prime Minister, John Howard, and a complete changeover of the department's top leadership. As well as serious organizational problems (such as a 'rotten culture'), the report identified an 'urgent need' to establish a system to record and check the fingerprints and biometric data of immigration detainees (*Canberra Times* 15 July 2005). It also found flaws in the four-year contract with Global Systems Limited to run the detention systems (*Courier Mail* 15 July 2005). As in our other countries, the post-9/11 era brought discussion of identity cards, something that the prime minister refused to rule out in the Summer of 2005 (*Australian Associated Press* 15 July 2005).

In New Zealand, the immigration function has also been historically important for nation-building, and continued to be so—for example, with a wave of entrants admitted from Hong Kong when it reverted to Chinese control in 1997. The responsible agency is Immigration New Zealand, answering to the Department of Labour. The agency assesses applications from people who wish to visit, work, study, or live permanently in the country, monitors travellers arriving in New Zealand without the required documents, takes action against breaches of immigration law, and ensures that people without permission to remain in New Zealand leave when they are supposed to. The agency also manages the New Zealand refugee programme and decides whether people can be recognized as refugees under the UN Convention on the Status of Refugees. The Department of Internal Affairs, particularly the New Zealand Passports Office, also plays a role, proclaiming proudly on its website that New Zealand 'prides itself on having one of the best passports in the world'.

A key system relating to immigration control was developed by the Australian company CPS Systems. By the beginning of 2004 more than half of all airline passengers entering New Zealand were being screened using the new Advanced Passenger Processing system, which went live in August 2003. The system lets airlines' overseas check-in staff electronically send passengers' passport information and travel itineraries to immigration officers in New Zealand, who can then electronically advise airline staff if they want the airline to refuse a passenger permission to board their flight. It is designed to prevent people with invalid visas, stolen passports, and criminal records from boarding flights to New Zealand, the intention being that by summer 2004, all passengers would be screened.

The US deadline for its visa waiver country partners to introduce electronic passports was a major spur to the Internal Affairs Department, which estimated the cost to New Zealand travellers of losing that visa-free status at around NZ$80 million a year (*NZ Infotech Weekly* 2 May 2005). By 2005, the Internal Affairs Department was trialing electronic passports with cabin crews flying between Los Angeles and Sydney. The project was put back, however, by the US announcement of a delay to its deadline until October 2006. The NZ electronic passports contain passport details, a digital photograph and a cleaned digital image designed for facial recognition software. A digital signature by the Department of Internal Affairs was embedded in the chip to make it 'tamper-proof'. The contract of NZ$1 million dollars to supply the underlying passport technology was won by Hewlett-Packard, with the US firm Entrust providing the encryption technology and the Malaysian firm Iris Corporation Berhad supplying software encoders, readers, and software to write information on the chips. In July 2005, Internal Affairs chose the Canadian Bank Note Company's ID services group as its lead technology partner to develop the microchip-based biometric passport system. The company, a 100-year-old manufacturer of security documents and bank notes, listed on the Toronto Stock Exchange, was already three years into a contract to manufacture NZ passports (*Dominion Post* 5 July 2004). The trial seemed to be successful, even though in October 2005 the Customs Service were (perhaps belatedly) looking for a company to supply electronic equipment to actually read the new e-passports, not included in the original Hewlett-Packard contract. By 2005, the NZ Passports Office was claiming on its website that all its passports issued met the ICAO and USA visa waiver requirements 'except for the inclusion of an electronic chip containing biometric identifiers'. The site said that 'New Zealand must now incorporate a chip', although with no clear schedule for how this was to be done.

In Japan, immigration control has been important in a different fashion, namely in preserving the ethnic homogeneity of the country, while still admitting foreign workers. The function is managed by the Immigration Bureau (IB) in the Ministry of Justice, which administers the registration and deportation of foreign nationals and 'aliens' and controls embarkation and disembarkation of the 14,000 foreign nationals visiting Japan and 42,000 Japanese citizens leaving Japan every day. The immigration services employed over 2,600 staff in 2002 across eight regional immigration bureaus, five district offices, seventy-eight branch offices, and three immigration detention centres. Rising numbers of deportees (55,000 in 2004) and visa overstayers (200,000 in 2005) are a key issue in Japanese immigration policy.

Officials told us proudly that 'everything is electronic in immigration control in Japan'. All records needed for passport control are in a database, including a 'black list' of records of foreigners not allowed entry. However, some aspects of immigration control were very much less automated. Even well into the mid-2000s immigration branches were unable to process any of the information submitted by foreign visitors such as name, nationality, passport number, or other personal data. Instead, the forms completed by visitors were mailed to the Ministry's Tokyo headquarters where they were entered into a central computer, a process which took over a week. Often, officials were unable to answer questions from investigative authorities, customs, and international agencies on foreigners entering Japan because their immigration forms were still in the mail. The procedure to acquire a re-entry permit (required if a foreign national on a long-term visa were to exit and re-enter Japan during the visa period) needed a visit to the regional immigration office to fill in a form repeating the information on the visa (with no option to either do it at the airport or at the central ministry or on the Internet). The form then had to be taken to a desk where an official handed a form needing a stamp, with the applicant going to a 'convenience' store in another part of the building to pay for and obtain the stamp, and then taking it back to the original official who hands over the re-entry permit—with no computers involved at any stage. Even records on individuals who in the past were deported after committing crimes were only available by fax from the particular local immigration bureau that carried out the deportation (*Yomiuri Shimbun* 12 June 2005). In November 2001, the Ministry of Justice announced as part of an anti-terrorism drive a plan to bring forward a reinforcement of the system so as to allow immigration officials to input data on foreign visitors when they enter the country, a process that still took at least a week at the time. The Ministry asked the Diet for 310 million yen (about US$2.5 million) for the system.

The Immigration Bureau has what officials admitted was 'in practice' a long-term relationship with Fujitsu and Hitachi. The IB tries to avoid a situation in which only one company can do its IT maintenance, asking at bidding time for a system that other companies can maintain. As with the other Japanese agencies discussed here, the IB maintains little specialized expertise in-house, believing it is 'not necessary to have IT expertise to operate a system'. They also do not write a detailed specification at con-tracting time. There is a section of the Ministry of Justice that considers IT issues but each system is developed within a section. Interagency working is not considered a problem. As one official put it to us: 'Each system is developed according to policy, so there is no need to cross between sys-tems'.

In terms of new systems, the IB is developing one system that is a US import—the APIS discussed previously, which was developed in the USA and Australia. It will involve getting information from flights of passen-gers coming into Japan from the airlines in advance. In 2000, Japan began to experiment with a voluntary identification scheme, following a law passed by the Diet in 1999 to require local governments to offer residents a chip-based ID card within five years (*Card Technology* May 2000), but the scheme was extremely unpopular. Finally, in January 2005, the Justice Ministry announced plans to introduce chip-loaded ID cards for Japanese citizens who make overseas trips. The cards contained an integrated circuit chip containing personal information, such as facial portrait and fingerprints, but no biometric data.

In 2005, the government also announced plans to introduce biometrics scanning at immigration checkpoints in 2006, requiring foreign visitors to be fingerprinted and photographed on arrival for security purposes. The move was said to be needed to tackle the rising number of visa overstayers and crimes committed by foreigners. Prime Minister Koizumi commented: 'Biometric scans are effective (in foiling) deported foreigners from reentering the country. Let's see a co-ordinated effort in trying to make Japan the safest country in the world' (*Asahi Shimbun* 2 July 2005). The biometric information is to be screened through watch lists provided by the Justice Ministry and the National Police Agency and would allow searchability of photos and fingerprints. The new law reversed an earlier decision made in 1998 to end the controversial fingerprinting of foreign nationals staying in Japan, a decision first made in 1992 for permanent residents, mainly long-term ethnic Korean residents. The only concession was that in the new version of the law Koreans with permanent resident status were excluded from being fingerprinted. The original legislation was part of the Alien Registration Law passed in 1952, which required any foreign national to provide a fingerprint when registering as a resident of Japan.

Conclusions

The administration of immigration policy has changed radically in the decade from the mid-1990s, and with it the character of its supporting IT. Many immigration systems still remain paper-bound in some of our countries, and the early 1990s experiments to introduce electronic routes for pre-registered frequent travellers are still of pretty marginal influence. But the longer-run impacts of globalization and the more near-term responses to 9/11 and terrorism have decisively switched the likely future of immigration IT. In open countries like the USA, the UK, and the Netherlands, the agencies administering border controls are now seeking to change the systems central to their operations from being a low-tech backwater to being a high-tech vanguard area. In different ways immigration agencies in our large countries are carving out paths to a new frontier of biometric electronic surveillance, pre-emptive state action at a distance, and more intensive international concertation.

Immigration, of course, has always been a sphere of international cooperation, but with only limited effects on immigration control processes and technologies throughout the long era of paper-based documentation. The current push towards high-tech solutions requires an intensification of technical cooperation. Standard-setting by the ICAO and by the EU has achieved considerable advances—notably the benefits that the Netherlands has made from the most successful EU-wide system, EURODAC and the Schengen arrangements for pooled border controls. The frankly assertive stance adopted by the USA after 9/11 and the 'war on terror' has also impelled much faster movement towards US-imposed common standards, as countries shy away from the economic damage that could follow from not meeting new American standards.

There are no guarantees that the new wave of IT will in fact work as anticipated, because new technologies may not work as planned, organizational limits may be pushed, alternative technology solutions may arrive, and conflicts of different standards may well occur. Public and political reactions to the envisaged surveillance may also trigger displacement effects and policy changes. But the long dawn of immigration high-tech IT is highly unlikely to be reversed, however things pan out in practice.

9

New Public Management Is Dead—Long Live Digital-Era Government

Defining periods in the evolution of any complex system, such as public management systems in advanced industrial countries, is a tricky task. New developments accrete and accumulate while older trends are still playing out and apparently flourishing. Relatively established ideas move from leading-edge countries or sectors to implementation in previous laggard areas, even as the same ideas are being repudiated or reversed in the erstwhile pioneering locations. And a confusing welter of changes goes on simultaneously, amongst which it is difficult to distinguish ephemeral and hyped-up innovations from those that are fundamental and longer-lasting.

Despite these substantial difficulties, it seems clear that a significant change has taken place in the public management systems of the influential advanced countries studied here. In all seven, government administration has undergone a sustained period of organizational change in response to technological developments. Governments have seen the potential for transformation in their interactions with citizens, businesses, and other governments. These changes have varied in their effect—indeed, as we have shown, the reality of government IT has often failed to live up to the expectations of policymakers or stand up against comparisons with other sectors, but they challenge profoundly conventional approaches to understanding public administration, discussed in Chapter 1. The continuing development of government IT systems and the vast array of relationships between government agencies and global corporations in providing them constitute the reality of modernization and rationalization in the modern world.

In this chapter, we take a step back and attempt to delineate what is, we argue, an emergent paradigm in public administration. The whole thrust of this book has been to stress that government IT changes are no longer peripheral or routine aspects of contemporary public management and public policy changes, but increasingly important and determinant influences upon what is feasible. IT and information system influences are as salient in current public sector management as they are fundamental in contemporary Weberian rationalization processes. We see this influence of IT systems as having effects not in any direct technologically determined way but via a wide range of cognitive, behavioural, organizational, political, and cultural changes that are linked to information systems broadly construed. The changes we discuss are by no means inevitable and indeed in the Afterword we discuss a number of alternative scenarios for public management change within states in the digital era, as these changes interact with the legacies of earlier public management reform movements. In this chapter, we set out this new constellation of ideas and modernization changes as a coherent picture of what could be the future for public management, terming this new reform transition, 'digital-era governance' (DEG). The label highlights the central role that IT and information system changes now play in a wide-ranging series of alterations in how public services are organized as business processes and delivered to citizens or customers.

Both to understand why DEG has arisen and to identify its salient features, it helps to define it by comparison and contrast with its immediate predecessor, new public management. The first section returns to the discussion initiated in Chapter 4, reviewing a general argument about how and why NPM ultimately stagnated, despite its substantial contributions to broadening and deepening modern administrative and organizational technologies. The second part outlines the contrasting lineaments of DEG and itemizes its major components and how they interrelate. The third section considers how the transition from NPM to digital era governance can be characterized as a whole (e.g. as a U-turn or a set of 'tacking' changes) and highlights the unique opportunities for genuine modernization open for the next decade or so. DEG processes could achieve productivity and effectiveness improvements while simultaneously simplifying the state apparatus and expanding citizen control of their own affairs. The opportunity to secure such a 'golden mix' of objectives simultaneously does not occur often in public management.

9.1 The Crisis of New Public Management

As a cognitive and reform schema, NPM is still afloat. And a minority of its component elements (reviewed in Chapter 4) are still actively developing. But key parts of the NPM reform message have been reversed because they lead to policy disasters. And other large parts are stalled. Often these past innovations are incapable now of being easily reversed. But even their strongest advocates now expect them to have little impact on altering the overall effectiveness of government. NPM practices are extensively institutionalized and will continue—just as NPM itself did not displace large elements of previous public management orthodoxies, sometimes characterized as 'progressive public administration' or PPA (Hood 1994, Chapter 7). And NPM ideas are still gaining influence in previously rather resistant countries, such as Japan (Yamamato 2003) or India (Chakraverti 2004). But NPM is no longer new. Rather it is a two-decades old set of public management ideas now. Even analysts sympathetic to NPM have been driven to acknowledge that it is 'middle-aged' and generates adverse by-product outcomes, while still resisting evidence of its senescence (Hood and Peters 2004).

Standing back from the more detailed picture, we examine here the general reasons for the stabilization and wearing thin of the NPM innovation wave, and perhaps also the reasons for NPM's restricted impact in other countries outside the core cases. Figure 9.1 shows that any new regime or style in public management is at first chiefly assessed in terms of its direct effect on achieving an improved level of social problem-solving, shown as flow 1. For any sustained programme of innovation,

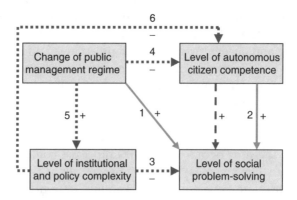

Figure 9.1. Mapping the direct and by-product effects from the NPM changes in public management regimes

such as NPM, this effect must be positive in some respect and some degree—for if it were not so, if the change had no positive impacts on social welfare at all, the policy-sifting and selection process in advanced liberal democracies might be expected to knock the change out of contention or to severely delay its implementation (Becker 1985).

In addition, there are several possible reasons why even initiatives with relatively tenuous claims to improve social welfare net of the transaction costs of the change may nonetheless have some positive impacts. For public choice theorists, even a stochastic process of policy change might be valuable in disrupting sclerotic tendencies inside the public sector and (temporarily) improving agencies' responsiveness. Some sociological observers suggest that much policy regime change has a chiefly symbolic significance, providing a stimulus for organizations to conform to 'modern' or normatively endorsed influences (Meyer and Scott 1978). In the public sector similar processes plus high levels of political direction imply that many agencies will extensively adopt changes, even where they are 'inauthentic' for them (e.g. because changes are applied in a standardized way across all state organizations). Party alternation in government can also produce a somewhat cyclical pattern of public sector governance changes, first emphasizing one set of priorities and then a rival one. Where this kind of zigzag guidance pattern develops a new policy regime, it may have some corrective re-balancing effects for an initial period.

However, with any public sector management reform agenda, it is normal for initially hyped changes, in which high hopes and political capital are invested, to prove more patchy in securing substantial improvements than anticipated. The aging of a reform programme also automatically thrusts the problems it has ameliorated into history, leaving its own flaws and shortcomings as the natural focus of political and administrative concerns. But often more important in the down-rating of reform hopes is a realization that looking only at the direct, intended impacts of policy changes can lead decision-makers to pay insufficient attention to less welcome 'by-product' or indirect effects. These problems are often represented in rationalist accounts as unusual, one-off, unexpected, or incapable of prior prediction, an approach that Hood and Peters (2004) broadly apply to NPM's entering an alleged 'age of paradox'.

There are good reasons to suppose that these often-neglected side implications of major initiatives running via civil society are absolutely inherent, even in societies with the most extensive state sectors. Scott (1978) argues strongly that statist reformers almost necessarily have a coarse-grained picture of social life, one that excludes 'metzis', the very detailed, practical and often informal knowledge and capacities that allow citizens (and enterprises) to effectively manage their lives. Hence, rationalist reforms often 'fail to improve the human condition' as their protagonists expect, because the major changes pushed through also erode essential minor practices essential for a well-functioning society. Figure 9.1 shows that autonomous citizen capabilities for coping with societal problems can powerfully define the final level of success achieved, indicated by the positive flow 2. In addition, the figure shows that the level of institutional and policy complexity will always have a considerable negative influence on the level of social problem-solving, flow 3. The impact of much recent public choice literature has been to cast doubt on the previous neo-classical economics assumption of a perfect administrative agent, and to emphasize the inherent transaction and transition costs (in terms of shirking, shaping, or rent seeking) in opting for public sector policy solutions, even with relatively vigorous intra-governmental 'markets' (Horn 1996; Kraan 1996; Breton 1999).

Turning to the implementation of NPM, the accumulation of difficulties with its solutions can be traced to the fact that NPM changes themselves had powerful adverse impacts on citizens' autonomous capacities, shown as flow 4 in Figure 9.1, and on the level of institutional and policy complexity, shown as flow 5. Even small effects that reduce citizens' competences can have dramatic multiplier effects. Yet there is every reason to suppose that new policy regimes will normally reduce citizen competences, especially in their early days. New policy and administrative concepts and terminologies are introduced, often at variance with established public understandings. And new agencies, procedures, methods of operating, and systems for allocating scarce public benefits appear, jarring with people's previous expectations. NPM proclaimed a strong customer orientation and there is evidence of some significant improvements in agencies' modes of operating on detailed issues like complaints handling (as in the 1990s UK's 'citizens charter' initiatives). Some substantial sections of the public also took advantage of enhanced choice opportunities (as in switching amongst alternative suppliers in privatized industries). Yet these changes came with a downside. 'Modernised governments are more responsive to groups of citizens. But there is a cost in capacity for collective action, when the public service is differentiated and fragmented' (OECD 2004: 4).

And because NPM was internally a very complex movement, with many management-strengthening elements, more autonomous managements could often construe what customers wanted in their own way. In a key study of Texas local governments' use of contracting, O'Toole and Meir (2004) found a negative association with the end-quality of services delivered. Some NPM-orientated managements even persuaded themselves that their own business objectives are what consumers also want, in the same way that some analysts could write seriously of 'marketing as increased accountability to customers' (Moore 1995: 186). Sometimes bizarre results could follow, as in the 1999 collapse of the UK Passport Agency, where management efforts to introduce new IT shaving £1 off a £27 passport fee precipitated a disaster. In a few months, 35,000 mailbags of unopened mail accumulated, more than 1 million phone calls went unanswered, and virtual agency paralysis ensued for a time (NAO 1999*b*). The ensuing political row made clear that the reliability of the service is actually a quality far more important to passport holders than a small cost reduction. (Rebuilding the agency's systems has subsequently pushed the price of a UK passport up to £51, an increase of over 75 per cent in five years, with virtually no adverse political fallout. Current UK government plans envisage a charge of £89 for a passport and identity card by 2007.) And critics argued that in the NPM heyday cost-cutting by contractors often meant quality-shading on areas vital for consumers, as with US airport security before the 9/11 massacre (Moss and Eaton 2001; Moynihan and Roberts 2002) or with the growth of hospital-acquired infections in UK hospitals, partly because outsourced cleaning contracts lead to dirtier wards. Consumers may care a great deal about this kind of quality-shading, but they confront severe collective action problems in communicating this to managements unless evidence of problems emerges forcefully. NPM's dictums of strong managerial action, rapid service changes, and the substitution of political controls by business processes hence all contributed to somewhat reducing citizens' autonomous problem-solving capabilities, a negative influence (flow 4) consequently lowering flow 3's positive contribution, to create a net negative effect.

New policy regimes also tend to increase institutional and policy complexity. The transactions costs of changes concentrate in the early years, when the new arrangements are by definition not routinized and administrative actors are required to undertake exceptional levels of policy learning. Policy succession is also rarely complete, so that the new regime tends to overlay pre-existing arrangements and procedures. The characteristic pattern of development in modern technological systems is also towards further specialization of subsystems. So, the direct ameliorative effects of new initiatives on social problem-solving are generally offset to some extent by countervailing increases in problem complexity. This development is adverse because policy complexity is one of the key in-hibitors on effective social problem-solving, magnifying information de-mands, boosting the number of clearance points needed for progressing solutions, and creating in particular increased coordination problems. Note that coordination difficulties are not necessarily premised upon direct conflicts of interest between actors. Problems of synchronization, design fit, assignment, and realization problems with innovation attri-butes can recur even in situations where all actors accept a common interest in achieving shared goals (Milgrom and Roberts 1992: 90).

NPM's focus on disaggregation and competition automatically in-creased the numbers of administrative units and created more complex and dynamic interrelationships amongst them compared with previous PPA systems. Moynihan and Roberts (2004: 141) offer a startling example of a complex design map of the highly agencified US homeland security area before the DHS reorganization and the subsequent December 2004 Bush reform to create an overall intelligence coordinator. Some NPM reforms touted specifically as increasing transparency have ended up in-stead creating bizarre new layers of impenetrability, as with accruals accounting. Barton (2004: 281) shows that the literally fantastic financial statements for the Australian Defence Forces make it 'appear to be the most profitable enterprise in the nation', whose 'profits and dividends far exceed those of . . . the largest private corporations'—a status achieved with 'negligible direct government investment in military equipment as they have been largely funded from accumulated surpluses accruing over many years. How can this be, given that the department is almost entirely dependent upon an annual budget appropriation for its defence services?' (Little wonder then that although a few NPM countries lead the way to accruals budgeting, many OECD countries remain content with older cash-based systems.) Similarly, layering new incentivization initiatives on top of, but in partial conflict with, public interest ethos devices (such as life-long career paths for civil servants) created more complex systems than had existed here to fore. Hence, again NPM boosted policy complex-ity and impaired to some degree social problem-solving—a positive (flow 5) plus a negative (flow 3) creating a net negative impact on the dependent variable.

In addition, increased policy complexity has negative effects on levels of citizen competence, shown as flow 6 in Figure 9.1. The more difficult it is for citizens to understand internal state arrangements and operate appro-priate access points to represent their interests politically and administra-tively, the more their autonomous capabilities to solve policy problems may be eroded. This loop may operate in particularly forceful ways in some areas, as suggested in Illich's controversial general argument (1977) that the industrialization, professionalization, or technicalization of social life all have fast and dramatic effects in eroding autonomous citizen competences to cope with their own problems, which the formalized systems of provision cannot actually match by providing replacement solutions. If this loop is present, then again a negative (flow 6) plus a positive (flow 3) yields a net negative effect on social problem-solving. There is good evidence from New Zealand and the UK especially that NPM changes creating additional complexity eroded citizens' problem-solving capacities, notwithstanding the commitment to improving customer service supposed to be fundamental to the movement.

We can sum up Figure 9.1 in slightly more formal terms: $\Delta S = f(\Delta R, \Delta O, \Delta X)$ where Δ stands for 'change in', S denotes social problem-solving, R the level of direct policy regime change, O the level of citizen competence in the issue area, and X the level of institutional and policy complexity. Holding all other contextual factors except the regime change equal, and assigning lower case letters to serve as parameter labels we get:

$$\Delta S = aR - oR - x_1 R - x_2 R$$

which says that the change in social problem-solving is the sum of the direct effect of the regime switch (whose efficacy is given by a and magnitude by R) minus the mediated side effects operating though reduced citizen competence (o) and increased policy complexity directly (x_1) and indirectly (x_2).

Finally, Figure 9.1 adds some important feedback loops from the level of social problem-solving achieved to other variables. With NPM as with any other change in public management regimes, successful problem-solving increases citizen competences and tends to reduce policy complexity, as issues become more benign and tractable. Worsening levels of ability to cope with problems can spiral into vicious circles or even crises, eroding citizens' confidence in their abilities to handle life-issues and greatly boosting difficulties in achieving institutional and policy coordination. We could easily incorporate feedback effects lagged by one relevant period in the equation above.

Note that in itself Figure 9.1 leaves moot the overall impact of NPM. In this case (as always), there were displaced side effects of these two primary kinds, and typically these side effects (and any interaction effects) to some extent offset any direct welfare gains achieved. But these propositions are consistent with NPM having a wide range of overall net effects. A strong and direct impact of NPM on social problem-solving might easily dwarf the mediated side effects. But on the other hand, a less impressive positive main effect might not be enough to stop overall social welfare being eroded. Our contention here is only that these two kinds of adverse by-product effects of NPM have contributed strongly to its waning momentum and to the stalling of its impetus (briefly reviewed in Chapter 4).

9.2 The Emergence of Digital Era Governance

There are a scattering of proposals for characterizing the post-NPM wave of management changes that is currently under way. Many seem overly optimistic, looking forward to 'banishing bureaucracy' (Osborne and Plastrik 1997) or achieving a 'post-bureaucratic' administration (Hekscher and Donnellon 1994; Kernaghan 2000). In the EU, the idea of administrative convergence has partly been seen as blunting NPM's impacts, creating counter-vailing shifts, especially in regulatory areas (Wood 2004). Our take here highlights the central importance of IT-based changes in management systems and in methods of interacting with citizens and other services users in civil society, in underpinning and integrating current bureaucratic adaptations.

As with any management regime succession, some elements of the post-NPM period's style of public management are set by what went before, both in terms of continuities for elements that have worked better or still have development potential, and in terms of reversing what worked less well and re-emphasizing priorities that NPM tended to neglect. However, we want to make a more ambitious argument here—that the unifying and distinguishing features of the current development of public sector organizational and managerial change mainly revolve around IT changes and alterations in information systems. Of course, we noted in Chapters 1 and 2 that IT systems have been important elements in shaping changes in public administration for several decades now, with the first-wave impact of automated data processes abolishing many thousands of clerical positions and subsequent waves producing smaller but recurrent savings and more significant alterations in administrative decision processes (Margetts 1999). Yet the waves of IT change that occurred before the late 1990s had very limited transformative impacts. Office automation processes were extensively adapted to and fitted in with the pre-existing organizational culture of public sector agencies. And once functions were routinized to the point of being handled automatically, organizational cultures tended to downgrade their importance for managerial performance. Agencies became highly dependent on their IT infrastructures, but this did not shape their modes of operating as much as might have been expected. What is different in the current period is the growth of the Internet, e-mail, and the web, and the generalization of IT systems from affecting back-office processes only to conditioning in important ways the whole terms of relation between government agencies and civil society.

By DEG we signify a whole complex of changes, which have IT and information-handling changes at their centre, but which spread much more widely and take place in many more dimensions simultaneously than was the case with previous IT influences. For the first time it now makes sense to characterize the broad sweep of current public management regime change in terms which refer to new information-handling potentialities that make feasible a transition to fully digital modes of operating for many government sector agencies. The advent of the digital era is now the most general, pervasive, and structurally distinctive influence on how governance arrangements are changing in advanced industrial states. Note that our position here remains very different from those accounts implausibly predicting e-government utopias, or already claiming the construction of a 'virtual state' (Fountain 2001; Accenture 2004). By contrast to these accounts, we stress that DEG is a movement of the digital era in society at large. But DEG is not a solely or even primarily about digital changes within the government apparatus itself.

A wide range of processes are involved in the shift to DEG changes' primacy, and Figure 9.2 shows that we are suggesting a technological colouration of these processes, but not any simple technological determination of them. The feeding through of technological changes in government in itself has no direct effects upon policy outcomes in the figure. Instead, IT changes work through indirectly in several different ways. The first are organizational culture changes inside the government sector.

Digital era changes have already triggered numerous significant shifts— a large-scale switchover to e-mail in internal and external communications; the rising salience of websites and intranets in organizational information networks; the development of electronic services for different client groups; the growth of electronic procurement systems; a fundamental transition from paper-based to electronic record-keeping and so on. A tipping point in many organizations' development towards digital agency status is when they move over from files and documentation

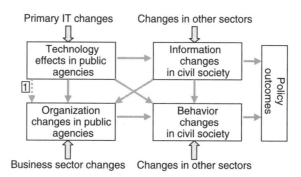

Figure 9.2. The centrality of IT changes in contemporary public management change

Note[1]: Organizational change brought about via increased IT outsourcing.

recognizably the same as those in Weber's day, where the authoritative version of policy is recorded on paper, to holding the authoritative version electronically (usually on an intranet) and simply printing off paper copies as needed. This transition reflects the ineradicability of serious 'version control' problems in any mixed paper/electronic systems. Full digital agency status is potentially achievable by many government agencies in advanced states, especially at the central or federal government tier and in regulatory areas, but of course less so for delivery agencies. In former NPM countries, there is an influential additional pathway for organizational change, the impact of large-scale contractor involvement in delivering IT-related administration processes on the organizational arrangements and cultures of the agencies they supply, denoted as flow 1 in Figure 9.2.

Contemporary IT technology changes also operate via shifts in societal information-handling norms and patterns, as modes of informing consumers and involving them with corporations change across leading-edge sectors. Particularly influential for government have been the disintermediation changes affecting the most cognate or similar private sector services industries, such as banking, insurance, comparator specialists, travel firms, and even electronic merchandizers. Similarly the B2B interactions in fields like procurement spill over directly into what civil society actors expect of government. As consumers' and corporations' behaviours in the private sector change, so there are direct demands for government information and transaction practices to shift in parallel ways. The lags involved here are considerable, of the order of half a decade, but there are strong similarities in the patterns of diffusion of innovations. Figure 9.2 shows that changes in information systems and alterations in citizen behaviours, partly shaped by government IT and organizational changes, are the key pathways by which alterations in policy outcomes are accomplished.

At every point in Figure 9.2 the impact of digital era governance shifts is also externally conditioned. The key influences on primary IT changes are commercial, the demands from the business sector for new capabilities and then the oligopolistic (or in software near-monopolistic) supply-side responses. The major external influences on state organizational changes remain business managerialism, although a different vintage from the now dated NPM influences, with many current effects also shaped strongly by digital-era influences. Societal information systems are integrally linked and civil society behavioural changes reflect much more general contextual shifts.

In more specific terms the impact of digital-era governance practices can be considered under three main themes. The first theme is partly a reaction against NPM's emerging problems and partly reflects digital-era opportunities. But the other two themes are essentially at a tangent to NPM practices, not convergent with them but quite different in orientation. These top-level themes are:

- *Reintegration.* The key opportunities for exploiting digital-era technology opportunities lie in putting back together many of the elements that NPM separated out into discrete corporate hierarchies, offloading onto citizens and other civil society actors the burden of integrating public services into useable packages. Reintegration approaches are not simple reruns of the old centralization phases of centralization/ decentralization cycles. Nor are they just variations on a unchanging menu of administrative possibilities stretching back to cameralist times, as the more despairing of contemporary commentators sometimes seem to suggest (Hood 1998). Rather they represent an antithetical (and partly synthesizing) response to the NPM experience.

- *Needs-based holism.* In contrast to the narrow joined-up-governance changes included in the reintegration theme, holistic reforms seek to simplify and change the entire relationship between agencies and their clients. Creating larger and more encompassing administrative blocs is linked with 'end-to-end' re-engineering of processes, stripping out unnecessary steps, compliance costs, checks and forms. It also stresses developing a more 'agile' government that can respond speedily and flexibly to changes in the social environment.

- *Digitization changes*, broadly construed. To realize contemporary productivity gains from IT and related organizational changes requires a far more fundamental take-up of the opportunities opened up by a transition to fully digital operations. Instead of electronic channels being seen as supplementary to conventional administrative and business processes, they become genuinely transformative, moving towards a situation where the agency '*becomes* its website', as a senior official in the Australian Tax Office described this process to us.

We fill out this broad-brush picture by saying a few words about the underlying components in each of the three themes, shown in Figure 9.3.

There are nine main *reintegration components* in Figure 9.3, all of which stress gathering back together the disparate functions and clusters of expertise that under NPM were fragmented into single-function agencies and spread across complex inter-organizational networks. However, the forms of reintegration are different from pre-NPM structures and some completely new patterns (such as shared services) are emerging.

The rollback of agencification and fragmentation has been achieved in the UK via mergers, re-assimilations of agencies into cohesive departmental groups, culls of quasi-governmental agencies, and the re-imposition of cooperative community-based structures on micro-local agencies previously encouraged to be unrestrictedly competitive. All these were prominent features of Labour government policies from 1997 onwards. However, the last years of Blair's government saw a re-emergence of measures to strengthen the corporate management and partial discretion of some local hospitals and schools under 'earned autonomy' principles, along with a concern to differentiate previously 'bog standard' public sector provision. But despite a surprisingly vigorous and continuous churn of agency creations and extinctions, the strong overall trend in UK central government was for a substantial reduction in agency numbers over time.

Joined-up governance (JUG) has been a central element of reintegration in the UK under the Blair government, and its main lineaments and problems have been well described already (6 et al. 2002; Pollitt 2003; 6 2004; Policy and Innovation Unit 2000). We focus narrowly here on major departmental amalgamations at central or federal levels—such as the creation of the Department of Homeland Security in the USA, responding to the previous deficiencies of agency fragmentation highlighted by the 9/11 terrorist massacre (Wise 2002); the merging of employment service and welfare benefits operations in the UK's Department of Work and Pensions; and the integration of the Inland Revenue and HM Customs and Excise

Theme	Component
Reintegration	Rollback of agencification and fragmentation
	Joined-up governance (JUG)
	Re-governmentalization
	Reinstating or re-strengthening central processes
	Radically squeezing production costs
	Re-engineering back-office function sand service delivery chains
	Procurement concentration and specialization
	Shared services on a 'mixed economy' basis
	Network simplification and 'small worlds'
Needs-based holism	Interactive information-giving and seeking
	Client-based or needs-based reorganization
	One-stop provision, ask-once processes
	Data ware housing
	End-to-end service re-engineering
	Agile government processes *(e.g., exceptions—handling, real-time fore casting and preparedness, responses to the unexpected)*
	Sustainability
Digitization processes	Electronic service delivery and e-government
	Web-based utility computing
	New forms of automate dprocesses *(e.g., zero touch technologies, ZTT or radio frequency identification RFID)*
	Radical disintermediation (cut out the middle man)
	Active channel streaming and customer segmentation
	Mandated channel reductions
	Facilitating isocratic administration *(e.g., co-production of services, quasi-voluntary compliance, do-it-your self forms, and tax-paying)*
	Moving towards open-book government

Figure 9.3. The key components of digital-era governance

into a single UK national tax agency. These seemingly conventional (outwardly almost 1970s era) changes in fact have a novel character chiefly because of the IT convergences involved in them. For instance, the merger of two previously separate UK tax agencies into one (HM Revenue and Customs) rests on an extensive IT integration programme (see Chapter 6).

Re-governmentalization involves the re-absorption into the public sector of activities that had previously been outsourced to the private sector. The biggest example so far has been the transfer of some 28,000 airport security staff from private contractors in the USA to the federal civil service, required by the Senate as the only sure corrective to the problems highlighted by 9/11 massacre, where the suicide hijackers passed through privatized airport security systems (see Moynihan and Roberts 2002). The de facto re-nationalization of Railtrack's infrastructure provision functions in the UK railways after the company went bankrupt in Summer

2000 is the second leading example. The government first replaced Railtrack with a government-owned, not-for-profit infrastructure company Network Rail, answering to a Strategic Rail Authority (SRA). But then in 2004 it abolished the SRA, made Network Rail more explicitly a public agency, and imposed direct Department of Transport control on it (House of Commons Transport Select Committee 2004).

Re-establishing or re-strengthening central processes has been important in the lagged appreciation that NPM's fragmenting changes have duplicated multiple hierarchies. NPM's focus on creating new or enhanced corporate management processes across dozens of agencies meant replicating on a smaller scale, and re-accomplishing over and over, some very similar generic functions, such as non-standard procurement, recruitment and human relations, or e-government operations. Varied initiatives have begun to re-impose a degree of order on the erstwhile anarchy of competing separate initiatives from the NPM era, especially in the IT area with the Canadian and US Federal Enterprise Architecture programs. In the UK, centralized e-change programmes have been extensively funded (see Chapter 4) and from 2005, the e-government unit began trying to reduce duplication in areas like the over-provision of websites. However, these large-country initiatives lag years behind effective governmentwide programmes launched by small countries like Singapore and Finland that were more resistant to NPM influences in the past, and hence have had stronger central processes from the outset.

Radically squeezing process costs emerged as a sub-theme of the Bush administration's FEAP efforts, but acquired much greater political prominence in the UK in 2004 when both the Labour government and the main opposition parties outlined plans for quantum reductions of at least 80,000 civil servants (out of a total of 530,000) over a five-year period (see Gershon 2004). The big reductions are concentrated in high IT-use departments, with 30,000 staff targeted in the Department of Work and Pensions and 15,000 from the merging of two national tax agencies. A longer-term civil service internal analysis foresaw saving 150,000 jobs, cutting civil service numbers by a quarter. Most of these changes would be achieved by the next three elements, with the aim of shifting resources to 'front-line' staff.

Re-engineering back-office functions partly aims to realize the productivity improvements offered by newer IT, consolidating 'legacy' labyrinths of discrete mainframe facilities and associated administrative units, which grew up piecemeal in the 1970s and 1980s and were never simplified in the 1990s. In the NPM countries, where IT system messes were merely outsourced but not modernized or redesigned, this potential is considerable.

The other part of this programme involves the redesign of back-office functions, a development facilitated by the system integrator corporations' concern to streamline the demands upon them, which in most cases has proved to mean persuading government agencies to scrap historic processes devoid of current rationale. Business process systematization may be undertaken either by agencies directly or by outsourced contractors on their behalf, as in the growing moves towards either a single agency-level IT contracts with a single systems-integrator firm or with a cooperative multi-firm team, often replacing myriads of cross-cutting contracts for discrete systems and processes. Yet the past rhetoric of NPM now has such a life of its own that even clear-cut reintegration moves like this are often strangely represented as somehow a further diffusion of power from agencies into 'networked governance' arrangements (Goldsmith and Eggers 2004*b*).

Procurement concentration and specialization has progressed considerably in the USA, both as a result of changes in the National Performance Review period and in IT especially with the growth of GWACs, which accounted for 39 per cent of American public sector civil IT procurement by 2003. But in the NPM core countries these ideas were neglected. In New Zealand, government outsourced its key competencies in contracts-drafting to private sector lawyers and consultants, as chief executives on short-term contracts themselves covered their positions against risks, more concerned with ensuring process-proofing and a clear audit trail than with contracting innovatively. In the UK, the NPM era produced a considerable duplication of procurement functions across departments and agencies. A 2004 efficiency review conducted for the Treasury concluded that £20 billions of cost savings could be made within four years from a range of measures, including a shift to smarter procurement carried out by a few major procurement centres, instead of independently by 270 departments and agencies at national level (Gershon 2004). The high rate of change involved in the NPM search for new ways of involving private capital in public services also meant that many government organizations made serial decentralized mistakes in running first privatizations, next PFI processes, and then public–private partnerships (PPPs). By 2002, when the PFI process was supposed to be mature, the UK National Audit Office found that still only one in six agencies had provision to share in re-financing gains with their PFI contractors (NAO 2002*d*).

Shared services initiatives pull together aspects of some of the last four trends in radical efforts to cut duplication by encouraging smaller departments and agencies to use commonly provided back office or more policy-relevant services, like human relations, IT services, or financial services, even perhaps what were seen as highly *sui generis* functions, such as citizen redress (NAO 2005). Instead of the old model of centralized provision that was mandatory for subordinate agencies, and often unresponsive and inflexible in operation, the current shared services provision uses much more flexible models. Agencies with a proven capability in one area are encouraged to provide the same service on a contract basis to other agencies with similar needs, with multiple providers ensuring that a customer agency experiencing poor levels of service can always switch to an alternative supplier. The GWAC contracts for procuring simple IT are an important forerunner here (see Chapter 4), but shared services are being extended to much more sophisticated professional services areas. In the UK, a 'mixed economy' model may develop under the Gershon review process, with a few central government 'hubs' for procurement and other services competing with a limited number of major outsourcing operations run by consultancies (like Acenture) or possibly big IT providers who can sell more wholesale 'business process outsourcing' solutions. Such an outcome with perhaps as few as seven or eight main providers of shared services is very different from the pre-NPM era of large hierarchical departments, and in the UK, a more integrated civil service. But the emerging pattern is also very different from an NPM boom period, when at its height, some 300 UK central agencies were repetitively carrying out the same functions, often at an uneconomically small scale.

Network simplification and 'small worlds' involves a recognition that the characteristic problem of modern bureaucracy is not budget-maximizing officials trying to expand their budgets and turfs. Instead, the bureau-shaping model (Dunleavy 1991) implies that a growing problem will be officials setting up boutique-bureaucracies, creating complex top tiers of regulatory or guidance agencies for highly articulated networks of public agencies and quasi- or non-governmental bodies (see Hood, James, and Scott 2000; James 2000). The multi-way fragmentation of the UK rail industry provides one of the most exaggerated NPM outcomes here, with at one time in the late 1990s three separate regulators covering rail infrastructure investment, rail safety, and the licensing of train companies. Streamlining regulatory overview and simplifying underlying networks can stop the creation of multiple management teams in highly balkanized policy areas, each partly making more work for others to handle. At the same time, there is again no return to the highly simplified and regular lattice networks with strong siloing characteristic of the golden age of the progressive public administration era that preceded NPM. Instead the 'small worlds' literature on network connectivity suggests that an optimum degree of linkaging can be achieved when a regular lattice of local links between close neighbour organizations is supplemented by a relatively small number of random or cross-cutting long-range links joining up further apart or even remote policy sectors (Watts and Strogatz 1998).

There are seven main components of *needs-based holism* in Figure 9.3, all of them going far beyond the conventional bounds of JUG processes, discussed above. Needs-based holism involves a whole-scale attempt to re-prioritize away from the NPM stress on business process management and towards a genuinely citizen-based, services-based, or needs-based foundation for organization (see 6 et al. 2003). Its implications run throughout the public sector networks involved—dictating new macro-structures, new fine-grain reorganizations, re-evaluations of processes and fundamental changes of management styles and information systems, and new modes of responding agilely to emerging problems. New integrating political authority structures are key stimuli for holistic change, because 'history suggests that substantial improvements in public services stem from broader forces in society—from political movements and community action' (Hambleton 2004: 2).

Interactive information-seeking and giving is fundamental for the emergence of all the other needs-based holism elements. This discovery was a long time coming in the public sector. In Chapter 4, we showed that governments for a long time accepted uncritically a five-phase model of e-government's development, in which passive information giving was dismissed as an elementary first phase, a 'billboards' phase that should be bypassed as swiftly as possible en route to the 'golden' applications of e-government in transactional uses. It took more than a decade for the government sector to stumble long after the private sector in different countries to a realization that in fact search applications (the foundations for Google's empire) and sophisticated information arbitrage would be every bit as critical in public sector applications. The basis for second-stage and better-founded informational applications of e-gov and other modern communications (such as Web-enabled call centres) was the realization that citizens and enterprises themselves have far more information about *their own* situations than government could ever acquire. The job of government information systems then is to let citizens and businesses with this unrivalled knowledge find within the government apparatus how to code and report the few salient features relevant for public agencies, and if necessary, to make the most appropriate decisions for them in the light of the applicable rules and regulations. Hood (1983) also stressed that government agencies need 'detector' mechanisms as much as they do 'effectors', so that how public agencies do information-seeking has as much importance as how they do delivery. Interactive mechanisms (such as using call centres and phone forms or online e-services rather than paper-based forms) automatically facilitate agency staff and systems taking a more holistic view of people's needs and preferences.

Client-based or function-based reorganisation revives the now very old fashioned practice (dating back to the Haldane report and Luther Gullick) of reintegrating agencies around a single client group, instead of the NPM focus on discrete business processes. A good example is the Pensions Service inside the UK's Department of Work and Pension, which pulls together all benefits for old people in a distinct administration. Alternatively, a macro-functional or macro-programme rationale has proved key in the USA's new Department of Homeland Security, which pulls together some twenty-two federal agencies that previously operated separately for decades under successive public management regimes.

One-stop provision takes various forms, including one-stop shops (where multiple administrative services are provided by the same co-located staff), one-stop windows (where only the customer interface is integrated), and web-integrated services (where the customer transparency and cross-services integration is primarily electronic). The impulse in all one-stop provision is for government agencies to proactively mesh together provision across erstwhile separate fiefdoms, so as to resolve 'lead agency' and duplication problems and to reduce the previously high-cognitive burdens and compliance costs placed on citizens or businesses in the NPM heyday. Key examples have been the pulling together of previously separated employment and benefits services for working age people in the UK, again in a new kind of client-focused agency, Job Centre Plus, following a pattern initiated much earlier by the pioneering Australian Centre-link agency (Select Committee on Work and Pensions 2002; Halligan 2004). 'Ask once' methods involve a commitment by government to reusing already collected information, rather than recursively gathering the same information many times, as happened under NPM's fragmented and supersiloed administrative systems.

Data warehousing sounds simple but in the context of most national-level taxation, social security, immigration, or security/intelligence systems in the largest countries, it is both a long way off and has radical implications. The normal administrative situation has been that different bits of information are being held on separate, often mutually incompatible systems, with data matches either difficult to do at all or having to be triggered by specific search requests. Instead, data warehousing makes case-by-case data available across multiple benefits, taxes, or security fields in a proactive way that can allow government agencies to anticipate citizens' needs or the key risks to policy. And using feasible algorithms agencies can then proactively try to match their services to meet citizens' needs or risks.

End-to-end service re-engineering draws on these innovations to look for radically different service-provision models. Under previous public management regimes, agencies often had perverse incentives to differentiate their services and processes. Despite moving the administrative furniture around a great deal, NPM reformers were actually very reluctant to undertake more fundamental questioning of administrative processes, because of the focus on short-term managerialist savings. Indeed, in the fragmented New Zealand system, re-engineering would pose impossible demands, for instance requiring agency chiefs to envisage their own organization's amalgamation or to contemplate a change programme extending far beyond their own short term of office. The key stimuli for taking a broader view have been all the processes above, plus the migration of key government information systems to the web, which dramatizes and makes public the interconnectedness of provision. An end-to-end approach ensures that project teams focus through the whole process without artificially demarcating their analysis at existing agency boundaries. A common aim now, even within single agencies, is to radically cut the length of government forms (see NAO 2003c). One Canadian social security official recounted to us how a task force asked to reduce a thirty-page state pensions-claiming form by half found that they could actually go much further. By pulling together information from existing IT systems previously held separately they could in fact replace the form completely, with a welcome letter and a statement of entitlement.

Agile government processes focus on achieving speed with flexibility and responsiveness, in the process making government decision-making competitive with best practice in the business sector (Dunleavy, Yared, and Bastow 2003). Two recent examples illustrate the power of the agile government case here. The first is the field of international aviation security, where the standard planning assumption for more than thirty years from the 1970s to fall 2001 was that potential airplane hijackers or bombers wanted to safeguard their own lives. So, hijackers were resisted by closing down escape options by banning countries taking in hijacked planes. And bombers were countered by matching all bags on planes to passengers. Suicide bombings and attacks were increasingly common in other contexts (such as civil conflicts in Sri Lanka) for up to five years before the 9/11 massacre. But the cultural assumptions underlying international aircraft security practices were not updated, so that the previous system collapsed in September 2001 under a determined assault by nineteen barely armed suicide hijackers.

The second example concerns the performance of the generally admired French public health care system, during a two-week Mediterranean-style heatwave affecting all of France during July/August 2003. With constant temperatures of over 40 degrees centigrade, many old and chronically sick people became severely distressed at the same time as summer holidays left hospitals poorly staffed and relatives away. National monitoring of the crisis failed to work, professions and trade union calls for action were dismissed as alarmist at the end of the first week, and no recalls of staff were issued until too late. French hospitals have few air-conditioned wards, so cooling off elderly or sick people was hard, and an estimated 10,000–14,000 additional deaths were charted in the heatwave period.

In both these cases, heavily invested and well-staffed policy systems handling perfectly foreseeable problems failed because of inflexibilities and slow response times, reflecting cultural barriers to re-orientating policy systems' inertial courses so as to cope effectively with a changed environment. By contrast, a stress on agility comes out of the private sector IT world, where the problems of companies becoming constrained by past investments and losing flexibility to carry out tasks in a different manner within a useful timeframe has been longer appreciated. The agile government concept denies the commonly held PPA view that government agencies operate in environments that are stable over the long term, with incubated solutions and a premium on achieving agreement amongst diverse stakeholders (Polsby 1984). Picked up first in the defence sphere, agile government focuses on achieving a public management and decision-making system that is capable of quickly reconfiguring to changing needs and responding to a volatile or turbulent external environment. As the US Navy Secretary said in October 2002: 'We need an organization that is very adaptive, that is very agile and is quick. Instead of having cycles that take years, we need cycles that take months... because the threat changes' (quoted Dunleavy, Yared, and Bastow, (2003: 3). Two key pieces of agility structures are real-time monitoring, forecasting, and prediction systems, cutting lag times for decision-makers, and systems that can achieve the tricky feat of 'expecting the unexpected', or at least being able to accommodate exceptions to what had previously been practiced or embedded in standard operating procedures in a flexible and rapid-adaptive way.

Sustainability may seem at first sight a completely left-field interjection into this set of criteria, since environmental pressures and environmentalist movements are undoubtedly the key origins of the modern push on these lines. Yet although the distinctiveness of this element is strong, it also fits closely with a more needs-orientated approach to agency operations. NPM was generally a movement that was careless of energy use and environmental impacts, with its focus on a narrowly corporate performance orientation in which negative externality effects were characteristically ignored. How far this process addressed environmental concerns was chiefly politically determined—it had progressive impacts only in so far as there were powerful environmental agencies specifically charged with advancing aspects of sustainability in their own targets and performance standards. However, the broader approach of needs-based holism of taking citizens' and enterprises' needs seriously and addressing them in the round, fits closely with the key demands of environmentalist groups that sustainability be 'mainstreamed' and become part of the intrinsic operation of all public sector agencies (Dryzek et al. 2003) rather than a restricted concern of a subset of not very powerful regulatory agencies, as it was under NPM.

The third theme, *digitization changes*, is the most closely connected to the impacts of web, Internet, and e-mail on public agencies, and the component changes set out here are often partially captured under the e-government label. Yet simple or direct technological impacts here are often over-hyped, with surprising levels of credence given to IT or e-government utopias produced by IT corporations or industry interest groups. In fact, the chief impacts of digitization processes are achieved via organizational and cultural changes inside the government sector, plus behavioural shifts by civil society actors outside—changes in which technology shifts play relatively small if critical roles (Margetts and Dunleavy 2002).

Electronic services delivery (ESD) covers the substantial potential for most paper-based administrative processes to be converted to e-government processes. Many post-NPM governments have adopted relatively ambitious programmes and targets, as with the UK's pledge to put 100 per cent of central and local government services online by the end of 2005, backed by a £1 billion investment (NAO 1999a, 2002c). In fact, citizens' take-up of e-services here has lagged considerably behind expectations, but once initiated has still shown rapid growth, as in the UK income tax area (NAO 2000, 2002a). With US household Internet access approaching 70 per cent, and even relative laggard countries like the UK reaching 51 per cent access, the business rationale and customer impetus for better ESD in government keeps strengthening.

Web-based utility computing denotes a trend towards simpler computing and IT tasks being made available packaged in such a way that either smaller government agencies can purchase 'on demand' over the web in a market with diverse suppliers (including suppliers of advice); or agencies could pick from a preset menu of services provided by their main contractor and defined in terms of modern capabilities (within the current state of knowledge) rather than in terms of procuring particular sets of hardware and software. At a limit either of these routes might open futures where smaller agencies no longer have to do complex IT pre-planning of their own. To some degree, the standardization of packages and the improvement of standard pack software has prefigured this potentially emergent trend, especially in civil service systems like the American federal administration, where more staff have stronger technical capabilities or fewer technical reservations than in Japan or the UK. However, critics argue that similar predictions of fully modularized IT and networks have been current for a long time, without any strongly convergent trend for anything like 'utility' computing to develop, even among small agencies. Thus, a question mark seems justified at the present time over the scenarios where agencies could buy ICT services in the same manner as gas, electricity, or other utilities. But the potential for development in this track is still strong.

Centralized, state-directed IT procurement covers initiatives, such as the £13 billion programme inaugurated by the UK government in 2001 to remedy poor use of IT in the National Health Service, which by 2004 saw the specification of servicewide systems and contracts to be taken up by individual NHS trusts and agencies. Here, the clarification and eventually imposition of a central network concept and design by a remarkably strong contracts team (operating in the public sector but largely recruited from the private sector) proved to be vital in overcoming more than a decade and a half of paralysis under previous NPM arrangements.

New forms of automated processes encompass in particular the 'zero touch technology' (ZTT) approach, pioneered in the private sector by companies like CISCO, where the ideal is that no human intervention is needed in a sale or administrative operation. There are huge areas of potential application in well-designed and modern public agency operations. For instance, the surveillance and control system for the London congestion charge is an almost ZTT process. Once the entry of a particular car has been paid for, its number plate is automatically counted as valid in the monitoring machinery, or turned up as an apparent exception if not paid for, with the vast majority of cases not requiring staff attention. In 2004, the

UK transport department outlined a plan for universal road charging based on satellite tracking of all vehicles using geo-positioning satellite (GPS) data. And with extensive mobile phone ownership more anonymous systems are being developed to aid public agency management of human behaviours, for instance, detecting traffic hold-ups and flow patterns on major highways and in city centres by monitoring the flow of mobile phones through different cell-net blocks. In other sectors there are also many applications for auto-monitoring, like policing where automatic number plate recognition and even face-scanning are spreading, immigration, where borders are electronically monitored by automatic sensors, and environmental management, where cheap mobile phone–based auto sensors (costing as little as US$15 each) can pervasively monitor water or pollution levels and replace manually inspected gauges and instrumentation. Radio frequency identification (RFID) chips also open up radically new systems of inventory control and omnipresent goods-tracking, in government sector organizations as much as in private firms.

Radical disintermediation denotes the potential for Web-based processes (including equivalent digital TV or mobile phone links) to allow citizens, businesses, and other civil society actors to connect directly to state systems, without passing through the previously universal gatekeepers in the form of civil service or agency personnel. Of course, Web-based or other automated systems in practice need substantial back-up and help desk systems. But the most innovative qualities of disintermediation changes is that civil society actors who know their own situations very well are able to autonomously sift and select what they may receive from government. Disintermediation is essentially accomplished only when citizens or consumers of public services change their behaviours in line with facilitating shifts by government agencies and officials. The potential for mismatches here is considerable, and there has inevitably been a learning curve in which some options are not actually offered in a useable form by the bureaucracy, or where viable options offered to citizens are taken up only partially or slowly.

But when genuine innovations are allowed to happen the changes can be considerable. For example, transport authorities in London in 1998 decided to install charging technology in underground rail stations and buses for using a smart card (called Oystercard), which allowed users to put credit on their card and then pay for any form of mass-transit journeys by swiping the card past an automatic reader. At first the 350,000 existing holders of paper season tickets were switched to the electronic card, but then card users grew in four years to more than 2.2 million, with large cost savings in ticketing staff, big reductions in peak hour queuing times, and increased use of mass transit by passengers, for whom the ticket-acquisition phase no longer featured in their journeys. Adding a Web-based card issuing service and the ability to 'top-up' cards credit online completed the disintermediation picture for customers.

Active channel-streaming and customer segmentation occurs when governments face up to the extra costs and difficulties of multi-channel access, abandoning the common initial position of simply adding electronic service channels to existing capacity, and of providing universalistic electronic channels. Instead, they move to a strategy of actively managing displacement of service users to electronic channels. There are two main options here, the first focusing on developing customer segmentation processes as strongly in the public sector as in the private business sector. This strategy fits closely with providing highly differentiated, meant-to-be-interrogated electronic information systems for citizens and enterprises in place of the older style, standardized broadcast information. Customer segmentation is also an essential step in the second key element of active channel-streaming, namely incentivizing people to switch via providing e-services with lower costs or greatly improved functionality. For example, in 2006, the mayor of London heavily promoted the use of pre-pay versions of the Oystercard (see above) by dramatically increasing prices on conventional ticket sales but keeping those on electronic transactions at the previous year's prices. The logic here is that strong incentives are needed to overcome the 'transaction' costs to consumers of moving from a familiar but very expensive to operate payment system (the 'farebox' methods) to a new but much cheaper alternative. Once this step transition has been encouraged the incentives for electronic customers can be reduced, and very few are likely to switch back once they have actually experienced the convenience of the new methods.

Mandated channel reductions or legally compelling people or businesses to change how they transact with government agencies remains an option in other applications, especially for regulatory compliance or tax and essential service payments (Margetts and Yared 2003). Elected politicians have been very reluctant to visibly be seen closing down previously established or well-used application or payment routes. But running multiple channels in tandem is potentially a highly expensive operation, especially in tax and social security applications where operating costs have already been squeezed in many areas to small proportions of the sums being transacted (see Chapters 6 and 7). As e-service usage rates rise and phone-based public services proliferate for harder-to-reach groups, so the pressure to move citizens and especially enterprises towards electronic-only access will increase. For instance, the UK tax department (HMRC) has already legally moved large businesses on to electronic-only payments and regulatory systems. And many customs systems have de facto been electronic-only for more than a decade now, with paper submission remaining as an expensive à la carte exception used by a minute fraction of freight traffic.

Facilitating isocratic administration is a ponderous label denoting a shift from agency-centred to citizen-centred (or business-centred or stakeholder-centred) processes, where citizens or businesses substantially run their own interactions with government. Isocracy is self-government, going beyond simple disintermediation. The self-administration concept reflects greater acceptance of the importance of quasi-voluntary and self-directed compliance with government in liberal democracies (Braithwaite 2002). The key new role for government's administrative apparatus is not necessarily directly collecting taxes or enforcing compliance in a detailed way—a capacity which the pared down systems of advanced industrial states probably no longer possess in the face of anything like widespread or organized citizen resistance. Instead, tax agencies' key roles are much more holding the ring and solving the assurance problem for people who are initially predisposed to cooperate, but are anxious not to be 'suckered' into isolated cooperation when others can defect without penalty (Levi 1997). Systems aimed at facilitating quasi-voluntary compliance (such as self-manageable tax accounts for citizens and businesses) are still widely resisted by conservative tax agencies, however, on the grounds that they would also make more manifest the limitations of external compliance-enforcing capabilities. In other areas of government though the principles of citizens *co-producing services* are well appreciated and deeper-rooted; for instance, in public health where active cooperation is the key for any communicable diseases control. And in environmental services, essential innovations like differentiated waste disposal are co-produced throughout—citizens actually do all the sorting of different types of household waste prior to its being simply collected by agencies or contractors.

Moving towards open book government means shifting from 'closed files' government on the Weberian pattern to allowing citizens to look at their own medical files and monitor their own treatment, or to actively manage their own tax account, exploiting holistic government, data warehousing, and greater self-administration. Creating data protection and freedom of information regimes is also crucial in persuading public opinion to accept facilitating changes, such as identity cards, long resisted on civil liberties

241

grounds in some large advanced societies. Increasing transparency has been a long-run trend in Western governments, since well before the NPM wave (OECD 2004). Digital-era governance processes add a new impetus for a more agile and customer-centred approach, opening up a prospect for citizens or businesses to easily track and self-monitor the processing of their applications or cases. Fully open book systems are still some way off, but there are reasonable templates of how they might operate in smaller countries such as Sweden, and even models of 'open book' corporations in some parts of the private sector (Martin 1999, Chapter 4).

9.3 The Potential of the Switch to DEG

Comparing across Figure 9.3 (on page 229) with the components of NPM (discussed in Chapter 4) shows some instances of DEG processes that directly reverse NPM changes, and many others which are clearly radically different from NPM priorities and orientations. But it is important to recognize that the relationship between the two movements in public management change is not necessarily a simply oppositional one, like the U-turn image shown in Figure 9.4a, where everything that was developed in the previous period is simply reversed 180 degrees, so that the effect of the reversal is to reinstate the status quo ante. Nothing in our account here should be interpreted as supporting some weighty academic authors whose work often suggests that change in public management is simply symbolic. In these accounts, one phase of change is likely to be as effective as any other, since the basis for change is the persuasive power of its proponents' rhetoric (Hood 1994). Alternatively, the change process itself is a 'ritual' of modernization, testing not improvements in effectiveness per se (which are unknowable), but simply the responsiveness of government sector organizations to political controls and a succession of new 'fashions' in public management, each as well- or ill-founded as the next (Meyer and Scott 1978). Equally, our account does not support the more prevalent low-level structuralist views in which there are a fixed repertoire of solutions in public administration, each of which tends to be cycled through in search of correctives for the problems of a previous phase of 'reform' efforts (Hood 1998). Hood's typology of alternative broad streams in the 'art of the state' is useful, but there is also a despairing quality about it, an implied cynicism about genuine advance in organizational analysis where *plus ça change, plus c'est la même chose.*

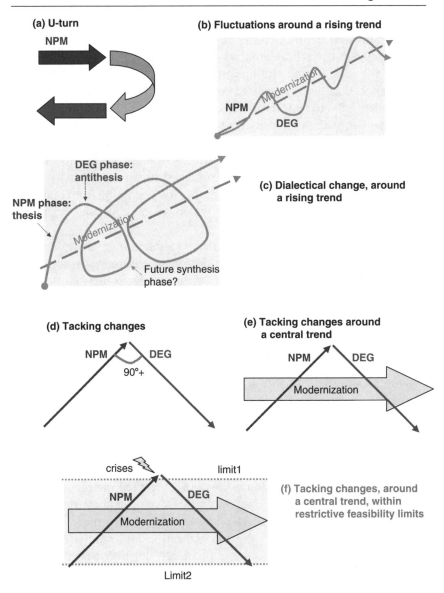

Figure 9.4. Alternative ways of envisioning the inter-relationship between NPM and DEG changes

The other parts of Figure 9.4 show a number of less cyclical views of the transition from NPM to DEG, each of which recognizes the possibility of both progressions and reversions in any phase of public management change, while yet being more optimistic about an underlying pattern of

243

overall progress or modernization. Figure 9.4b shows a pattern of a steady, long-run upward trend in effectiveness (shown on the vertical axis) over time (shown on the horizontal axis), but also with a series of strong cyclical wobbles around the upwards trend, with phases of short-term effectiveness declines interspersed between periods of strong effectiveness growth. The NPM to DEG transition could be seen as the bottom of one of these wobbles, with NPM being over-pushed in countries like the UK and New Zealand to create a period of regression, but DEG processes then kicking in to revive progress again. The cyclical nature of the wobbles here seems objectionable, however, in suggesting an automaticity about the processes involved and a smooth or inevitable phasing from one stage of the cycle to another, neither of which seems applicable to public management change.

A third image shown in Figure 9.4c shows a much more dialectical and strife-prone cyclical process, with periods of strong progress (thesis) succeeded by far more marked periods of declining effectiveness (antithesis), apparently writing off many previous gains only for a later period to integrate together the problems or crises with the initial change push in a new synthesis that opens up a new period of rapid advance. This image has some advantages in suggesting the importance of the conflicts over strategic directions amongst political and administrative actors. But it also suggests an automatic quality and seems to require a much stronger set of mechanisms to explain why such a violent pattern of change is sustained over time.

We believe that a 'tacking' image derived from the way that sailing boats make progress better captures what is going on. As Figure 9.4d shows tacking often involves very radical alterations of course, apparently partly going back in the same direction as previously travelled where the angle of change is a sharp one, but in fact over successive tacks showing a strong underlying direction of travel. This last aspect is shown more clearly in Figure 9.4e as being towards the modernization and rationalization of public management apparatuses and processes. But note that this direction of travel is a chosen or subjectively defined one, and that by definition there is no 'wind' or underlying impulse for change running in the same direction. (If there were, then the sailing boat would not need to tack at all, but could simply 'run before the wind' with straight sails.) Whatever the fundamental impulses or driving forces for change in the external environment, the tacking image makes clear that the direction of travel must always be chosen by political and administrative actors, and sustained by making periodic painful course adjustments. Figure 9.4f completes the picture by suggesting a stronger mechanism for course reversals in the form of externally fixed feasibility limits, where transgressing these limits precipitates crises that signal strongly to decision-makers the need to change course—thereby providing a strong mechanism to impel radical course corrections, with all the extra work and difficult reassessment that they entail. Of course, a final order of difficulty occurs where the feasibility limits themselves vary in restrictiveness over time, sometime necessitating shorter tacks and sometimes permitting longer ones (inherently the most common situation for real-life sailboats steering in shallow or coastal waters).

The switch from NPM to DEG involves, therefore, a series of painful changes and reappraisals, a sharp change of direction orthogonal to the NPM course, just as NPM itself implied a substantial reversal of some aspects of its predecessor (PPA). Of course, NPM itself became fully established in only a few 'heartland' countries (like the UK and New Zealand) and had a very partial and delayed impact elsewhere, in most cases adding to or supplementing PPA practices rather than fully displacing or reversing them. In the same way the impact of DEG practices will be partly achieved by NPM changes drying up, by supplementing NPM practices, by reversing some of them, and by DEG innovations that build on NPM changes to create wholly new approaches.

There are several substantial grounds for optimism about the scope and scale of DEG changes over the next fifteen years to 2020. First, the changes summarized in Figure 9.3 encompass as wide a range of possible components as those incorporated in the NPM movement, and within an equivalently powerful set of organizing themes capable of being worked through in an ordered and coherent way. Second, there is already strong evidence from the experience of private sector industry in the USA and less strong evidence from Europe that the development of IT since 1995 has helped firms to achieve strong productivity growth, especially in the most heavily IT-using and high-tech industries, but also more generally. These changes followed a long period of previous heavy investment in IT by corporations that analysts had a great deal of difficulty showing was positively linked to either growth or profitability. Figure 9.5 shows a highly simplified model of how these major productivity changes have apparently built into a self-sustaining process of major change. The heavy investment in IT-based modernization achieved positive effects only when linked to clear leadership that helped firms to define their roles and ambitions and incorporated IT changes in a wider pattern of organizational changes, flattening hierarchies, and cutting organizational costs radically. Cost reductions in turn generated the first feedback loop numbered 1 in the Figure, freeing up resources to sustain the investment process and create new foundations for expansion and further organisational changes. Leadership influence feeding through e-changes also increased organisation's responsiveness and helped trigger significant customer behaviour shifts, especially into using the web for information-seeking and (later) for transactions, which in turn generated the feedback loop numbered 2 in Figure 9.5, where disintermediation effects created additional resources to sustain new investment and organizational changes.

Similar processes of self-sustaining change are feasible with digital-era governance shifts, so that Figure 9.5 not only captures something of the existing impact of the new 'industrial revolution' amongst private firms, but also expresses synoptically the considerable potential of DEG processes in the public sector. There are substantial extra difficulties in creating self-sustaining changes within government, such as the tendency for early digitalization changes to create extra demands and costs for agencies while mixed channels capacities are built up initially. And the critically important phases for government organizations will be to push through customer behaviour changes successfully, in itself a difficult task to manage for corporations but one made all the harder for agencies that have little experience or expertise in achieving planned behavioural shifts. Creating the right kind of feedback loops will be vital to reaching a self-sustaining pattern of DEG changes, and as in the private sector,

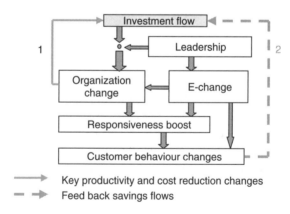

Figure 9.5. Achieving a self-reinforcing cycle of 'digital era' organizational changes

e-changes should be seen as strictly supplementary to the impact of initial investments, effective organizational and sectoral leadership, and detailed change management strategies.

Despite these difficulties, Figure 9.6 also shows a reworking of Figure 9.1, this time assessing the potential for digital-era governance to create a politically self-sustaining process of change. The key difference here is that almost uniquely in the annals of public management changes DEG processes have the capability to radically simplify the internal workings of the state apparatus, cutting institutional complexity, and increasing the inter-visibility of government organizations to each other. Fully implemented DEG changes should also have the effect of increasing citizens' and businesses' capacity to solve their own problems, essentially by simplifying information search and transactional processes radically, as well as greatly reducing the perceived institutional complexity of the government sector. So, with all the of the key feedback arrows switched to positive in Figure 9.6 the previous tendency for all public management changes to accumulate adverse by-product effects that sap their progress and cause them to peter out need not apply.

In addition, DEG processes lend themselves to an evolutionary 'build-and-learn' approach (Dunleavy and Margetts 1999) and entail a culturally different treatment from the 'big bang' implementations of large-scale ICT projects during the 1980s and 1990s (Margetts 1999). The focus here would not be on any instantaneous realization of every element of the DEG approach, any more than the full menu of NPM changes discussed in Chapter 4 emerged at a single time and place. But cumulatively over around the next decade and a half, the clear potential exists for the

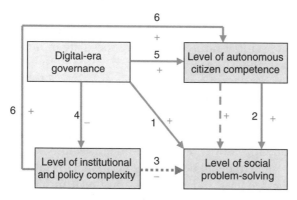

Figure 9.6. The potentially beneficial impacts of DEG changes on social problem-solving

construction of a digital state, founded on the writing off and redirecting of the intellectual capital of the NPM era in the light of new capabilities for organizational development that IT and technology changes make feasible.

Conclusions

Most social scientists are sceptical of claims that technology changes entail alterations of social behaviour. But in the little over a decade that it has existed the development of the Internet and the web has already fundamentally changed how global industries (like the music industry or tourism) operate. The web's direct and mediated impacts are still changing the social behaviour of hundreds of millions of people every year in one aspect or another. So is it any surprise that these shifts should also have a range of significant effects also within public management and state administration? Our central argument is that while the impacts of technological change are never direct and are always filtered and conditioned by organizational, social, and political processes, nonetheless, they have been and will be substantial in the sphere of government also.

The growth of the Internet and the web have contributed to the obsolescing of NPM, its fading importance in defining the future directions of change. Perhaps this change would have happened anyway, as the newness of NPM drains away and its visible difficulties accumulate. But the growth of the Internet and web have also helped to illuminate a possible future that we have labelled DEG. As with NPM, a wide range of specific DEG changes nest within some core but flexible principles (of reintegration, holism, and digitalization). This parallel suggests that in the same way as NPM the already existing DEG trends can be developed and sustained for a substantial future period. We speculate in more detail about future trends in the Afterword, pointing out that both government and the IT industry may need to change their practices quite radically if the best results are to be attained.

Despite this inevitable indeterminancy, we believe that the current period holds out the promise of a potential transition to a more genuinely integrated and citizen-orientated government, whose organizational operations are visible in detail both to the personnel operating in the fewer, broader public agencies and to citizens and civil society organizations. A certain penumbra of fashions and regressions will almost inevitably surround the swing to DEG strategies in leading-edge countries. But a strong underlying upward modernization momentum can still persist and achieve cumulative improvements, moving to a radically less complex institutional and policy landscape—engineered for simplicity and automaticity in routine operations; and designed also for agility and responsiveness in service delivery and government's monitoring of the risk-environment. Digital-era changes inside the government machine would be closely meshed with and run strictly in parallel with increases in citizens' autonomous capabilities for solving social problems. They would go with the grain of what civil society stakeholders are doing anyway, as the digital era unfolds further. For public managers the trick will be to help make it so.

Afterword: Looking Ahead on Technology Trends, Industry Organization, and Government IT

Most academic work in the social sciences is backwards looking—it tells you what was, sticks to the evidence and essentially refines hindsight. There are good scholarly reasons for this approach and the few bits of genuine social science futures work have the same patchy record as other futurology. But here, with the formal analysis and chapters complete, we want to venture a few more speculative thoughts, not just on where we have been in the organization of government IT but also on where we may go next. We look first at some of the most feasible 'next-wave' technology-driven changes, then at how the world market for government IT may change in the next two decades, and finally at alternative scenarios of how governments may handle the development of their IT systems.

Our study period has coincided with a massive increase in interest in government IT (albeit from an astonishingly low-starting point), as the spread of central government e-government initiatives across the world took on some aspects of the earlier *dot.com* boom in e-commerce. Although this 'e-government boom' never reached a peak from which it could crash, the 2000s have seen a slowing down as governments start to come to terms with the problematic features of decades of government IT in terms of crumbling legacy systems and complex networks of contract relationships.

Information technology has now spread right across government, including professional bureaucracies that had typically been laggard in using IT, despite their criticality for welfare state delivery (e.g. the UK National

Health Service). Government's IT-heavy departments were, and still are, machine bureaucracies, particularly the tax, welfare, and immigration departments covered in this book. But the skills required of personnel in these agencies have irrevocably changed, right to the highest levels. Acceptance of this necessity, along with the development of an IT profession and the professionalization of IT procurement staff came late to several of our case study countries, but it has come and there is no going back. Unlike the organizational changes associated with the NPM era, digital-era technologies are having radical impacts on societal behaviour anyway, regardless of what governments choose. Societal and commercial change will exert a continual pressure on government organizations of all kinds to innovate. And the rapid development and societal spread of the Internet and web-based technology with growing interactive and potentially 'expert' services for citizens via the Web have particular relevance for professional bureaucracies.

A key theme for the coming decades in all our case study countries will be identity management, as more advanced online governmental interactions with citizens and businesses rely on the transfer of personal data and extensive authentication procedures. In our three case study areas—tax, social security, and immigration—technological trends are requiring ever greater innovation in terms of reliable identification and authentication techniques, as governments struggle to tackle new types of online fraud (particularly in taxation and social security) and to strengthen border control (in immigration). In the UK, the government's proposed identity card scheme relies heavily on expensive, largely untried, and apparently flawed forms of biometric identification, which are likely to ratchet up the cost of information systems and introduce new complications into administration as police, immigration officials, and government officials in general struggle to build them into existing processes.

Digital-era technologies have brought change across all the four 'tools' of government policy discussed in Chapter 1 (Hood 1983; Hood and Margetts 2006). With the remarkable and rapid expansion of e-commerce, governments face new competition for nodality in the online world, as private sector organizations develop ever more sophisticated methods of ensuring that their products and services are visible and accessible online. We have discussed various developments here which potentially strengthen governments' authority resource, particularly in terms of border control, and this seems likely to be a key area for innovation in the future. At the same time, sustained and radical outsourcing in some countries (particularly the UK) has engendered a wholesale shift away from organizational capacity in terms of 'people power' and towards the buying of equipment and skills (organized expertise) with 'treasure'. The distinctive ways in which national governments employ digital technologies across the tools of government will have the potential to engineer fluctuation in the relative ease with which they can be used, ensuring variation in permutations of the tool mix and implying a range of possible outcomes from the scenarios outlined below.

Five Feasible Technology Trends

We have identified five feasible technology-driven changes with particular relevance for government over the coming decades, as follows:

- web-based utility IT for some agencies;
- a shared-services mixed economy;
- spread of zero trend technologies (ZTT);
- semantic Web;
- graphical interface to governmental services.

Utility computing is a business model whereby a service provider makes available computer resources to their clients and charges them for the usage rather than hardware or software. As for gas or electricity, computing resources such as storage, data registers, and utilization of software are metered and charged to the user on that basis. There would seem to be potential for medium and small agencies to rely principally on web-based services and software supplied in this fashion, cutting software, updating and maintenance costs, particularly with modularization and standardization. Progress here will worsen the gap with large agencies' 'legacy IT', deeply accentuating the difference between large and small agencies, and highlighting the need for larger agencies to 'grasp the nettle' of taking control of their own IT needs.

Shared services indicates the sharing of some functions, particularly IT, across a small number of agencies. The NPM era massively reduplicated management hierarchies—with very poor economies of scale in IT. Our study of seven countries has highlighted emergent trends for a new shared-services mixed economy with agencies contracting for professional services amongst a handful competing intra-government providers and private sector providers—a model pursued to some extent in the USA, highlighted as a key theme of the UK's e-government strategy of 2005, and developed less consciously in the Netherlands and Canada.

The notion of shared services could be extended to cover more than just IT, for example, general government tasks such as procurement, contracting, citizen redress, IT services, policy research services, web provision, PR and marketing. Some of these functions, citizen redress for example, might involve third-sector or NGO suppliers also.

The *spread of ZTT* is something that has been clear in the private sector from the late 1990s and is growing in importance for government. ZTT automates radically, removing human intervention completely from some processes, such as paying pensions or other benefits when citizens become eligible, or automatically renewing road tax when data feeds are made from insurance company and garage databases. ZTT is radically cheaper, communicating via sensors with intelligent automatic appraisal in physical uses. In social management, a rapid growth of charging technologies could potentially solve some public goods/club goods supply problems and deliver labour cost and dis-intermediation savings. ZTT can evoke major problems of identity management, but there have been many successful anonymous uses, such as the traffic congestion charging scheme introduced by London in 2003, new ticketing systems for transport in cities (such as the Oyster card in London), and congestion management via mobile phone unobtrusive measures. These type of initiatives are far easier to implement and arouse far less public disquiet than systems which 'deeply' identify individuals or rely on historical records, such as satellite-based road charging or biometric-based IDs (as discussed in Chapter 8), which involve intense authentication transactions with major acceptance issues.

The *semantic Web* is the next version of the World Wide Web, currently being developed by a research group under the direction of the original author of the Web, Tim Berners Lee. The intention is to create a universal medium for information exchange by giving computer-understandable meaning (semantics) to the content of documents on the Web, thereby extending the Web through the use of standards, mark-up languages, and related processing tools. The semantic web has major ramifications for the development of scientific expertise and knowledge and some professional communities, as major research resources become available in an easily processable way. Were governments able to reliquish control of their data to the extent that it could be marked up in computer readable form, the semantic Web could also have enormous possibilities for government applications, as it creates the potential for extracting data from relevant government sources and putting it together for individuals or businesses in an easily understandable way, supplanting the need for centralized registers. The first wave of online governmental services has been driven by widespread societal use of the Internet and the Web and has had most impact on machine bureaucracies. If the semantic Web gains currency, the next wave would come via the scientific community and could be expected to have most impact upon professional bureaucracies, particularly in the health sector.

A *graphical interface* to governmental services could help to overcome the substantial low-literacy group that is not served by current text-heavy government access. Online gaming applications can already sustain up to 40,000 simultaneous users with broader education ranges, using heavily graphical interfaces and dynamic multimedia content. Developments in the semantic web makes extensive use of graphical images to present data, in particular using maps as a way of illustrating the distributions of key variables. The first area for government might be expert systems, such as pensions check up and advice, or preliminary health checks online. Government progress may lag behind the corporate sector (as with the other developments discussed in this book), but the potential here is great.

The Organization of the IT Industry

Government's capacity in any of our case study countries to enjoy the benefits of these technology-driven trends will be heavily reliant on IT corporations. We started the research project that led to this book looking for policy transfer, hypothesizing that global computer services providers operating within policy sectors across countries would have huge incentives to offer standardized systems to their customers (see Dunleavy and Margetts 1995). In fact, we have found little evidence of policy standardization; rather, the largest providers appear to be offering and developing bespoke systems to some national governments, reaping the financial benefits of tailor-made solutions and enhancing the likelihood that governments will be locked into their long-term relationships.

This tendency of IT corporations to deliver bespoke solutions has ensured that national 'contract regimes' and markets of computer services providers have survived. IBM or EDS, and the other companies we have studied, undoubtedly share resources and internal information systems across their global structures. But they have few incentives to standardize governmental systems across the countries in which they operate, although success in a sector in one country may be a reputational advantage in gaining business in another. Indeed, in most of our countries, the local

IBM operation was considered almost as a domestic player. It is hard to see a direct incentive for these companies to encourage their governmental partners to take advantage of cheap 'off-the-peg' utility computing. And they may resist moves towards shared services across multiple departments and agencies, particularly when such a development would jeopardize long-standing and highly profitable single-agency relationships. The evidence presented in this book has shown how some contracting regimes will do little to incentivize corporations to deliver cutting edge technology to government agencies. Governments which have denuded themselves of IT expertise will find it hard to keep apace of technological innovation and to recognize the potential benefits of new developments.

Governments have a range of mechanisms at their disposal in terms of maximizing the benefits of their contract relationships. For example, the companies suffer reputational scars in some countries (particularly Canada), when government IT projects run aground and other countries take a corporatist approach (such as the Netherlands), compared with the extraordinary generosity with which the larger global IT corporations have been treated by the UK government. These differences between countries are likely to be accentuated in the future. Corporations will penetrate and spread in markets where it is easiest to do so and can be held at bay where governments choose otherwise, as evidenced in Canada, the USA, and the Netherlands.

However, there are some signs of disquiet in the IT industry itself concerning the developments discussed in this book. Even from the mid-1990s in the UK, some IT corporations have warned against the more radical forms of government outsourcing (Margetts 1999). As noted in Chapter 6, when Cap Gemini won the massive contract for taxation IT in the UK, their share price went down. And Japanese companies have come to accept that their years of domestic dominance do not aid them, indeed work against their capacity to gain a foothold in the global outsourcing market. While the IT industry gathered around the new plans for an identity card scheme in the UK, some key players were voicing concern and even funding research which argued against the cost and shape of the scheme. In the countries where the most wholesale outsourcing has taken place (the UK, New Zealand, and Japan), intelligent corporations may come to welcome digital-era initiatives, where governmental agencies attempt to rebuild internal expertise and explore different outsourcing approaches such as the more relational contracting models used in the Netherlands.

Scenarios for How Governments Handle Next Stage IT Development

Socialized as we are into disparaging the idea of technologically determinist processes of social change, most social scientists will be initially sceptical about the transformative potential of the next phase of public administration changes. And it is important to stress that there is nothing automatic about the constellation of DEG processes set out above being widely adopted. For instance, the history of earlier IT-based change in private corporations before the mid-1990s shows very different pressures acting on companies about whether IT-related changes are seen as inescapable modernization expenses (which may or may not increase productivity or shareholder value), or on the other hand are expected to at least cumulate in substantial bottom-line changes in these critical variables over a run of years. There is every reason to expect government systems to show an equivalent degree of variation around the outline of trends sketched above. Current cohorts of administrators and politicians have been socialized in a more or less NPM-influenced environment, and many have committed themselves very heavily to at least part of NPM's (disaggregation + competition + incentivization) agenda. The managerial and political vision needed to fully embrace the digital era agenda is still likely to be in scarce supply, whatever the welfare-maximizing logic of making a radical break with NPM approaches.

We can picture current possibilities in a summary form in terms of two dimensions:

- the extent of digital era changes in public management, whether radical (transformative change) or far more modest, catch-up change lagging behind private corporations and civil society; and
- the pattern of change, depending on the extent to which DEG processes sit within and reinforce an NPM momentum, or are recognized as a distinct new paradigm of public sector management. An intermediate outcome is that they cut across NPM in an inconsistent way, but without creating a clear alternative pattern of their own.

Figure A.1 shows that the intersection of these categories yields four feasible outcomes, with two empty cells in debarred combinations (shown shaded).

1. *The transition to a digital state scenario* (shown in the upper right hand corner) represents the full implementation of DEG changes sketched

	Digital-era governance changes:		
Extent of changes	*Occur within NPM paradigm*	*Cut across NPM*	*Supersede NPM*
Radical/transformative	2. Digital NPM scenario	Infeasible	1. Transition to a digital state
Slow/partial	3. State residualization	4. Policy mess	Infeasible

Figure A.1. Alternative scenarios for change

above. It assumes that NPM orientations can be relatively quickly abandoned and new holistic, reintegrating, and web/digital process changes can be quickly recognized and cumulatively developed to create radical but coherently implemented changes.

2. *The digital NPM scenario* would occur if the range of feasible DEG changes was filtered and sifted by a cohort of bureaucratic and political decision-makers still committed to NPM perspectives, but the extent of change was nonetheless considerable—for instance, because of the need to cut public sector costs or realize substantial public service productivity improvements. Radical outsourcing changes (perhaps linked to exporting routine government jobs to LDCs, such as call centres) could be used to achieve some DEG effects in a back-office focused way, without realizing the broader holistic effects or changing the fundamentally siloed nature of government or the terms of relations with civil society stakeholders. This kind of selective implementation would probably lead to little progress in citizen/state interactions, except where governments can legally compel shifts to electronic services.

3. *State residualization* would kick in where DEG processes are adopted half-heartedly and only within an NPM framework—for example, by governments and agencies resisting the logic of reintegration and allowing IT corporations with outsourced contracts to dictate the pace of change. Here government's failure to grasp inescapable, digital-era challenges gives another twist to a spiral of governmental decline which NPM partly responds to but has also facilitated. Public agencies could become marginalized from modern society—less accessible, less networked, less nodal, and a by-word for primitive organizational structures and lagging, expensive organizational technologies. Political pressures could then mount for the sphere of governmental action to be pared down to the absolute minimum, for instance interacting only with social groups least able to communicate using Web-based methods—the old, the poor, the sick, and

so on. There is even a potential for disintermediation processes to cut government agencies out of the visible spectrum entirely—for instance, if banks or supermarkets pay government for the right to deliver welfare benefits, while another contractor organizes the determination of eligibility. The clear danger could be that government's nodality—its ability to receive information free from societal actors and to broadcast messages which are accorded special attention by them (Hood 1983)—will radically decrease. But because nodality is a very cheap resource, if it is depleted or lost then governments would need to use other resources—such as compulsion or finance (treasure and authority in Hood's terms) to compensate, triggering a further increase in the relatively high cost of public services.

4. *A policy mess outcome* would occur where DEG changes are only tepidly implemented, in a way that cuts across any NPM inheritance but without specifying a clear alternative approach. Trying to push through some DEG changes while retaining a highly fragmented NPM structure and anti-holist procedures, as New Zealand has been doing since 2000, is unlikely to work. Unless DEG processes are accepted as central elements of restructuring, they can be marginalized or rejected—for instance, because managers and agencies have strong incentives to resist disintermediation. Despite the great potential for DEG processes, a kind of deadlock is possible in which they occur too slowly or too piecemeal to counteract the deadweight of 'legacy' organizations and systems left from years of NPM or pre-NPM arrangements. A degraded form of DEG development is possible, where most aspects of the new paradigm happen only partially, happen late, and happen inconclusively. Government bureaucracies slowly add web-based and Internet-based capabilities to their existing operational mix, but they continue to lag years or even decades behind private corporations in their internal work processes—still addicted to paper, to seeing people in person, to recording things in paper filing registries, to not accepting each others' administrative processes, and so on. Here, adding in DEG processes could end up adding to the complications of transacting with government for citizens and of understanding what is happening inside the public sector for policymakers or central agencies.

Even if DEG-type changes are apparently implemented as envisaged in scenario 1, there are also many voices warning of potentially adverse consequences and even policy disasters ahead. Civil liberties groups critique data warehousing without adequate individual privacy rights, especially when linked to ever more intrinsically personal identifiers, such as biometric data and genetic information. At the same time government agencies' capabilities may be enhanced by the continuous (real-time) tracking of mobile phones' or cars' positions and the use of face-recognition software along with CCTV in urban areas, combined with enormously enhanced massive IT storage and search capabilities. The spread of RFID chips in perhaps every private sector product could also expand police or government agencies' forensic abilities. These developments could yet create a universal surveillance apparatus unparalleled in human history, engendering pervasive reductions in privacy without transmuting into any genuinely enhanced service provision for the public at large. And DEG changes are also as vulnerable as any previous initiatives to problems of rhetorical self-deception, political hyperactivism and initiatives for initiatives' sake, as perhaps the UK's controversies over introducing identity cards demonstrate.

Whichever scenarios emerge, it is clear that IT has not proved—and will not prove—a straightforward rationalizing force for government. The scenarios we present engender similar hopes and similar fears to those felt by Weber for bureaucratic modernization. Modern governments are armed with a new array of policy tools for solving social problems, the nature of which are heavily linked to technological development. In using them they are inextricably bound to IT corporations, now a permanent part of the governmental landscape. For better or worse, richer or poorer, governments do not face the technological future alone.

Bibliography

6, Perri, Leat, D., Seltzer, K., and Stoker, G. (2002). *Towards Holistic Government: The New Reform Agenda*. Basingstoke, UK: Palgrave.

6, Perri, (2004). 'Joined-up Government in the Western World in Comparative Perspective: A Preliminary Literature Review and Explanation', *Journal of Public Administration Research and Theory*, 14: 103–38.

Accenture (2002). *eGovernment Leadership: Realizing the Vision*. London: Accenture, The Government Executive Series.

—— (2003). *eGovernment Leadership: Engaging the Customer*. London: Accenture, The Government Executive Series.

—— (2004). *eGovernment Leadership: High Performance, Maximum Value*. London: Accenture, The Government Executive Series.

—— (2005). *Leadership in Customer Service: New Expectations, New Experiences*. London: Accenture, The Government Executive Series.

Albrow, M. (1970). *Bureaucracy*. London: Pall Mall.

Alexander, C. and Pal, L. (1998). *Digital Democracy: Policy and Politics in the Wired World*. Toronto: Oxford University Press.

Allard, T. (2000). 'Paid $1m a Year But IT Hit Squad Can't Deliver Savings'. *Sydney Morning Herald*, 7 September: 3.

ANAO (Australian National Audit Office) (2000). *Implementation of Whole-of-Government Information Technology Infrastructure Consolidation and Outsourcing Initiative*. Report No. 9. Canberra: AusInfo. Available at: www.anao.gov.au

Anessi-Pessina, E., Cantù, E., and Jommi, C. (2004). 'Phasing out Market Mechanisms in the Italian National Health Service', *Public Money and Management*, 24(5): 309–46.

Atkinson, R. D. and Leigh, A. (2003). 'Customer-Orientated e-Government: Can We Ever Get There?', in G. E. Curtine, M. H. Sommer, and V. Vis-Sommer (eds.), *The World of E-Government*. Binghamton, NY: Haworth Press, pp. 159–81.

ATO (Australian Taxation Office) (2003). *Channel Strategy: Assessment of Current Channel Usage*, 26 May (No longer available online.)

Aucoin, P. (1996). *The New Public Management: Canada in Comparative Perspective*. Ottawa: Institute for Research on Public Policy.

—— (1998). 'Accountability in Public Management: Making Performance Count'. Paper to the 'Revitalising the Public Service' conference, Canadian Centre for Management Development, Ottawa, November.

Bardach, E. (1998). *Getting Agencies to Work Together: The Practice and Theory of Managerial Craftsmanship*. Washington, DC: Brookings Institution Press.

Barrett, P. (2001). 'Managing and Monitoring Privatization and Outsourcing Initiatives—Challenges in Maintaining Accountability', Mimeo Speech 7 January. Available at: www.anao.gov.au

Barton, A. D. (2004). 'How to Profit from Defence: A Study in the Misapplication of Business Accounting to the Public Sector in Australia', *Financial Accountability and Management*, 20(3): 281–304.

Barzelay, M. (2000). *The New Public Management: Improving Research and Policy Dialogue*. Berkeley, CA: University of California Press.

Bastow, S., Dunleavy, P., Margetts, H., and Tinkler, J. (2000). 'The Advent of a "Digital State" and Government-Business Relations'. Paper to the UK Political Studies Association Conference, London School of Economics, April.

Becker, G. (1985). 'Public Policies, Pressure Groups and Dead Weight Costs', *Journal of Public Economics*, 28(2): 329–47.

Bellamy, C. and Taylor, J. (1998). *Governing in the Information Age*. Buckingham, UK: Open University Press.

Bhatta, G. (2003). *Post NPM Themes in Public Sector Governance*. Working Paper 17. Wellington, NZ: State Services Commission. Available at: http://www.ssc.govt.nz/upload/downloadable_files/Working_Paper_17.pdf

Boston, J., Martin, J., Pallot, J., and Walsh, P. (1996). *Public Management: The New Zealand Model*. Auckland, NZ: Oxford University Press.

Bozeman, B. (2002). *Government Management of Information Mega-Technology: Lessons from the Internal Revenue Service's Tax Systems Modernization*. Arlington, VA: The PricewaterhouseCoopers Endowment for The Business of Government, New Ways to Manage Series.

Braithwaite, J. (2002). *Restorative Justice and Responsive Regulation*. New York: Oxford University Press.

Breton, A. (1998). *Competitive Government*. Cambridge: Cambridge University Press.

Broughton, C. and Chalmers, J. (2001). 'Reconsidering the Revolution? Australian Public Sector Administration in 2000', *Australian Journal of Public Administration*, 60(1): 81–8.

Canberra Connect (2001). 'Canberra Connect Marketing Plan'. Canberra: Mimeo ACT Government.

CITU (Central IT Unit) (2000). *Information Age Government: Benchmarking Electronic Service Delivery*. London: CITU.

Chakravati, S. (2004). 'Management Mantras: Make Way for New Public Administration', *Times of India*, 14 July, Editorial. Available at: http://timesofindia.indiatimes.com/articleshow/msid-776848,prtpage-1.cms

Ciborra, C. U. (1993). *Teams, Markets and Systems: Business Innovation and Information Technology*. Cambridge: Cambridge University Press.

CSD (Civil Service Department) (1978). *Longer Term Review of Administrative Computing in Central Government*. London: HMSO.

Cohen, M., March, J., and Olsen, J. (1983). 'A Garbage Can Model of Organizational Choice', *Administrative Sciences Quarterly*, 17: 1–25.

Cullen, S. (1994). *IT Outsourcing: The Myths Exploded*. Melbourne: Cullen.

—— (1997). *Information Technology Outsourcing Survey*. Melbourne: Deloitte Touche.

Cullen, S., Willcocks, L., and Seddon, P. (2001). *Information Technology Outsourcing Practices in Australia*. Melbourne: Deloitte Touche Tohmatsu.

Davis, G. and Wood, T. (1998). 'Is There a Future for Contracting in the Australian Public Sector?', *Australian Journal of Public Administration*, 57(4): 85–97.

Davis, R. (1999). *The Web of Politics: The Internet's Impact on the American Political System*. New York: Oxford University Press.

Davis, S. (2004). *The Enhanced US Border Surveillance System: An Assessment of the Implications of US-VISIT*. London: Privacy International.

De Bruijn, H. (2002). *Managing Performance in the Public Sector*. London: Routledge.

Denning, P. J. (2001). 'The Profession of IT: Who Are We?', *Communications of the ACM*, 44(2): 15–19.

Derthick, M. (1990). *Agency Under Stress: The Social Security Administration in American Government*. Washington, DC: Brookings Institution Press.

DOCITA (Department of Communications, Information Technology and the Arts) (2000*a*). *Government Online: The Commonwealth Government's Strategy*. Canberra: DOCITA.

—— (2000*b*). *Government Online Newsletter*. September, Issue 2. Canberra: DOCITA.

Domberger, S. (1998). *The Contracting Organization*. Oxford: Oxford University Press.

Douglas, M. (1986). *How Institutions Think*. Syracuse, NJ: Syracuse University Press.

Dryzek, J. S., Downes, D., Hunold, C., and Schlosberg, D. with Hans-Kristian, H. (2003). *Green States and Social Movements: Environmentalism in the United States, United Kingdom, Germany, and Norway*. Oxford: Oxford University Press.

Dunleavy, P. (1991). *Democracy, Bureaucracy and Public Choice*. Hemel Hempstead, UK: Harvester Wheatsheaf.

—— (1994). 'The Globalization of Public Services Production: Can Government Be "Best in World"?', *Public Policy and Administration*, 9(2): 36–65. Revised version published in A. Massey (ed.) (1996). *Marketization and Globalization of Government Services*. London: Macmillan.

—— (1995). 'Policy Disasters: Explaining the UK's Record', *Public Policy and Administration*, 10(2): 52–70.

Dunleavy, P. and Hood, C. (1994). 'From Old Public Administration to New Public Management', *Public Money and Management*, 14(3): 9–16.

Dunleavy, P. and Margetts, H. (1999). *Government on the Web*. UK National Audit Office report HC 87 Session 1999–2000. London: The Stationary Office. Available at: www.nao.gov.uk and www.governmentontheweb.org

—— —— (2000). 'The Advent of Digital Government: Public Bureaucracies and the State in the Internet Age'. Paper to the American Political Science Association, Omni Shoreham Hotel, Washington, DC, September. Available at: www.governmentontheweb.org

Dunleavy, P., and Margetts, H. (2002). *Government on the Web II*. UK National Audit Office report HC 748 Session 2001–2002. London: The Stationary Office. Available at: www.nao.gov.uk and www.governmentontheweb.org

Dunleavy, P., Margetts, H., Bastow, S., and Tinkler, J. (2000). 'The Digital State and Government-Business Relations in the Information Age'. Paper to the UK Political Studies Association, London School of Economics, April.

Dunleavy, P., Margetts, H., Bastow, S., and Yared, H. (2001). 'Policy Learning and Public Sector Information Technology: Contractual and E-government Changes in the UK, Australia and New Zealand'. Paper to the American Political Science Association, Hilton Hotel, San Francisco, September 2000.

Dunleavy, P., Yared, H., and Bastow, S. (2003). *Government Agility: The Scope for Improving Public Sector Performance*. Report for AT Kearney, 5 August.

Dutch Ministry of Finance (1999). *Taxes in a World Without Distance*. Available at: www.minfin.nl/uk/taxation/tax

Economist Intelligence Unit (2002). *The 2002 e-Readiness Rankings*. Available at: www.eiu.com

EDS (Electronic Data Systems) (2000). 'The First Whole-of-Government Outsourcing Contract in the World'. Available at: www.eds.com/case_studies/govsoau.pdf

—— (2001). 'Factsheet'. Available from 'About Us' at: www.eds.com

Edwards, P., Shaoul, J., Stafford, A., and Arblaster, L. (2004). *Evaluating the Operation of PFI in Roads and Hospitals*. ACCA Research Report No. 84. London: Association of Chartered and Certified Accountants. Summary available at: http://www.accaglobal.com/research/summaries/2270443

European Commission (2005*a*). *Second Annual Report to the Council and the European Parliament on the Activities of the EURODAC Central Unit*, June.

European Commission (2005*b*). eGovernment Factsheet: Netherlands—eServices for citizens. Available at: www.europa.eu.int/idabc/en/document/1237/422

Ferdinand, P. (2000). 'The Internet, Democracy and Democratisation', *Democratization*, 7(1): 1–17.

Fountain, J. (2001). *Building the Virtual State: Information Technology and Institutional Change*. Washington, DC: Brookings Institution Press.

Franda, M. (2002). *Launching into Cyberspace: Internet Development and Politics in Five World Regions*. Boulder, CO: Lynne Rienner.

Furukawa, S. (2001). 'Electronic Governance in Japan: Implications for Politicians and Public Servants'. Paper to the International Congress of Administrative Sciences, Athens, July.

GAO (General Accounting Office) (1991*a*). *SSA Computers: Long-Range Vision Needed to Guide Future Systems Modernization Efforts*. GAO/IMTEC-91-44. Washington, DC: GAO.

Garvey, G. (1993). *Facing the Bureaucracy: Living and Dying in a Public Agency*. San Francisco, CA: Jossey-Bass Publishers.

Gershon, Sir P. (2004). *Releasing Resources to the Front-Line: Independent Review of Public Sector Efficiency*. London: HM Treasury.

Goldsmith, S. and Eggers, W. D. (2004*a*). *Governing by Network: The New Shape of the Public Sector*. Washington, DC: Brookings Institution Press.

Goldsmith, S. and Eggers, W. D. (2004*b*). 'Rewiring Government'. *Federal Computer Week*, 13 December. Available at: http://www.fcw.com

Goles, T. and Chin, W. (2002). 'Relational Exchange Theory and IS Outsourcing: Developing a Scale to Measure Relationship Factors', in R. Hirschheim, A. Heinzl, and J. Dibbern (eds.), *Information Systems Outsourcing: Enduring Themes, Emergent Patterns, and Future Directions*. Berlin: Springer-Verlag, pp. 221–50.

Grace Commission (1983). *The President's Private Sector Survey on Cost Control. A Report to the President*. Washington, DC: Government Printing Office.

Gulick, L. (1937). 'Notes on the Theory of Organization', in L. Gulick and L. F. Urwick (eds.), *Papers on the Science of Administration*. New York: Institute of Public Administration, Columbia University, pp. 3–40.

Haldane Report (1918). *Report of the Machinery of Government Committee of the Ministry of Reconstruction*. London: The Stationary Office.

Halligan, J. (2001*a*). 'Paradoxes in Reform in Australia and New Zealand', in J. J. Hesse, C. Hood, and B. Guy Peters (eds.), *Paradoxes in Public Sector Reform*. Berlin: Duncker and Humboldt, pp. 97–125.

—— (2001*b*). 'Implications of the Humphrey Report', *Canberra Bulletin of Public Administration*, 99/March: 1–4.

—— (2004). 'The Quasi-Autonomous Agency in an Ambiguous Environment: The Centrelink Case', *Public Administration and Development*, 24: 147–56.

Hambleton, R. (2004). 'Beyond New Public Management—City Leadership, Democratic Renewal and the Politics of Place'. Paper to the City Futures International Conference, Chicago, Illinois, July 2004. Available at: http://www.uic.edu/cuppa/cityfutures/papers/webpapers/cityfuturespapers/session8_1/8_1beyondnew.pdf

Harvard Policy Group on Network-Enabled Services and Government (2000). *Eight Imperatives for Leaders in a Networked World: Guidelines for the 2000 Election and Beyond*. Cambridge, MA: John F. Kennedy School of Government.

Hecksher, C. and Donnelon, A. (eds.) (1994). *The Post-Bureaucratic Organization: New Perspectives on Organizational Change*. Thousand Oaks, CA: Sage.

Heeks, R. and Davies, A. (1999). 'Different Approaches to Information Age Reform', in R. Heeks (ed.), *Reinventing Government in the Information Age: International Practice in IT-Enabled Public Sector Reform*. London: Routledge, pp. 22–48.

—— (ed.) (1999). *Reinventing Government in the Information Age: International Practice in IT-Enabled Public Sector Reform*. London: Routledge.

Hirschman, A. (1970). *Exit, Voice and Loyalty*. Cambridge, MA: Harvard University Press.

Holmes, D. (1997). *Virtual Politics: Identity and Community in Cyberspace*. London: Sage.

Hood, C. (1983). *The Tools of Government*. Basingstoke, UK: Macmillan.

—— (1985). 'Contemporary Public Management: A New Global Paradigm?', *Public Policy and Administration*, 10(2): 104–17.

—— (1994). *Explaining Economic Policy Reversals*. Buckingham, UK: Open University Press.

Hood, C. (1998). *The Art of the State: Culture, Rhetoric and Public Management*. Oxford: Clarendon Press.

Hood, C. and Jackson, M. (1991). *Administrative Argument*. Aldershot, UK: Dartmouth.

Hood, C. and Margetts, H. (2006, forthcoming). *The Tools of Government*. Basingstoke, UK: Palgrave.

Hood, C. and Peters, B. Guy (2004). 'The Middle Aging of New Public Management: Into the Age of Paradox?', *Journal of Public Administration Research and Theory*, 14(3): 267–82.

Hood, C., James, O., and Scott, C. (2000). 'Regulation in Government: Has It Increased, Is It Increasing and Should It Be Diminished?', *Public Administration*, 78(2): 284–304.

Hori, M. (2004). 'Japanese Public Bureaucracy in the Era of Globalization', *Ritsumeikan Law Review*, International Edition, 21/March. Available at: www.lex.ritsumei.ac.jp

Horn, M. (1995). *The Political Economy of Public Administration: Institutional Choice in the Public Sector*. Cambridge: Cambridge University Press.

House of Commons Transport Select Committee (2004). *The Future of the Railways*. Seventh report. Volume 1, Session 2003–4 HC145. London: The Stationary Office.

House of Commons Work and Pensions Committee report (2005). *The Performance of the Child Support Agency*. HC 44 – I. London: The Stationary Office.

Humphrey, R. (2000). *Report of the Review of the Whole of Government Information Technology Outsourcing Initiative*. Canberra: Commonwealth of Australia.

IDC (International Digital Communications) (1993). *Facilities Management: The Nature of the Opportunity*. London: IDC.

Illich, I. (1977). *Limits to Medicine: Medical Nemesis: The Expropriation of Health*. Harmondsworth, UK: Penguin.

Immigration Bureau (2002). *Immigration: Internationalization in Accordance with the Rules 2002*. Immigration Control Guidebook. Tokyo: Immigration Bureau, Ministry of Justice.

Infodrome (1999). *Report on the Dutch Information Society*. Amsterdam: Infodrome. (No longer available online.)

Inland Revenue (2004). *Autumn Performance Report*. CM 6437. London: The Stationary Office.

ITANZ (Information Technology Association of New Zealand) (1999). 'Public and Private Sector Partnership—A New Concept for IT Procurement', Wellington, NZ: ITANZ.

James, O. (2000). 'Regulation Inside Government: Public Interest Justifications and Regulatory Failures', *Public Administration*, 78(2): 327–43.

—— (2003). *The Executive Agency Revolution in Whitehall: Public Interest Versus Bureau-Shaping Perspectives*. Basingstoke, UK: Palgrave Macmillan.

—— and Manning, N. (1996). 'Public Management Reform: A Global Perspective', *Politics*, 16(3): 143–9.

Jupp, V. (2003). 'Realizing the Vision of e-Government', in G. E. Curtine, M. H. Sommer, and V. Vis-Sommer (eds.), *The World of e-Government*. Binghamton, NY: Haworth Press, pp. 129–45.

Kaufman, H. (1976). *Are Government Organizations Immortal?* Washington, DC: The Brookings Institution Press.

Keliher, L. (1995). 'Core Executive Decision Making on High Technology Issues: The Case of the Alvey Report', in R. A. W. Rhodes and P. Dunleavy (eds.), *Prime Minister, Cabinet and Core Executive*. London: Macmillan, pp. 219–47.

Kern, T. and Willcocks, L. (2001). *The Relationship Advantage: Information Technology Sourcing and Management*. Oxford: Oxford University Press.

Kernaghan, K. (2000). 'The Post-Bureaucratic Organization and Public Service Values', *International Review of Administrative Sciences*, 66(1): 91–104.

Kickert, W. J. M. (1997). 'Public Governance in the Netherlands: An Alternative to Anglo-American Managerialism', *Public Administration*, 75(4): 731–53.

—— (2000). *Public Management Reforms in the Netherlands: Social Reconstruction of Reform Ideas and Underlying Frames of Reference*. Delft: Eburon.

Kirkpatrick, I., Ackroyd, S., and Walker, R. (2004). *The New Managerialism and Public Service Professions*. Basingstoke, UK: Palgrave.

Koga, T. (2003). 'Access to Government Information in Japan: A Long Way Toward Electronic Government?', *Government Information Quarterly*, 20: 47–62.

Koslowski, R. (2002). 'Information Technology, Migration and Border Control'. Paper to the Institute of Government Studies conference, University of California, Berkeley, April.

—— (2004). 'Intersections of Information Technology and Human Mobility: Globalization vs. Homeland Security '. Paper to the ESRC/SSRC Money and Migration After Globalization Colloquium, St Hughs College, University of Oxford, March 2004.

—— (2005). *Real Challenges for Virtual Borders: The Implementation of US-Visit*. Washington, DC: Migration Policy Institute.

Kraan, D.-J. (1996). *Budgetary Decisions*. Cambridge: Cambridge University Press.

Kurunmäki, L. (1999). 'Making an Accounting Entity: The Case of the Hospital in Finnish Health Care Reforms', *European Accounting Review*, 8(2): 219–37.

—— 'Professional vs. Financial Capital in the Field of Health Care: Struggles for the Redistribution of Power and Control', *Accounting, Organizations and Society*, 24(2): 95–125.

Lacity, M. and Wilcocks, L. (1998). 'An Empirical Investigation of Information Technology Outsourcing Practices: Lessons from Experience', *Management Information Systems Quarterly*, 22(3): 363–408.

—— —— (2000a). *Global IT Outsourcing: In Search of Business Advantage*. Chicester, UK: Wiley.

—— —— (2000b). *Inside Information Technology Outsourcing: A State-of-the-Art Report*. Oxford: Templeton Research, Templeton College.

Lawson, G. (1998). *NetState: Creating Electronic Government*. London: Demos.

Levi, M. (1997) *Consent, Dissent and Patriotism*. Cambridge: Cambridge University Press.

Liou, K. T. (2001). *Handbook of Public Management Practice and Reform*. New York: Dekker.

Longford, G. (2002). 'Rethinking E-Government: Dilemmas of Public Service, Citizenship and Democracy in the Digital Age'. Paper to The Workshop on Public Sector Innovation, University of Ottawa, February 2002.

Lord, R. (2000). *The Net Effect*. London: Random House.

Lucas Jnr, Henry C. (2002). *Strategies for Electronic Commerce and the Internet*. Cambridge, MA: MIT Press.

Lynn, L. (2000). 'Globalization and Administrative Reform: What Is Happening in Theory?' Paper to the International Research Symposium on Public Management, Erasmus University, Rotterdam, April 2000. Available at: http://harrisschool. uchicago.edu/pdf/wp_00_4.pdf

Manning, N. (2000). 'The New Public Management and Its Legacy'. World Bank discussion note. Available at: http://www1.worldbank.org/publicsector/civilservice/debate1.htm

March, J. and Olsen, J. (1976). *Ambiguity and Choice in Organizations*. Bergen: Bergen Universitetsforlaget.

Margetts, H. (1995). 'The Automated State', *Public Policy and Administration*, 10(2): 88–103.

—— (1996). *Computerisation in American and British Central Government 1975–1995: Policy-Making, Internal Regulation and Contracting in Information Technology*. PhD Dissertation, Department of Government, LSE, April 1996.

—— (1997). 'The National Performance Review: A New Humanist Public Management', in A. Massey (ed.), *Globalization and Marketization of Government Services*. Basingstoke, UK: Macmillan, pp. 47–70.

—— (1998). 'Computerising the Tools of Government', in I. Snellen and W. van de Donk (eds.), *Public Administration in an Information Age*. Amsterdam: IOS Press, pp. 441–57.

—— (1999). *Information Technology in Government: Britain and America*. London: Routledge.

—— (2000). 'Political Participation and Protest', in P. Dunleavy, A. Gamble, I. Holliday, and G. Peele (eds.), *Developments in British Politics 6*. London: Macmillan, pp. 185–202.

—— (2003). 'Electronic Government: Method or Madness'. An inaugural lecture, University College London, 13 February. Available at: www.ucl.ac.uk/spp

—— (2006). 'E-Government in Britain: A Decade On'. *Parliamentary Affairs*, 59(2): 250–65.

Margetts, H. and Dunleavy, P. (2002a). *Cultural Barriers to e-Government*. London: NAO.

—— —— (2002b). 'Better Services Through e-Government'. To accompany *Better Services through E-government*. For the UK National Audit Office, Session 2001–2 HC 704. London: The Stationary Office.

Margetts, H. and Yared, H. (2003). 'Incentivization of e-Government'. To accompany *Transforming Performance of HM Customs and Excise through Electronic Service*

Delivery. For the UK National Audit Office, Session 2003–4 HC 1267. London: The Stationary Office.

Margetts, H. and Dunleavy, P., Bastow, S., and Tinkler, J. (2003). 'Leaders and Followers: E-Government, Policy Innovation and Policy Transfer in the European Union'. Paper to the European Union Studies Association conference, Nashville, TN, March 2003.

Martin, C. (1999). *Net Future*. New York: McGraw-Hill.

Meyer, J. W. and Scott, R. W. (1978). *Organizational Environments: Ritual and Rationality*. Beverley Hills, CA: Sage.

Milgrom, P. and Roberts, J. (1992). *Economics, Organisation and Management*. Englewood Cliffs, NJ: Prentice-Hall.

Milne, J. (2002). 'Electronic Delivery of National Social Services: A Canadian Progress Report'. Presentation to the International Conference on Information Technology in Social Security, Valencia, Spain, October.

Minogue, M., Polidano, C., and Hulme, D. (eds.) (1998). *Beyond the New Public Management: Changing Ideas and Practices in Governance*. Cheltenham, UK: Edward Elgar.

Mintzberg, H. (1983*a*). *Power in and Around Organisations*. New York: Prentice-Hall.

—— (1983*b*). *Structure in Fives: Designing Effective Organisations*. Englewood Cliffs, NJ: Prentice-Hall.

Moore, M. H. (1995). *Creating Public Value: Strategic Management in Government*. Cambridge, MA: Harvard University Press.

Moran, M. (2003). *The British Regulatory State: High Modernism and Hyper-Innovation*. Oxford: Oxford University Press.

Moss, M. and Eaton, L. (2001). 'Security Firms Ever Mindful to Cut Costs'. *New York Times*, 15 November: B1.

Moynihan, D. P. and Roberts, A. S. (2002). 'Public Service Reform and the New Security Agenda', in D. P. Moynihan and A. S. Robert (eds.), *Governance and Public Security*. Syracuse, NY: Campbell Public Affairs Institute, Syracuse University, pp. 129–45. Available at: http://faculty.maxwell.syr.edu/asroberts/documents/chapters/MoynihanRoberts.pdf

NAO (UK National Audit Office) (1995*a*). *Inland Revenue: Market Testing the Information Technology Office*. HC 245 Session 1994–5. London: The Stationary Office.

—— (1995*b*). *Entry into the United Kingdom*. HC 204 Session 1994–5. London: The Stationary Office.

—— (1997). *The Contributions Agency: The Contract to Develop and Operate the Replacement National Insurance Recording System*. HC 12 Session 1997–8. London: The Stationary Office.

—— (1999*a*). *Government on the Web*. HC 87 Session 1998–9. London: The Stationary Office.

—— (1999*b*). *The UK Passports Agency: The Passport Delays of Summer 1999* (London: The Stationary Office), HC 812 Session 1998–9.

—— (2000a) *Inland Revenue/EDS Strategic Partnership: Award of New Work*. HC 35 Session 1999–00. London: The Stationary Office.

—— (2000b). *The Cancellation of the Benefits Payments Card Project*. HC 857 Session 1999–00. London: The Stationary Office.

—— (2001a). *Ministry of Defence: Maximizing the Benefits of Defence Equipment Co-operation*. HC 300 Session 2000–01. London: The Stationary Office.

—— (2001b). NIRS2: Contract Extension. HC 355 Session 2001–02. London: The Stationary Office.

—— (2002a). *e-Revenue*. HC 492 Session 2001–02. London: The Stationary Office.

—— (2002b). *Individual Learning Accounts*. HC 1235 Session 2002–03. London: The Stationary Office.

—— (2002c). *Government on the Web 2*. HC 764 Session 2001–02. London: The Stationary Office.

—— (2002d). *PFI Refinancing Update*. HC 1288 Session 2002–03. London: The Stationary Office.

—— (2003a). *New IT Systems for Magistrates' Courts: the Libra Project*. HC 327 Session 2002–03. London: The Stationary Office.

—— (2003b). *PFI Operational Performance*. HC 371 Session 2002–03. London: The Stationary Office.

—— (2003c). *PPP in Practice: National Savings and Investments' Deal with Siemens Business Services Four Years On*. HC 620 Session 2002–03. London: The Stationary Office.

—— (2003d). *Difficult Forms: How Government Agencies Interact with Citizens*. HC 1145 Session 2002–03. London: The Stationary Office.

NOIE (National Office for the Information Economy) (2001). 'Electronic Government in Australia's Information Economy'. Speech by the CEO, John Rimmer, 9 July. Available at: www.noie.gov.au/publications/speeches/Rimmer/Washington.htm

Nooteboom, B. (1999a). 'Innovation and Inter-Firm Linkages: New Implications for Policy', *Research Policy*, 28: 793–805.

—— (1999b). 'Trust as a Governance Device', in M. Casson and A. Godley (eds.), *Cultural Factors in Economic Growth*. Berlin: Springer, pp. 44–68.

NZ Minister for Information Technology's IT Advisory Group (1999). *The Knowledge Economy*. Wellington: Ernst & Young.

NZ Ministry for Social Policy (2001). *The Social Report 2001*. Wellington: Ministry of Social Policy.

NZ Ministry of Commerce (1998). *Electronic Commerce: The 'Freezer Ship' of the 21st Century*. Wellington: Ministry of Commerce.

NZ Ministry of Economic Development (2000). *E-Commerce: A Guide for New Zealand Business*. Wellington: Ministry of Economic Development.

—— (2001a). *New Zealand's Standards and Conformance System: A Guide for Business*. Wellington: Ministry for Economic Planning.

NZ Ministry of Economic Development (2001*b*). *Statistics on Information Technology in New Zealand*. Wellington: Ministry of Economic Development.

NZ Ministry of Justice (2000). *Report of the Ministerial Enquiry into INCIS*. Wellington: Ministry of Justice. Available at: www.justice.govt.nz/pubs/reports/2000/incis_rpt/index.html

NZ State Services Commission (2001). *government.nz@your.service*. Wellington: State Services Commission.

NZNAO (New Zealand National Audit Office) (1999). *Towards Service Excellence: The Responsiveness of Public Agencies to Their Clients*. Wellington: NZNAO.

—— (2000). *Governance and Oversight of Large Information Technology Projects*. Wellington: NZNAO.

OECD (Organisation for Economic Co-operation and Development) (2003). *The e-Government Imperative: Main Findings*. Policy brief. Paris: OECD.

—— (2004*a*). *Information Technology Outlook*. Paris: OECD.

—— (2004*b*). 'Modernizing Government: The Synthesis'. Paper to the Meeting of the Governance Committee, 29 October. Written by Alan Matheson. Paris: OECD.

—— (2005). *E-Government for Better Government*. Paper GOV/PGC 2005(1). Written by Edwin Lau. Paris: OECD.

OMB (Office of Management and Budget) (1994).

OPSS (Office of Public Service and Science) (1991). *Competing for Quality*. Cabinet Office, Cm 1730. London: HMSO.

Osborne, D. and Gaebler, T. (1992). *Reinventing Government: How the Entrepreneurial Spirit Is Transforming the Public Sector*. Reading, MA: Addison Wesley.

Osborne, D. and Plastrik, P. (1997). *Banishing Bureaucracy: Five Strategies for Reinventing Government*. Reading, MA: Addison Wesley.

OTA (Office of Technology Assessment) (1986). *Social Security Administration and Information Technology, Special Report*. OTA-CIT-311. Washington, DC: GPO.

O'Toole, L. J. and Meier, K. J. (2004). 'Parkinson's Law and the New Public Management? Contracting Determinants and Service-Quality Consequences in Public Education', *Public Administration Review*, 64(3): 342–52.

Overman, S. and Boyd, K. (1994). 'Best Practice Research and Postbureaucratic Reform', *Journal of Public Administration Research and Theory*, 4(1): 67–83.

Pascal, B. (1909–14). *Thoughts*. New York: P.F. Collier and Son Company.

Peled, A. (2001). 'Do Computers Cut Red Tape', *American Review of Public Administration*, 31(4): 414–35.

Peters, G. and Savoie, D. (eds.) (1998). *Taking Stock: Assessing Public Sector Reforms*. Montreal: Canadian Centre for Management Development/McGill Queen's University Press.

Policy and Innovation Unit (2000). *Wiring It up: Whitehall's Management of Cross-Cutting Polices and Services*. London: Cabinet Office. Available at: http://www.pm.gov.uk/files/pdf/coiwire.pdf

Pocock, J. G. A. (1973). *Politics, Language and Time*. New York: Athenaeum.

Polidano, C., Minogue, M., and Hulme, D. (eds.) (1998). *Beyond the New Public Management: Changing Ideas and Practices in Governance*. Cheltenham, UK: Edward Elgar.

Pollitt, C. (1993). *Managerialism and the Public Services*, 2nd edn. Oxford: Blackwell.

—— (2003). 'Joined-up Government: A Survey', *Political Studies Review*, 1(1): 34–49.

Pollitt, C. and Boukhaert, G. (2000). *Public Management Reform: A Comparative Analysis*. Oxford: Oxford University Press.

Pollitt, C., Birchall, J. and Pearson, K. (1998). *Decentralising Public Service Management*. Basingstoke, UK: Macmillan.

Pollock, A. (2004). *NHS plc: The Privatisation of our Health Care*. London: Verso.

Polsby, N. (1984). *Political Innovation in American: The Politics of Policy Initiation*. New Haven, CT: Yale University Press.

Power, M. (1994). *The Audit Explosion*. London: Demos.

Prebble, M. (1993). *New Zealand: The Turnaround Economy*. London: Institute of Directors.

Pusey, M. (1992). *Economic Rationalism in Canberra: The Nation Building State Changes Its Mind*. Sydney: Allen and Unwin.

Quinn, J. (1992). *Intelligent Enterprise*. New York: Free Press.

Ragin, C. (2000). *Fuzzy-Set Social Science*. Chicago, IL: University of Chicago Press.

—— (1994). *Constructing Social Research. The Unity and Diversity of Method*. Thousand Oaks, CA: Pine Forge Press.

—— (1987). *The Comparative Method. Moving Beyond Qualitative and Quantitative Strategies*. Berkeley, CA: University of California Press.

—— and Griffin, L. (eds.) (1994). 'Formal Methods of Qualitative Analysis', *Special Issue of Sociological Methods and Research*, 23(1).

Ritzer, G. (1993). *The McDonaldization of Society*. Thousand Oaks, CA: Pine Forge Press.

Rose, N. (1999). *Powers of Freedom: Reframing Political Thought*. Cambridge: Cambridge University Press.

Savas, E. (1987). *Privatization: The Key to Better Government*. Chatham House, NJ: Chatham House.

—— (2000). *Privatization and Public-Private Partnerships*. Chatham House, NJ: Chatham House.

Savoie, D. (1995). 'What is Wrong with the New Public Management?', *Canadian Public Administration*, 38(1): 112–21.

Schick, A. (1996). *The Spirit of Reform: Managing the New Zealand State Sector in a Time of Change*. Wellington: State Services Commission. See also a summary of the report and commentaries by R. Mulgan and J. Martin in *Public Sector* (1996), 19(4): 2–13.

—— (1998). 'Why Most Developing Countries Should Not Try New Zealand's Reforms', *World Bank Research Observer International*, 13: 23–31.

Scott, J. C. (1998). *Seeing like a State: How Certain Schemes to Improve the Human Condition Have Failed*. New Haven, CT: Yale University Press.

Seddon, P. B. (2001). 'The Australian Government's Clustered-Agency IT Outsourcing Experiment', *Communications of the Association for Information Systems*, 5/ article 13. Available (to CAIS subscribers only) at: http://cais.isworld.org/contents. asp

Select Committee on Work and Pensions (2002). *The 'ONE' Pilots and the Lessons for Jobcentre Plus*. 13 March. First report session 2001–2. Available at: http://www. publications.parliament.uk/pa/cm200102/cmselect/cmworpen/426/42602.htm

Silberman, B. S. (1993). *Cages of Reason: The Rise of the Rational State in France, Japan, the United States, and Great Britain*. Chicago, IL: University of Chicago Press.

Simon, H. A. (1973). 'Applying Information Technology to Organization Design', *Public Administration Review*, 33: 268–78.

Singapore Government (2000). *e-Government Action Plan*. Available at: www.ida. gov.sg

Skålén P. (2004). 'New Public Management Reform and the Construction of Organizational Identities', *International Journal of Public Sector Management*, 17(3): 251–63.

SSA (Social Security Administration) (1982). *Systems Modernization Program*. Baltimore, MD: Office of Systems, SSA.

—— (1994). *The Social Security Administration's Information Systems Plan*. Baltimore, MD: Office of Systems Planning and Integration, SSA.

Strassman, P. (1990). *The Business Value of Computers*. Connecticut, CT: The Information Economics Press.

—— (1995). 'Outsourcing: A Game for Losers', *ComputerWorld*, 29 August, 29(34): 75.

—— (1997). *The Squandered Computer: Evaluating the Business Alignment of Information Technologies*. New Canaan, CT: Information Economics Press.

Sunstein, C. (2002). *Republic.com*. Princeton, NJ: Princeton University Press.

Talbot, C. (2004). 'Executive Agencies: Have They Improved Management in Government?', *Public Money and Management*, 24(2): 104–12.

Taylor Nelson Sofres (2003). *Government Online: An International Perspective*. London: Taylor Nelson Sofres.

Treasury and Civil Service Select Committee (1994). *The Role of the Civil Service: Fifth Report*, Volume 1. London: The Stationary Office.

Treasury Board of Canada (1998). *An Enhanced Framework for the Management of Information Technology Projects*. Ottawa: Treasury Board.

Turpin, C. (1972). *Government Contracts*. Harmondsworth, UK: Penguin.

UNPAN (United Nations Online Network in Public Administration and Finance) (2004). *Best Practices in the European Countries: The Netherlands*. Available at: http://unpan1.un.org/intradoc/groups/public/documents/CAIMED/UNPAN019 388.pdf

Upton, S. (2000). 'Quo Vadis New Zealand'. Mimeo speech to a parliamentary seminar, Wellington.

Van de Walle, S., Sterck, M., Van Dooren, W., Bouckaert, G. and Pommer, E. (2004). 'Public Administration'. *Public Performance: An International Comparison of Education, Health Care, Law and Order and Public Administration*. The Hague: Social and Cultural Planning Office.

Walsh, K. (1995). *Public Services and Market Mechanisms: Competition, Contracting and the New Public* Management. Basingstoke, UK: Macmillan.

Watts, D. and Strogatz, S. (1998). 'Collective Dynamics of Small World Networks', *Nature*, 393: 440–2.

West, D. (2000). 'Assessing e-Government: The Internet, Democracy and Service Delivery by State and Federal Governments'. Available at: www.insidepolitics. org/policyreports.html

West, D. M. (2005). *Digital Government: Technology and Public Sector Performance*. Princeton, NJ: Princeton University Press.

Whittaker, S. (2001). 'Making the Web Work: I Before E—No Exceptions'. Paper available at: www.eds.com

Wilhelm, A. G. (2000). *Democracy in the Digital Age: Challenges to Political Life in Cyberspace*. New York: Routledge.

Willcocks, L. and Fitzgerald, G. (1994). *A Business Guide to Outsourcing Information Technology*. London: Business Intelligence.

Williamson, O. (1975). *Markets and Hierarchies: Analysis and Anti-Trust Implications*. New York: Free Press.

—— (1993). 'Calculativeness, Trust and Economic Organization', *Journal of Law and Economics*, 36: 453–86.

Wise, C. R. (2002). 'Special Report: Organizing for Homeland Security', *Public Administration Review*, 62(2): 131–44.

Wood, G. (2004). 'New Public Management and Europeanization: Convergence or Nestedness?', in P. Dibben, G. Wood, and I. Roper (eds.), *Contesting Public Sector Reforms: Critical Perspectives, Rational Debates*. Basingstoke, UK: Palgrave Macmillan, pp. 167–78.

World Bank Group (2003). *Supporting Institutional Reforms in Tax and Customs: Integrating Tax and Customs Administrations*. PLS Ramboll on behalf of the World Bank Group, January.

World Markets Research Centre (2001). *Global E-Government Survey*. London: World Markets Research Centre.

Yamamoto, H. (2003). *New Public Management: Japan's Practice*. IIPS Policy Paper 293e. Tokyo: Institute for International Policy Studies.

Yates, A. (2001). 'Risk Management in the Commonwealth's IT Initiative', *Canberra Bulletin of Public Administration*, 99(March): 5–7.

Zifcak, S. (1994). *New Managerialism: Administrative Reform in Whitehall and Canberra*. Milton Keynes: Open University Press.

Newspapers, Magazines, and Websites

Accountancy Age (www.accountancyage.com)

Asahi Shimbun (www.asahi.com/english/english.html)

Australian, The (www.theaustralian.news.com.au)

Australian Associated Press (www.aap.com.au)

Aviation Week and Space Technology (www.aviationnow.com/avnow/news/channel_awst.jsp)

Business Week (www.businessweek.com)

Business Wire (www.businesswire.com)

Canada News Wire (http://www.canadanewswire.ca/en/)

Canberra Connect (www.canberraconnect.act.gov.au)

Canberra Times (www.canberra.yourguide.com.au/home.asp)

Card Technology (www.cardtechnology.com)

Chicago Daily Herald (www.dailyherald.com)

Computer Weekly (www.computerweekly.com)

ComputerWorld Canada (www.itworldcanada.com/Pages/Docbase/Browse Publication.aspx?Publication=ComputerWorld)

Computing (www.computing.co.uk)

Courier Mail (www.couriermail.news.com.au)

Datamonitor's ComputerWire (www.computerwire.com)

Dominion Post (www.dominionpost.com)

Edmonton Journal (www.canada.com/edmontonjournal/index.html)

eGovernment Observatory News (www.europa.eu.int/idabc/en/chapter/194)

Extel Examiner (now called *AFX News*, www.afxnews.com)

Financial Post (www.canada.com/nationalpost/financialpost/index.html)

Financial Times (www.ft.com)

Government Computer News (www.gcn.com)

Government Computing (www.kablenet.com)

Guardian (www.guardian.co.uk)

idg.net (www.idg.net)

Independent (www.independent.co.uk)

Infotech Weekly (now called *Stuff*, www.stuff.co.nz)
Inter Press Service (www.ips.org)
Kable/Kabledirect (www.kablenet.com)
London Free Press (www.lfpress.com)
Montreal Gazette (www.canada.com/montrealgazette/index.html)
National Journal Group (www.nationaljournal.com)
New Statesman (www.newstatesman.com)
New Zealand Herald (www.nzherald.co.nz)
Nikkei Weekly (www.nni.nikkei.co.jp/FR/TNW/)
Ottawa Citizen (www.canada.com/ottawacitizen/index.html)
PBI Media (now called *Access Intelligence*, www.pbimedia.com/index.html)
Sunday Telegraph (www.telegraph.co.uk)
Sunday Times (www.timesonline.co.uk)
Times (www.timesonline.co.uk)
Toronto Star (www.thestar.com)
Vancouver Sun (www.canada.com/vancouversun)
VNU Net (www.vnunet.com)
Washington Post (www.washingtonpost.com)
Winnipeg Sun (www.winnipegsun.com)
Yomiuri Shimbun (www.yomiuri.co.jp/dy)

Index

Additional labels in italics indicate where government agencies and programmes came from our seven case study countries: *Aus* Australia; *Can* Canada; *Japan*; *Neth* Netherlands; *NZ* New Zealand; *UK*; *USA*.